The Cultural Politics of the
New American Studies

[handwritten inscription:] For Mark & Annette, overlords overly with all your help with the digital format for this book & the into doodle & to Gary & Joanne, Enduring friendship! John & Kristin.

The Cultural Politics of the New American Studies

John Carlos Rowe

O

OPEN HUMANITIES PRESS

An imprint of MPublishing – University of Michigan Library, Ann Arbor

2012

First edition published by OPEN HUMANITIES PRESS 2012

Freely available online at http://hdl.handle.net/2027/spo.10945585.0001.001

ISBN-10 1-60785-243-8

ISBN-13 978-1-60785-243-8

OPEN HUMANITIES PRESS is an international, scholar-led open access publishing collective whose mission is to make leading works of contemporary critical thought freely available worldwide. Books published under the OPEN HUMANITIES PRESS imprint at MPublishing are produced through a unique partnership between OHP's editorial board and the University of Michigan Library, which provides a library-based managing and production support infrastructure to facilitate scholars to publish leading research in book form.

MPublishing
www.publishing.umich.edu

O
OPEN HUMANITIES PRESS
www.openhumanitiespress.org

Contents

In Memory of Edward Said

Preface

This book proposes that we consider the relationship of our many different activities as scholar-teachers in terms of our work for greater social justice and equality. Although this goal is not limited to scholars in the humanities and social sciences, it is more obviously related to our work than to other disciplines. Our scholarship is tested primarily by our students and occasionally by legislators and others framing public policies. We both study and practice "cultural politics", especially as I define this phrase in this book. My claim contradicts those who argue that knowledge must be "free" of politics. Knowledge is never free of political values, and it is wisest for us to encourage our students to debate the political connotations of whatever field they study. When such political implications are ignored or denied, they continue to operate but in secret, more dangerous ways. Of course, we must "teach the conflicts", not just advocate for our own political positions, however persuasive we may find them.

I also believe that in many academic disciplines there is a necessary continuity between academic and public debates, as well as between scholarly and social activism. In this book, I offer examples of how I have engaged these debates and pursued activist goals since 1991. I am not an important or influential political activist, and it is one of my central arguments that ordinary scholars do make a difference in the public sphere and can be even more influential once they recognize their abilities to do so. The monumental changes in world history are built upon very small acts, whose coordination may be both the result of profound organization and historical fortune. It is easy to be discouraged today by the marginal positions so many academics appear to occupy amid the broader social, political, and economic forces of globalization. It is more difficult, but far more hopeful and productive, for us to find the points of intersection where our work complements labor by others in the interests of achieving greater equality for all.

All of the chapters in this book are based on essays published in journals, scholarly books, and newspapers in the U.S., Germany, Egypt, and the United Kingdom. Each chapter differs greatly from its first publication, in most cases because the history separating its original publication and its appearance in this book is addressed. I have made specific efforts in several chapters (chapters 1, 2, 3, 5, 8, and 9) to retain the historical contexts prompting their original publication and to comment on the intervening history. Sometimes these changes are specifically indicated, as in chapters 2, 3, and 8; in other cases, these changes are integrated into a unified argument, as in chapters 1, 5, and 9. I am trying to represent the historical dimension of scholarship when it enters explicitly the political and public spheres. In one sense, scholarship must be timely; in another sense, scholarship must mark and record the passage of historical time.

I am grateful to many friends who have inspired me with their own activism as scholar-teachers. This book is dedicated to Edward Said, who continues to teach me. When I first came up with the idea for publishing this book in digital format, my good friend, Mark Poster, introduced me to Gary Hall, whose work has also had a profound influence on me. Randy Bass at Georgetown University, Reinhard Isensee at the Humboldt University (Berlin), and Matthias Oppermann at Bielefeld University have led the way in digital scholarship and encouraged me to complete this book. Other friends have set a very high standard for me to follow with regard to activism: Colin Dayan and Hortense Spillers at Vanderbilt University, Ruth Wilson Gilmore at the City University of New York, Henry Giroux at McMaster University, Abdul JanMohamed at the University of California, Berkeley, Curtis Marez and Shelley Streeby at the University of California, San Diego, Donald Pease at Dartmouth College, Wilfried Raussert at Bielefeld University, Marita Sturken and Dana Polan at New York University and Winfried Fluck at the Free University (Berlin). My colleagues in American Studies and Ethnicity at the University of Southern California are well-known for their abilities to connect scholarship, teaching, and activism. Sarah Banet-Weiser, Richard Berg, Philip Ethington, Macarena Gomez-Barris, Sarah Gualtieri, Jack Halberstam, David Lloyd, Tania Modleski, Tara McPherson, Maria Elena Martinez, Manuel Pastor, Laura Pulido, Leland Saito, George Sánchez, and Janelle Wong have taught me more about "cultural politics" than I can ever repay.

My thanks to the editors and publishers for permission to reprint significantly revised versions of the essays first published by them: Chapter 1, "Edward Said and American Studies", first published by *American Quarterly* 56:1 (March 2004), 33–47; Chapter 2, first published as "The 'Vietnam-Effect' in the Persian Gulf War," *Cultural Critique*, special issue, "The Economies of War," 19 (Fall 1991), 121–39; Chapter 3, first published as "Images from Fallujah Will Stir Debate, But... Won't Alter Policy", Op-Ed, *Newsday* (April 2, 2004), A49; Chapter 4, "Areas of Concern: Area Studies and the New American Studies", first published in *Alif: Journal of Comparative Poetics* (Egypt) 31 (2010), special issue on "The Other Americas"; Chapter 5, "Culture, U.S. Imperialism, and Globalization", first published in *American Literary History* 16:4 (Winter 2004), 575–595; Chapter 6, "Reading *Reading Lolita in Tehran* in Idaho", first published in *American Quarterly* 59:2 (June 2007), 253–275; Chapter 7, "The Death of Francis Scott Key and Other Elegies: Music and the New American Studies", *Cornbread and Cuchifritos*, eds. Wilfried Raussert and Michelle Habell-Pallán (Trier: Wissenschaftlicher Verlag Trier, 2011), 27–40; Chapter 8, "Visualizing Barack Obama", first published in *Journal of Visual Culture* 8:2 (August 2009), 207–210; Chapter 9, first published as "The Dramatization of *Mao II* and the War on Terrorism", *South Atlantic Quarterly* 103:1 (Fall 2003), pp. 21–43 and "Global Horizons in Don DeLillo's *Falling Man* (2007)", *Don DeLillo: Mao II, Underworld and Falling Man*, ed. Stacey Olster (London: Continuum, 2011), 121–134.

The Cultural Politics of the New American Studies

Now what? Barack Obama's election was a great success. A person of great integrity and political skills replaced George W. Bush. In his memoir, *Decision Points* (2010), George W. Bush defends water-boarding and other forms of torture for "saving lives", as well as his decision to invade Iraq on the erroneous evidence of Iraqi "weapons of mass destruction" for "making the world a safer place without Saddam Hussein".[1] The 2010 mid-term elections have given Republicans a majority in the House of Representatives, promising a politically divided Congress for the remaining two years of President Obama's first term. President Obama's popularity has dropped to 47%, well below the enormous popularity he enjoyed in his first 100 days in office. Republicans, especially advocates of the Tea Party or Tea Party Express, appear to be resurgent, successfully defending their foreign policy mistakes under George W. Bush and redirecting their responsibility for the current economic recession to President Obama and the Democrats. In the Republicans' political statements, government bailouts of Wall Street and the costs of "Obamacare" have caused our economic and social problems, not two costly and unnecessary foreign wars or unregulated capitalism. We are at a critical point in U.S. politics, when scholarly knowledge is needed more than ever to clarify history and enable citizens to make intelligent decisions.

Most of the people reading this book contributed to Barack Obama's victory, as well as criticized the policies of the George W. Bush administration. Indeed, one of the few positive lessons from the past decade is that a relatively free intellectual class is one of our best protections against fascism or other dictatorial usurpations. During the Second Gulf War, our invasion and occupation of Iraq, and our ongoing war in Afghanistan and Pakistan, academics were among the most consistently critical of our policies and the best informed regarding the long history of U.S. imperialism as background to our foreign policies, which were justified by the Bush Administration as "exceptions" to an otherwise "anti-imperialist", democratic U.S. For a variety of reasons, intellectuals with academic appointments turned out to be even more courageous than the usually celebrated "public intellectuals", many of whom defended U.S. policies in the post-9/11 era. Todd Gitlin's nationalist sentiments, of course, preceded 9/11 but Don DeLillo's surprisingly sentimental defense of beleaguered New Yorkers and his general indictment of global terrorism in his *Harper's* essay "In the Ruins of the Future: Reflections on Terror and Loss in the Shadow of September" (December 2001), and his novel, *Falling Man* (2007) surprised many fans of his canny interpretation of the U.S. role in global disorder in *Mao II* (1991). In the past decade we also witnessed the proliferation of neo-conservative public intellectuals, many supported by private think-tanks as they rotated out of government positions in Republican administrations or relied on their own tenured positions in colleges and universities to defend Bush's foreign policies, Wall Street's unregulated, late modern capitalism, and to fuel populist anxieties about "illegal immigrants" as internal enemies.

The emergence of neo-conservative public intellectuals from the academic ranks dates back to the "culture wars" of the late 1980s and early 1990s. Richard Rorty, Samuel Huntington, and Stephen Ambrose were spinoffs of Allan Bloom, E. D. Hirsch, Jr., Dinesh D'Souza, and Francis Fukuyama. As print and broadcast journalism tempered its criticism of our foreign policies under George W. Bush thanks in part to mergers and acquisitions in these media and the general "Murdoch Effect", academic criticism joined with political organizations like Moveon.org to preserve some semblance of anti-war and anti-imperialist activism. As hundreds of thousands of Iraqi civilians were murdered in sectarian violence and millions of Iraqis emigrated to Jordan, Syria, and other countries, changing dramatically the geopolitical shape of postwar Iraq while U.S. occupying forces allowed such violence to continue unabated, a few brave academics tried to challenge the public's mood of war's "inevitable violence" by risking their own lives to visit and report on the shattered lives and neighborhoods of Iraq.

Mark Levine's book, *Why They Don't Hate Us: Lifting the Veil on the Axis of Evil* (2005), grew out of just this sort of eyewitness travel outside the

U.S. State Department and military channels to war-torn Iraq.[2] Levine's work is complemented by the consistent criticism of U.S. imperialism and neo-imperialism by a wide range of American Studies scholars, including Donald Pease and Amy Kaplan, who criticize how the Bush Administration built what might be termed "State Exceptionalism" to justify both our invasion of Iraq and the subsequent human rights' abuses from Abu Ghraib to Guantanamo integral to this foreign policy.[3] Much of this new work on U.S. imperialism draws upon the anti-imperialist scholarship of Richard Drinnon, Richard Slotkin, Ronald Takaki, Annette Kolodny, and other American Studies' scholars of the 1960s and 1970s, who understood how colonial expansion and accompanying racial subalternity are central to U.S. nationalism, no matter who occupies the Executive branch of the government. Much of President Obama's global popularity depends on his appeal to a new American Exceptionalism and on the presumption that nationalism transcends ethnic and racial identities. The repeated refrain of his campaign that only in America could Barack Hussein Obama be elected President impresses me as a gentler version of the older and more dangerous exceptionalisms American Studies has criticized so effectively.

We still have important obligations as scholarly activists to continue our criticism of U.S. imperialism in the ongoing occupation of Iraq, the expansion of the war in Afghanistan and Pakistan, meliorist policies in the Israeli-Palestinian conflict, and the U.S. "empire of military bases" that continues to grow.[4] U.S. neo-imperialism also includes policies of strategic neglect, including the ongoing crises in Haiti, Darfur and Somalia, Zimbabwe, and other African political and human rights' crises barely visible in the U.S. media and State Department policies.[5] Although U.S. policies appear to be thawing toward Cuba, we continue to wait for regime changes, as we did in Vietnam so long ago, expecting that Fidel Castro's diminished powers or death, like Ho Chi Minh's death in Vietnam and Saddam Hussein's execution in Iraq, will result in sudden political transformations. A new policy toward Cuba is urgently needed, as is more public debate about our role in the Caribbean and broader Latin America. Given the importance of the history of Cuba-U.S. relations in the hemispheric scope of the new American Studies, we must push as scholars and activists for more than merely symbolic acts by the U.S. state toward Cuba, Haiti, and other hemispheric sites of traditional conflict with the U.S.

President Obama also needs to address the current political crisis in Iran, defending the rights of the Iranian opposition while avoiding the usual platitudes about how Iran should "follow" the model of U.S. democracy and its civil religion. Despite our constitutional separation of church and state, our political history has been profoundly shaped by religious interests, perhaps no more powerfully than in the past few decades. Our complaints about "theocratic" Iran should be tempered by our own reverence for the "Puritan Origins" of U.S. democracy and the persistence of these religious values in the Protestant work-ethic and various forms of capitalist rationalization of economic inequities. We should also be aware of the long history of religious persecution in the U.S., whose original colonists so famously immigrated to the Western Hemisphere in quest of religious freedom and tolerance. Yet colonial and national U.S. history is full of the religious persecution of peoples practicing indigenous religions, Catholicism, Caribbean Voodoo and North American Hoodoo, Mormonism, Buddhism, Confucianism, Sufism, Jainism, Islam, and many other religions.

To be sure, the Obama administration in two years has changed significantly our global reputation. President Obama's speech in Cairo, "A New Beginning", on June 4, 2009 is a powerful indication of these new, good intentions.[6] But none of this should dissuade us from the necessary criticism of Obama's practical policies. U.S. troops remain in Iraq, despite the much-publicized withdrawal of U.S. combat forces in September 2010. The Obama administration has widened the unwinnable war in Afghanistan and Pakistan against the Taliban while maintaining support for the corrupt administration of President Karzai, thus ignoring the lessons of history for the region and of the more general "Vietnam-Effect". The recent assassination of Osama bin Laden by U.S. Navy Seals operating covertly in Abbottabad, Pakistan affirms our commitment to violent, military solutions and our disregard for the sovereignty of our client-state, Pakistan. The Palestinian-Israeli conflict is at one of its most volatile stalemates of the past fifty years. Although scheduled for closure, Guantanamo remains open, its prisoners now destined to be sent to foreign countries like Palau and Bermuda, in yet another instance of U.S.

"outsourcing", while those prisoners released have often rejoined al-Qaeda or other terrorist organizations after their long incarcerations by the U.S. Further information about how our government tortured prisoners of war has been suppressed on grounds as specious as those employed by the Bush Administration.

Such macropolitical issues cannot be separated from the economic crisis the U.S. and many first-world nations are still struggling to overcome. The front cover of *Newsweek* for June 13, 2009 advertised Fareed Zakaria's "The Capitalist Manifesto", replete with a faux red leather binding and Soviet star. Tediously repeating slogans about "Capitalism with a Conscience", Zakaria dismisses strong evidence that Karl Marx's prediction is coming true, advocating instead economic "self-regulation" by Wall Street and Pennsylvania Avenue.[7] Predicated on a relentless will to grow without regard for the consequences, capitalism is collapsing from its own internal contradictions. What we are witnessing in the "global credit crisis", "subprime mortgage meltdown", or "financial regulatory failure" is in fact the consequence of economic surpluses used to produce further surpluses, rather than being reinvested in the human, social, and global system or prompting redistribution of wealth through improved wages, benefits, and working conditions for the proletariat. The modernization of China has resulted in its transformation into a modified capitalist economy that has produced extraordinary surpluses, often cited as one part of the global economic solution, but also strong evidence of what is wrong. Propping up bureaucratic Chinese Communism is a capitalist economy that has rapidly produced incredible class distinctions in China and now commands immense surplus wealth that will reconfigure economies around the globe under the guise of saving these economies from their own internal problems.

Ruth Wilson Gilmore has argued in *Golden Gulag: Prisons, Surplus, Crisis, and Opposition in Globalizing California* (2007) that the prison-industrial complex in California is just one example of how "criminality" has been redefined under the pressures from economic surpluses looking for new investment opportunities.[8] Motivating legislators looking for economic opportunities for their districts, these surpluses have contributed to a prison-industrial-legislative complex far more difficult to decipher than the relatively simple accounting tricks of hedge fund managers and other manipulators of surplus capital. Like Angela Davis and other activists committed to prison reform, Gilmore interprets the "carceral geographies" written on the bodies of inmates in the vast U.S. prison system to constitute neo-slavery, whose abolition faces economic entanglements between criminalization and capitalism as profound as those confronting nineteenth-century abolitionists. At what point does the globalizing of California intersect the Chinese factories, where exploited labor produces so many of the inexpensive imports to the U.S.?

William D. Cohan's *House of Cards: A Tale of Hubris and Wretched Excess on Wall Street* (2009) clearly analyzes how the investment banking firm of Bear Stearns could go from one of the most powerful investment companies in the world to bankruptcy in a matter of weeks.[9] The surpluses with which Bear Stearns "played the market" were never intended to help the poor, rebuild the infrastructure, or contribute to the U.S. "common wealth". In their greatest crisis, the Bear Stearns Board members worried first about their enormous bonuses, topping 25–35 million dollars annually, then as the investment firm buckled as its reputation failed, voiced concern for their "loyal employees". Finally pleading for U.S. government bailouts, they vaguely invoked patriotic commitments to the U.S. economy. But Bear Stearns' purpose in the everyday economy of Wall Street had nothing to do with jobs, wealth, or opportunities "trickling down" to the American people, especially those suffering at the bottom of a rapidly expanding class hierarchy; Bear Stearns worked only for its own sake, borrowing more and more money at an increasingly rapid rate for the sake of its balance sheet built on assets that, while substantial in their own right, increasingly appeared trivial when compared with the margin and other credit obligations of the firm. In the end, Bear Stearns was little more than its symbolic capital, which dwarfed its actual cash and material assets, and this symbolic capital could be sustained only by a reputation for ever-increasing growth that was unsustainable. Desperately trying to save the firm's reputation in the final weeks of its existence, Bear Stearns' executives seemed blithely unaware of the fact that their collapse was inevitable, whether sooner or later, according to the theory of surplus value.

Yet if late-modern capitalism is indeed collapsing, traditional Marxism is unlikely to reappear as a viable alternative. However vigorously the Left has challenged the bailouts and solutions to capitalism sponsored by Secretary of the Treasury Timothy Geithner and the Obama Administration as superficial efforts to address systemic problems, the Left still has not offered a socio-economic alternative to late-modern capitalism and its complement, the "war on terror". We may be witnessing the revival of the Keynesian economic policies tested in the most sustained way by Franklin Roosevelt, but Roosevelt's "New Deal" was not socialism, much less communism. As intellectuals, we need to remind people of the long history of efforts at collectivization, including its failures, and of the inherent relationship between collective labor and the basic social contract. At the same time, we need to revise dramatically the basic Marxian analysis of class divisions, class conflict, and industrial modernization.

Who today constitutes the "working class"? How is our labor alienated from us, and what are the processes of reification and other forms of mystification? What role does culture play in these "productive" processes of the late-modern or postmodern economy, and how have these economic practices reconfigured the global economy into a hierarchy of different national economies producing value in ways unimaginable to Karl Marx and Friedrich Engels? In many respects, our post-Marxian and neo-Marxian ideas remain too close to their modern sources.

How shall we do this work of criticizing the Obama Administration for continuing the imperial legacies of the U.S. state and propping up the rotten capitalist economy? American Studies is traditionally an activist field. We work for social change and greater justice in classrooms, at conferences, on the streets, on the web, and through the many political organizations to which we contribute. These activities are for most of us not discrete. We encourage our students to get involved in the causes they find compelling; we work more than most academics for "open classrooms" that include field work, community involvement, volunteer work, and internships as part of the course assignments. The meaning of cultural politics is not to be sought in a particular method but in the intersection of these activities in progressive politics committed to the demystification of such separate domains as politics, economics, education, and activism.

Traditional Marxism considered cultural practices to be epiphenomenal, part of the super-structural consequences of deeper economic processes. But culture is where value is defined and revised or sustained, especially in post-industrial societies in which cultural production is fundamental to their economies. Prevailing cultural values in U.S. culture make possible salaries for CEOs and celebrities in excess of 100 million dollars per year, as well as our tolerance of gun violence, pervasive poverty, inadequate health care, high unemployment, racism, sexism, and a host of other social failures. In this regard, the Myth-and-Symbol scholars were right to focus on cultural narratives that reified the most fantastic social inequities, even if the national myths they studied often spoke more to U.S. ideals than realities.

Cultural politics also refer to the processes through which the prevailing values of a society are internalized and lived by subjects who identify with the imagined community fashioned and reproduced by such narratives. Whether we mean the processes of interpellation through which subjects are managed by ideological state apparatuses, as Louis Althusser argued, or Slavoj Žižek's neo-Lacanian notions of internalization in post-ideological contexts, culture designates the symbolic system through which we constitute ourselves as subjects.[10] There is no "value" without culture; economic surplus, political power, personal identity, and social affiliation depend upon their deployment through the symbolic network we term "culture". Political critique is thus impossible without interpretation of this cultural matrix; analysis remains mere commentary on political particulars until it has taken into account how political practices rely on the rhetorical persuasion of culture.

Do such claims grant culture more importance than it deserves? Am I conflating culture with social, political, and economic forces that in fact operate according to their own rules and are merely *represented* in cultural systems? Such questions will always be debated, but my contention in this book is that at least since the 1960s, political and economic leaders have understood culture to be an essential field of power. Advertising in both political campaigns and the marketplace involves more than just winning votes and selling products, but providing the sort of legitimacy within an imagined community that grants the politician and corporation identity and authority. Of course without votes or sales, neither the politician nor the corporation would survive, but cultural circulation enables the sort of authority that promises re-election or the successful introduction of new products. Because subjects understand themselves primarily through cultural networks, culture can no longer be understood as merely a semiotic fantasy whose illusions can be dispelled but must be interpreted as fundamental to social, political, and personal relations. Cultural politics thus designates the interpretation of the cultural narratives that enable such fictions as the State, the market, the nation, and citizenship to be accepted as real. What matters in cultural politics is the articulation of a system of cultural representation that accomplishes a specific end or purpose, whose "value" may then be judged.

Such interpretations are not exclusively the work of scholars; representatives of the State, the market, the nation, and citizens offer frequent and competitive interpretations of this cultural narrative. We refer vaguely to "popular culture" and "mass media", sometimes merely to distinguish their works and forms from "high culture" and its specialized media. But such distinctions no longer have much relevance, except as vestigial traces of earlier periods defined by other media, such as print and orality. Contemporary scholars interpret cultural narratives along with other interpreters, all of whom compete for audiences. Don DeLillo's difficult novels differ from a performance by the Jonas Brothers; both their implied and actual audiences reflect these differences. But both forms of cultural representation exist on the same plane of "cultural politics": interpretations that situate their audiences in relation to an imagined community, market, and identity. As a medium, the Internet enables a wide range of different discursive, visual and aural practices, including avant-garde works targeting small audiences and others intended to reach the broadest possible market share.

The Cultural Politics of the New American Studies is thus an effort to comprehend these different interpretations in relation to the field of American Studies. In the exceptionalist understanding of "America" as a unique nation, this task would be difficult enough, but today we understand "American Studies" to encompass the different societies of the Western Hemisphere, their many different languages, the global intersections we identify loosely with the "Pacific Rim" and "Atlantic World", and the history of Western imperialisms and neo-imperialisms that continue to shape global realities.[11] *The Cultural Politics of the New American Studies* does not claim to deal with all of these issues and areas, because the discipline is no longer encyclopedic in its methods or scope. Instead, these many fields are understood in terms of their relevant intersections and historically significant contacts.

The chapters in this book are examples of the interpretations I have defined as "cultural politics", and they do a variety of activist work I try to identify in each chapter. The book is divided into two parts. Part I: Cultural Politics deals with issues and topics of immediate activist relevance. In this part, I ask how our work as scholars qualifies as "cultural politics", competing with the other, everyday acts of interpretation that construct the narratives of state, market, nation and citizen. Edward Said's dual role as a public intellectual and a distinguished scholar at a major university is used to introduce this part to encourage us to think anew about a distinction between these two social and political functions. Every scholar *is* a "public intellectual" in the digital era, but just what does this new role mean for those of us trained in the specific protocols of traditional scholarship?

In chapters two and three, I offer two personal examples of efforts to use scholarship to act in the public sphere in response to political crises: the First and Second Persian Gulf Wars, respectively. Although done in the spirit of Said's activism, my own efforts require a reinterpretation of Said's founding concept of "Orientalism" to understand better the transformation of Western Orientalism into the foreign policies of the U.S. as it justified the Vietnam War and then the First and Second Gulf Wars in relation to this "Vietnam-Effect". All three chapters suggest their mutual concern with the intellectual problem of interpreting U.S. nationalism in relation to Western imperialism and transnationalism. Chapter four turns from the activist questions of how we can best protest U.S. neo-imperialism to the more specific academic politics of the "area-studies" model for studying Latin America, Asia, and other regions. Recalling how the academic practices of area studies were developed by scholars, private foundations, and the U.S. state during World War II, I argue that some of the same issues facing us today in our protests of U.S. participation in foreign wars also haunt our academic disciplines. Nation and region-specific forms of knowledge may contribute, however unwittingly, to our imperial imaginary. "Cultural politics" thus includes critical accounts of the public sphere and academic protocols. It is not simply a question of choosing whether to demonstrate in the streets against war or write about the assumptions behind nation-specific knowledge, but of doing both in conjunction with each other.

Part II: Cultural Practices deals with more familiar cultural media: film and television (chapter 5), memoir and literary criticism (chapter 6), music (chapter 7), visual culture (chapter 8) and the novel (chapter 9). All of these media are in themselves instances of "cultural politics", so my interpretations do not depart from the focus on this topic in Part I. In Part II, I am also concerned with the conflict between nation-specific knowledge and global concerns, often arguing that the focus on the U.S. nation in a global era has had two troublesome consequences. In the aftermath of 9/11, U.S. nationalism has assumed a reactionary political quality that is curiously linked with an effort to internalize foreign problems. What I term in several chapters "hyper-nationalism" depends on the effort to import imaginatively foreign conflicts and render them in more manageable domestic terms: terrorism, religious intolerance, racism, sexism and class conflict. Many U.S. cultural works attempt to comprehend and imaginatively solve international problems by restaging them in U.S. national contexts. Tacitly such hyper-nationalism reinforces U.S. cultural and political imperialism by arguing that such domestic negotiations are models for the eventual and ideal democratization of other nations.

Alternatively, the popularity of an émigré writer's works in the U.S. is often motivated by our desire to recognize in such works a desire for U.S. citizenship and thus a validation of our social and political values. It is no coincidence that the émigré memoirs and novels of greatest interest to us come from the very regions where our national values are the most contested. The colonial subaltern who once reproduced the values of the imperial power in the colonized country has reappeared in U.S. neo-imperialism as a model citizen in the domestic U.S., testifying to the justice of contested foreign policies and rehabilitating old U.S. myths. Equally interesting is how older U.S. cultural narratives are interpreted by immigrant writers who have lived and worked both outside and inside the U.S. The vestigial colonialism in the European and U.S. literature Nafisi reads as a child in her upper-middle-class family in Tehran becomes a cultural source of freedom and rebellion in her adult opposition to the theocracy of the Republic of Iran. The flea-markets of Oakland are greeted by

Khaled Hosseini's Afghani characters in *The Kite Runner* as versions of the stands in the bazaars of Kabul before the rule of the Taliban.

Part II asks how we can criticize those cultural politics so deeply embedded in inherited behaviors, whether those of the immigrant to the U.S. or the U.S. citizen, whose identifications with a cultural narrative are crucial for their physical and psychological survival. The usual scholarly answers are still important: offer historical contexts and knowledge about all the communities involved; call attention to national myths and how they work and clarify cultural, religious and political differences. Yet there are limits to rational explanations, especially when the cultural narratives are powerful and venerable. As I suggest in chapter 7, alternative means must also be considered, including emotional, affective appeals, such as popular music makes, in order to challenge the emotive bonds we establish with the nation, market and identity. The nineteenth-century abolition of slavery would not have occurred without the powerful appeals that fugitive slave narratives, testimonies, and sentimental romances made to readers without direct experiences of slavery. By the same token, the mere appeal to feelings did not alone bring about the Emancipation Proclamation or the other legislation guaranteeing abolition. The coordination of different practices of cultural politics is thus a central subject of Part II.

Finally, the medium of this book is itself an important part of the cultural politics of the new American Studies. We are familiar with the ways late-modern capitalism has invaded all aspects of education. From incentive pay for and performance-related evaluations of teachers to charter schools and for-profit colleges and universities, education has become a business like any other in our own time. Extramurally funded research and criteria for promotion and tenure are closely tied to marketability, even in fields where the capitalist model makes little sense. Of course, education is *not* a business, even if the financial aspects of education are crucial for its success. Our products are not commodities, but human beings, whatever our specializations. Our success is not measured in test-scores, job security, or salaries, but in the quality of our students' minds and psyches. However vainglorious it may be to claim that we are trying to educate "good citizens", something of this ideal should guide our efforts, especially for those of us whose teaching and research focuses on the arts, humanities and social sciences. What better proof of our teaching and research can there be than the student who uses that knowledge to shape his or her social, economic, political and cultural experiences?

We should talk back to this corporatizing of the late-modern research university, in part because we have a better understanding of and greater access to the structures of academic power than most corporate administrators. We need, of course, to take the "American University" as an object of study in the new American Studies, and there are superb examples of such work already available from Bill Readings' *The University in Ruins* (1997) to Christopher Newfield's *Ivy and University: Business and the Making of the American University, 1880–1980* (2003) and *Unmaking the Public University: The Forty Year Assault on the Middle Class* (Harvard UP, 2008), work Newfield has acted upon by serving on the University of California's Budget and Planning Committee.[12] Readings and Newfield emphasize how the real problem in the late-modern university is not tenured radicals "politicizing" classrooms, but capitalism turning the university into a factory to produce new products and workers.

Politicized knowledge is far less dangerous than *capitalized* knowledge. Political positions and ideas can be debated and rejected, which is what occurs in most educational contexts. Irrational biases on the part of students and faculty can be evaluated negatively and when necessary protested as unjust, especially when our understanding of diverse political issues is crucial to historical, social, political and cultural education. *Economic* interests in education, excluding the study of Economics as a discipline, operate normally apart from pedagogy. Even the research that depends crucially upon funding is often separated from specific economic interests, even when the research is serving such ends. It is the *invisibility* of economic influence on teaching and scholarship that makes its power so insidious. While insisting upon the importance of "free inquiry" in both the classroom and laboratory, no college or university administrator would deny the necessity of extramural funding from government and private sources to assure fiscal stability.

Everyone knows that these funding sources regulate formally the ways we can use the funds and the kinds of projects that are supported. As long as we are paid salaries and benefits, we will be part of the economics of the contemporary university, but we can in fact work to resist the growing capitalization of knowledge and the economic valuation of such knowledge. One way to begin such work is to change the way we communicate our research to each other and the broader world. The time has come for us to abandon the vestigial elements of capitalism that govern the dissemination of our research and to make it accessible to everyone in the most affordable ways. *The Cultural Politics of the New American Studies* follows the model developed by Gary Hall in *Digitize This Book! The Politics of New Media or Why We Need Open Access Now* (2008), published in Kate Hayles' and Mark Poster's "Electronic Mediations" series by the University of Minnesota Press.[13]

I will not repeat here Hall's persuasive arguments, which are both theoretically sophisticated and practical responses to the crisis in scholarly publishing. My own volume is simply one contribution to Hall's larger project of "open access", but it is worth spelling out a few of the implications of this method of sharing knowledge in relation to the arguments of *The Cultural Politics of the New American Studies*. First, the publication of this book in digital format and its free availability to anyone who wishes to download it are acts of "cultural politics". As a political act, digital publication of a scholarly book seems a mere token gesture, hardly comparable to more serious activism. But the purpose of "open access" is not intended to compete with other acts of political activism, but merely to include the free dissemination of scholarly knowledge as one part of the work for greater social justice.

Will publishing the book on the Internet end global warfare, racism, or class inequities, or will it be accessible to the millions of people without any Internet access, computer hardware, or digital education? Of course not. But "open access" to scholarly knowledge has some immediate consequences worth considering. By refusing a market-based model for the success of our work, scholars can emphasize its intellectual purposes and make it available to a much larger potential audience. Will this *potential* audience have an impact on the sort of scholarship we produce? One of my purposes in this book is to suggest a much closer relationship between "high", "popular", and "mass" cultural work. These distinctions have been maintained largely by scholars, who have often placed the greatest value on "high" cultural work. The availability of our work to audiences outside strictly academic circles might change this hierarchy or at the very least prompt scholars to provide better justifications for their attention to high, popular, or mass cultural materials.

This book is also *not a book*. The chapters are revised essays, all of them published in journals, books and newspapers. In fact, this method of producing scholarly books in the humanities and social sciences is quite common. Few scholars have the luxury to write from start to finish a new book, despite the high value these fields place on the scholarly book. In most research universities and many liberal arts colleges, an Assistant Professor will not be promoted and tenured without a scholarly book, an Associate Professor not promoted without two or more scholarly books. Yet few scholars *read* new books from start to finish, unless we are reviewing the book in a journal. We surf other scholarly books, read chapters for class preparation or to write our own work, assemble parts of books with other essays for classroom readers, and in countless other ways "use" them.

Will you read this book from cover to cover, or will you download portions, speed-read others, ignore still more? How you use this book is up to your particular interests. I offer a sustained argument, offer several examples and thus demonstrate my ability to represent the sort of intellectual authority that justifies my work as a scholar-teacher. If we believe that our younger colleagues should still be asked to do such work of sustained argument and demonstrate their ability to disseminate that work in the seven years usually allowed for a tenure and promotion decision, then we should provide them with the means of sharing this work that are not tied exclusively to market conditions. Should "supply-and-demand" economics determine the fate of a Medievalist who has spent a decade earning a Ph.D. and has new work to share with well-trained specialists in his/ her field? Such scholarly communication will expose us even more than we are today to the Campus Watches of the world, as well as to those readers who take perverse satisfaction in our specialized, indecipherable prose. But it will also mobilize our scholarship in ways that will make it more responsive to the crises that every day demand our analytical and interpretive talents.

For Open Humanities Press and its equivalents to succeed, we will have to change the local academic protocols regarding the value of scholarship. What indeed is the difference between a refereed electronic book and a hardcopy or paperback book? Why must younger scholars compete in the marketplace of university or trade publishing to prove the value of their ideas? I want to suggest that we declare our scholarship free, distinct from corporate capitalism's valuation of everything, including intellectual property, and insist not just that you "steal this book!"—that worthy slogan of the 1960s—but that you *use* this book! Perhaps when prices for university press books drop from their now unaffordable heights to free downloads, we might read more of each others' work.

We might also find that our work participates more quickly and broadly in the new political and social movements facilitated by new technologies. Some will argue reasonably that we ought to remain apart from the political ferment of the present, offering the distance and perspective of careful deliberation, scholarly rigor, and documented evidence. But we have witnessed in the past how readily such scholarly distance has produced excess caution, in some cases ideological collaboration, that has contributed to the very terrors we had hoped knowledge would help us and our students overcome.

Cultural politics resulting in progressive social changes is the result of many different kinds of activities: traditional protest in the streets, social and political organization through the Internet, op-ed journalism, traditional scholarship in established journals and books, quickly deployed electronic scholarship in zines and new digital presses, popular music, film and television, visual and plastic arts and museum exhibitions. Rather than venerating those rare public intellectuals, like Edward Said, who have spoken the truth to power, every scholar should aspire to be a public intellectual, connecting his or her scholarship to the domestic and foreign policies that shape our lives every day. At the same time, scholars must be vigilant regarding the cultural politics employed to discourage progressive change, especially when it only pretends to advocate social equality and justice. The sites of power are no longer obvious; scholars can help map them and enable us all to challenge their authority.

I
Cultural Politics

CHAPTER 1

Edward Said and American Studies

How did exile become converted from a challenge
or a risk, or even from an active impingement on
[Auerbach's] selfhood, into a positive mission, whose
success would be a cultural act of great importance?

– Edward Said, *The World, the Text, and the Critic* (1983)

I first met Edward Said in 1976, when he came to the University of California, Irvine for what turned out to be one of many visits over the next twenty-five years. He was invited to Irvine primarily as a Critical Theorist, first by the School of Criticism and Theory, founded by Murray Krieger, and later by the Critical Theory Institute, a research group organized at Irvine in the early 1980s, for several occasional lectures, mini-seminars, and the 1989 Wellek Library Lectures. Several of the faculty members in the Critical Theory Institute, such as Alexander Gelley, Gabriele Schwab, J. Hillis Miller, and Wolfgang Iser were also in Comparative Literature, so Said's lectures and seminars usually drew a good proportion of Critical Theorists and Comparatists. Of course, Comparative Literature and Critical Theory were closely related at Irvine between 1975 and 2005, which may have been one of the many reasons we felt such close ties with Edward Said's work.

When Said delivered his Wellek Library Lectures on May 9, 10, and 11, 1989, he was Parr Professor of *English* and Comparative Literature at Columbia University, a fact lost on many people who viewed him primarily as a Comparatist and Critical Theorist.[14] Said's 1964 doctoral dissertation at Harvard was on "The Letters and Short Fiction of Joseph Conrad," and his subsequent writings include numerous essays and book chapters on major figures in nineteenth and twentieth-century English literature.[15]

Shakespeare, Milton, Defoe, Swift, Samuel Johnson, Sterne, Fielding, Blake, Austen, Wordsworth, Keats, Coleridge, George Eliot, Dickens, Gissing, Arnold, Hopkins, Hardy, Wilde, Shaw, Yeats, Conrad, Ford Madox Ford, Kipling, Joyce, T. E. Lawrence, and Orwell appear frequently in his books and essays. Even this partial list indicates both Said's thorough education in the elite literary culture of the modern Anglo-American university, often identified loosely with F. R. Leavis's *The Great Tradition* (1948), and the social criticism of an aesthetic ideology he drew from Swift, Sterne, Dickens, Gissing, Wilde, Shaw, and Conrad.

Yet when considered in terms of his contributions to American Studies and American literary study, Edward Said does not appear to figure centrally in fields secondary to his formal education in English and his increasing focus on non-European cultures, especially those constituting the Arab world, from *Orientalism* (1978) to the end of his career. Said refers frequently to T. S. Eliot and Henry James, especially in the early work *Beginnings: Intention and Method* (1975), but he treats both authors in keeping with their post-World War II incorporation into the English tradition.[16] Of the relatively few U.S. literary authors Said treats at any length, he quickly focuses on their scholarly reputations as representative Americans in order to link such exceptionalism with "the American quest for world sovereignty" (*R*, 364). His witty review of Ernest Hemingway's posthumously published *The Dangerous Summer* (1985)—Hemingway's return to the bullfighting culture he treated expertly in *Death in the Afternoon* (1932)—begins by invoking the platitude that "American writing" is distinguished by its "'how-to-ism,'" only to conclude that "the great problem of American writing" is that "the shock of recognition derived from knowledge and converted into how-to-ism can only occur once [...]. The second time around, it is dragged into the market" and commercialized.[17] Said is referring explicitly to the inferiority of *The Dangerous Summer* to the earlier *Death in the Afternoon*, but he is also arguing that the distinctiveness of Hemingway's identity is more an effect of the market than of his ineffable representation of American masculinity.

In his "Introduction" to the 1991 Vintage paperback of *Moby-Dick*, Said also focuses on American exceptionalism, agreeing with "Leon Howard, Newton Arvin, and Michael Paul Rogin" that "the irreducibly American quality of his life and work" (*R*, 358) distinguishes Melville's reputation and confirms the scholarly cliché that *Moby-Dick* is "the greatest and most eccentric work of literary art produced in the United States" (*R*, 356). Having paid homage to the Americanists, Said stresses *Moby-Dick*'s "Euripidean" plot and "connections to Homer, Dante, Bunyan, Cervantes, Goethe, Smollett," proceeding to an extended comparison of Melville and Conrad (*R*, 356, 358–359). Putting Melville in the comparative contexts of Europe and America, Said can then problematize the exceptionalist model of American literature by claiming: "I suppose it is true to say that only an American could have written *Moby-Dick*, if we mean by that only an author as prodigiously endowed as Melville could also have been, as an American, so obsessed with the range of human possibility" (*R*, 358). Said's rhetorical qualifications cause the reader to hesitate as well, so that the fiction of Melville's "Americanness" is effectively replaced by what Said concludes are the inherently transnational qualities of *Moby-Dick*: "The tremendous energies of this magnificent story of hunting the White Whale spill over national, aesthetic, and historical boundaries with massive force" (*R*, 358).

Another good example of how Said deconstructs American exceptionalism is his interpretation of R. P. Blackmur. Said views Blackmur's focus on "consciousness" in Henry James as symptomatic of Blackmur's own struggle to legitimate his authority "as a teacher, critic, and cultural force at Princeton right after World War Two" (*R*, 261), especially in an anti-intellectual and anti-aesthetic society that "obligates the artist" to realize imaginatively the whole cultural fabric "no longer carried by social institutions" (*R*, 260). Said also argues that the Jamesian sensibility or fine conscience that so appealed to Blackmur was part of that civilized heritage the American had to take up in the postwar period as part of a vaguely defined "American responsibility for the world after the dismantling of the old imperial structures" (*R*, 261). Said can thus identify "the imperialism latent in [Blackmur's] sense of the American creation of a new consciousness" while brilliantly diagnosing Blackmur's skepticism as a reaction to this new version of the white man's (call it the *American's*) burden: "All [Blackmur's] portraits of intellectuals and artists in the world are either morose, severely judgmental, or downright pessimistic: his lifelong fascination with Henry Adams is the strongest case in point" (*R*, 261–262).[18]

Taken by themselves, Said's writings on American authors and critics do not constitute a major contribution to American Studies, but weaving through even his earliest references to the U.S. is his central concern with the rise of the American Empire. Said's definition and criticism of U.S. imperialism developed throughout his career, and there are notable omissions and oddities in the ways he interprets the rise of the U.S. global hegemony. *Orientalism* is the work most frequently cited as a model for new American Studies committed to the critical study of the U.S. as an imperial power, but Said's classic work relatively backgrounds the complex nineteenth-century history of U.S. political, economic, and cultural involvements in the South Pacific, Japan, China, Africa, and the Arab world. Said's most sustained discussion of this history occurs in the final chapter, "Orientalism Now", where he emphasizes how "during the nineteenth century the United States was concerned with the Orient in ways that prepared for its later, overtly imperial concern" and proceeds to a brief discussion of "the founding of the American Oriental Society in 1842".[19] Said's criticism of imperialism in *Orientalism* focuses on the great *European* imperial powers of the eighteenth and nineteenth centuries—England, France, Spain, and Portugal—to understand in part the historical legacies and foreign policies taken over by the United States in the twentieth century. Said often characterized *Orientalism* as part of his own anti-war response to U.S. involvement in Vietnam, including his endorsement of Noam Chomsky's critique of the "instrumental connection between the Vietnam War and the notion of objective scholarship as it was applied to cover state-sponsored military research" (*O*, 11).[20] Nevertheless, the general argument of *Orientalism* stresses U.S. imperialism as a twentieth-century development, despite the substantial, even defining scholarship in American Studies of the late 1960s and early 1970s that studied the "internal colonialism" of slavery, Native American genocide, Manifest Destiny, and sustained conflicts with other colonial powers in North America such as Spain, France, Great Britain and Mexico.

Fifteen years after *Orientalism*, Said refers in *Culture and Imperialism* (1993) to an "imperial motif" that rivals "the European one" in nineteenth-century America and how such U.S. imperialism has been "memorably studied by Richard Slotkin, Patricia Limerick, and Michael Paul Rogin".[21] American Studies scholars could add many names to Said's

1993 list, including Ronald Takaki, Richard Drinnon, Robert Berkhofer, Reginald Horsman, and Annette Kolodny, but it is fair to conclude that *Culture and Imperialism* takes more seriously than *Orientalism* the study of how U.S. racial, gender, ethnic, and regional categories legitimated traditional imperialism. It might also be the case that Said's relative neglect in *Orientalism* of nineteenth-century U.S. imperialism, including the substantial scholarship done on the U.S. as an "internal colonizer", may have provided motivation for new scholarship in American Studies that since 1993 has focused increasingly on the relationship between internal and external modes of territorial expansion, economic exploitation, population control and cultural legitimation. Amy Kaplan acknowledges just this sort of indirect influence in the opening chapter of *The Anarchy of Empire in United States Culture* (2002): "I am indebted to Edward Said's *Culture and Imperialism* [...] which powerfully shows how the treasures of high culture in Europe bear the traces of their foundation in a remote geography of imperial violence".[22]

Culture and Imperialism certainly pays much greater attention to U.S. imperialism (and American Studies scholarship on this subject) than *Orientalism*, but Said's identification of the U.S. with neo-imperialism in the aftermath of decolonization is consistent in both works. "Freedom from Domination in the Future" is the final chapter of *Culture and Imperialism*, and it begins with "American Ascendancy: The Public Space at War", which deals primarily with U.S. global hegemony as it took shape in the post-World War II period (*CI*, 283–303). To be sure, Said makes references to earlier instances of U.S. imperialism, including the territorial expansion of Manifest Destiny and "offshore experiences [...] from the North African coast to the Philippines, China, Hawaii, and [...] the Caribbean and Central America" (289), as well as to "anti-imperialists like Mark Twain, William James, and Randolph Bourne" (287). But the explicitly utopian project of political reform Said proposes in his final chapter is set firmly in contrast to "the depressing truth" that cultural anti-imperialism "has not been effective" from the Spanish-American and Philippine-American Wars to Desert Storm, the military action that haunts the final pages of *Culture and Imperialism* with Said's awareness that: "Such views as opposed the United States attack on Iraq did nothing at all to stop, postpone, or lessen its horrendous force" (287).

Even Said's brief "A Note on Modernism" in *Culture and Imperialism* follows his periodization of traditional imperialism with primarily the British and French (and to a lesser extent imperial powers of Spain and Portugal who are in "decline" in the nineteenth century) and neo-imperialism with the U.S. (*CI*, 186–190). His version of cultural modernism does not go very far beyond the Anglo-Irish-Franco version he considers at greater length in *Beginnings*. Conrad, Forster, Joyce, Woolf, T. E. Lawrence, Malraux, Proust, Picasso, T. S. Eliot, Pound, and Thomas Mann (a nod to German colonialism) are Said's representatives of the cosmopolitan modernism that ambivalently represented non-European cultures either in conjunction with or as contesting the European will to global power (188–189). In these contexts, T. S. Eliot and Pound figure for Said less as "American" writers than as major figures in such cosmopolitanism, an assumption reinforced by their own carefully cultivated expatriate identities as British and Italian, respectively.

Edward Said is often named as the "founder" of Postcolonial Studies, a claim that has troubled me even as I acknowledge Said's great importance in advancing Postcolonial Studies as a diverse set of methodologies and overlapping, sometimes contentious, studies of different areas and groups, especially in the non-European and non-U.S. "peripheries" where the majority of the world's population lives and in many cases barely survives. In recent years and certainly influenced in part by Said's work, Postcolonial Studies has become a central methodology and topic of debate within the changing field of American Studies. Beginning with Lawrence Buell's "Are We Post-American Studies?" (1996) and including the essays in C. Richard King's *Postcolonial America* (2000) and in my *Post-Nationalist American Studies* (2000), discussions of how American and Postcolonial Studies can be related have been among the most lively and contentious in the academy.[23] In *The New American Studies* (2002), I offer my own analyses and solutions to these problems, because I believe that the future of both fields are crucially related and that mistaken efforts to struggle with each other for institutional power and space may have unexpectedly negative consequences for both fields.[24]

Said's ambivalent relationship to the history of Postcolonial Studies is instructive for those scholars interested in articulating a closer relationship between American Studies and Postcolonial Studies. One of the most important sources for Postcolonial Studies is the work done by South Asian scholars in groups like the Subaltern Studies Group of Historians, which has close affiliations with politically activist groups, including Marxist and feminist organizations. *Culture and Imperialism* cites the work of some Postcolonial Studies scholars, but Said pays scant attention to feminism and repeats his traditional distrust of Marxist politics. *Orientalism* is predicated on the European "feminization" of the "Orient", as well as the projection of European homophobia onto the "exotic East", but throughout his career Said acknowledges feminism more gesturally than substantially, rarely mentions gay studies and queer theories, and registers frequently his commitments to Marxian theories but his distrust of Marxian practice. As early as 1982, Gayatri Spivak challenged Said to take more seriously both feminism and post- or neo-Marxian theories by contending that Said's "calls for a criticism that would account for 'quotidian politics and the struggle for power'" must be supplemented by "feminist hermeneutics", which already "articulate the relationship between phallocracy and capital, as well as that between phallocracy and the organized Left".[25] In *The World, the Text, and the Critic* (1983), Said could admire Marx's *The Eighteenth Brumaire of Louis Bonaparte* as "brilliant and [...] compelling" while distancing himself from "Marxism" as just another label that inhibits the freedom of "critical consciousness".[26]

My uneasiness with the identification of Said as the origin of Postcolonial Studies stems in part from Said's own cultivation of his role as a Gramscian "organic intellectual", whose critical function Said identified in the early 1980s as operating "in that potential space inside civil society, acting on behalf of those alternative acts and alternative intentions whose advancement is a fundamental human and intellectual obligation" (*WTC*, 30). In my view, Said grafted Gramsci's organic intellectual with the modernist "cosmopolitan" in an effort to salvage an independent, often elite, metropolitan "critical consciousness" that became increasingly untenable in the light of poststructuralist critiques of the subject, postcolonial calls for collaborative multidisciplinary scholarship and political coalitions, and cultural studies' criticisms of the aesthetic ideology and its cult of "genius". In 1997, Said criticized Postcolonialism for "the realization of militant nationalism and of nation-states in which dictators [...] speak the language of self-determination and liberation". Under these circumstances, Said prefers the alternative "of the intellectual whose vocation is to speak the truth to power, to reject the official discourse of orthodoxy and authority, and to exist through irony and skepticism, [...] trying to articulate the silent testimony of lived suffering and stifled experience" (R, 526).

Said always stresses how his own transnational experiences help him shape an identity strategically "out of place", to borrow from the title of his autobiography, and thus capable of a "worldly" perspective often unavailable to intellectuals rooted in specific national or other social locations. In the concluding paragraph of *Out of Place*, Said turns such an outlook into an ontological category: "I occasionally experience myself as a cluster of flowing currents. I prefer this to the idea of a solid self, the identity to which so many attach so much significance. These currents .[...] are 'off' and may be out of place, but at least they are always in motion, in time, in place, in the form of all kinds of strange combinations [...]. A form of freedom, I'd like to think, even if I am far from being totally convinced that it is".[27] Said often found such worldliness in the best literature, comparative scholarship, and in strong predecessors, notably Erich Auerbach, but in ways that sometimes threatened to gloss over the very different historical, cultural, and sociopolitical circumstances involved (WTC, 5–9).[28] Said never explicitly connected this cosmopolitanism with Americanness or even with modernism, but it has very strong roots both in the myth of American selfhood criticized effectively by the American myth critics and in American expatriates' careful cultivation of their "otherness" abroad.

Many of Said's models for such cosmopolitanism were friends and colleagues at Columbia identified with the New York intellectuals.[29] Said's collection of essays, *Reflections on Exile and Other Essays*, is dedicated "To the memory of F. W. Dupee" and opens with a testament to their friendship, especially Dupee's "radical and open spirit" and his encouragement of Said's "interest in the new styles of French theorizing, in experimental fiction and poetry" (R, xiii). Although he acknowledges his "great affection for Trilling as an older colleague and friend", Said clearly includes Lionel Trilling with those New York intellectuals "among whose worst features were [...] a tiresome narcissism and a fatal propensity to self-important, rightward-tending shifts", as well as an "Anglophilia so endemic to the New York intellectual style" (xiii).[30] In contrast, Said represents Dupee as a left intellectual, committed to the "radical, anti-authoritarian politics of his early Trotskyist years", even though Dupee's scholarship and teaching in the years Said knew him certainly followed the high-cultural model of many other New York intellectuals (xiii). As a scholar, Dupee is certainly best remembered for his 1951 contribution to the "American Men of Letters" series, *Henry James: His Life and Writings*, which played a major part in the post-World War II revival of Henry James as central in the American literary tradition.[31] Nevertheless, it is "Fred Dupee who after 1967, when the great Arab debacle occurred, supported me in my lonely fight on behalf of the Palestinian cause", and "Dupee and his wife Andy were the only friends from my academic New York life ever actually to pay me a visit in Beirut, at that time (fall 1972) the center of revolutionary politics in the Middle East" (xiii).

Said's testament to his friendship with the Dupees is unquestionably personal and sincere, but it is also a means for Said to acknowledge his affiliation with the New York intellectuals while distancing himself from their Eurocentric cultural interests and conservative politics. The same conclusion might be drawn more broadly with respect to Said's frequent praise for New York City as "today [...] what Paris was a hundred years ago, the capital of our time", due largely to "its eccentricity and the peculiar mix of its attributes", especially as it contributes to his own sense of being "out of place" (*R*, xi). Remarkably, Said's admiration of Fred Dupee and his love of New York follow the logic of filiation and affiliation he analyzed so brilliantly in "Secular Criticism": "If a filial relationship was held together by natural bonds and natural forms of authority—involving obedience, fear, love, respect, and instinctual conflict—the new affiliative relationship changes these bonds into what seem to be transpersonal forms—such as guild consciousness, consensus, collegiality, professional respect, class, and the hegemony of the dominant culture" (*WTC*, 20).

I have focused thus far on how Edward Said ambivalently worked within the EuroAmerican worlds of culture, history, and higher education he so effectively criticized in his major writings. Succeeding within those systems was, of course, crucial for his critical consciousness, and his role as a public intellectual cannot be understood without analyzing his affiliations with the EuroAmerican modernists, the New York intellectuals, myths of the "American Adam," and the "traveling theory" that found such a welcome in the U.S. academy of the 1970s and 1980s. Much of Said's "critical consciousness" was thus deeply "American", just as he was himself not only a sometime scholar of American literature and culture but personally, existentially, and legally American. Indeed, his celebrity was also curiously and sometimes troublingly American, insofar as the international community of scholars both loved and reviled him for his ability to operate successfully within the specialized discourses of the university and still respond in several different mass and popular media. Said exemplified the ways the Enlightenment's cult of genius changed into one of celebrity in the postmodern era, and along the way how this transformation became closely identified with the American commercialism Said satirizes so eloquently in his essay on Hemingway, "How Not to Get Gored" (R, 238).

Scholars admired or condemned Said precisely because he was expected to assume the responsibilities of communicating our knowledge to the general public and of translating intellectual debates into public, even foreign, policies. Edward Said did this work brilliantly, but he also became the academy's sacrificial figure, far too charismatic in our imaginations for us ever to match his accomplishments and far too dangerous in his political actions for us to emulate. W. J. T. Mitchell points out in "Remembering Edward Said" that "Edward's public appearances were plagued by death threats that he dismissed (along with his cancer) as an annoying distraction, and (even worse) by questioners who wanted to lure him into anti-Semitic comments, or to characterize his criticisms of Israel as expressions of anti-Semitism".[32] Said was unquestionably courageous in the ways he responded to public, often dangerous, criticism and in the positive ways he responded to his Leukemia, but we also fitted to him the mask of mythic heroism in part to avoid our own responsibilities as intellectuals to carry our knowledge to a wider audience and to endure the eccentric responses such wisdom so often provokes. There are, of course, many other public intellectuals who have achieved their reputations in part as consequences of their distinguished scholarship, yet few achieved the sort of celebrity that in the case of Edward Said was a distinctively American version of sacrificial success.

The dangers of this cult of academic celebrity are underscored by the continuing debates regarding academic freedom and legislative efforts to limit such freedom, often on the grounds that "politics" do not "belong" in the classroom. The recent legislation in Arizona directed at undocumented workers included a bill banning Chicano/a Studies in the Tucson public schools on the grounds of its "anti-Americanism". In 2003–2004, there was considerable debate in Congress over H.R. 3077, the resolution popularly known as Congress's effort to "regulate postcolonial studies".[33] Passed by the House of Representatives on October 24, 2003, H. R. 3077 languished in a Senate subcommittee before quietly dying in 2004. The bill grew in part out of efforts by Martin Kramer's Middle East Forum and Daniel Pipe's Campus Watch to repress what these neo-conservatives consider the politicizing of knowledge by area studies and Postcolonial Studies. The Congressional hearings were viewed by many intellectuals as a new stage in the federal government's censorship under the guise of "national security". Named several times as the "founder of Postcolonial Studies" in Stanley Kurtz's report to the Subcommittee, Edward Said and *Orientalism* are central examples of what Kurtz terms the "anti-Americanism" now taught in U.S. universities. Kurtz, a "well known partisan from the Hoover Institute and *National Review*", recommends U.S. government regulation of "the Title VI funds given over to universities of the study of the rest of the world" (Prashad). The ease with which Kurtz incorrectly identifies Said as the "founder" of Postcolonial Studies and suggests thereby a conspiracy controlled by a single intellectual is what troubles me. New government interference in intellectual life has already resulted from the Bush Administration's appeals for "anti-terrorist" and new "Homeland Security", with or without scapegoats like Edward Said, but the ability of uninformed neo-conservatives to mount successful attacks of this sort hinge on their rhetoric of paranoia and conspiracy. How much better might it have been for Postcolonial and Area Studies had Kurtz been unable to single out the "perpetrators", because so many scholars had shared openly these paradigms of knowledge? In short, what would have happened if we had all said: "Yes, we are all Postcolonial scholars"?

Said's fame is based less on his arguments in such major academic books as *Beginnings, Orientalism,* and *Culture and Imperialism,* few of which have been read by Said's most vituperative public critics, than on his advocacy of the politics of self-determination and cultural representation by the peoples of the Arab world. Within this world, there are of course Said's own Egyptian, Palestinian, and Lebanese filiations; he has argued vigorously on behalf of the Palestinians' rights to their own homeland and accompanying economic, political, and cultural autonomy. In this respect, he has criticized consistently and coherently U.S. foreign policies that have unilaterally supported Israeli imperialism toward the Palestinian people, especially evident in the conduct of the Israeli government and its military in the current crisis. One of the consequences of the internationalizing of American Studies as a discipline is that we must take responsibility for the conduct of the U.S. outside its borders, and Said's advocacy of Palestinian rights generally includes his criticism of U.S. governmental policies, media representations of Palestinians primarily as "terrorists", and Orientalist scholarship that have contributed to the current undeclared war between Israel and Palestine.[34]

Said's extensive scholarship and journalism on the politics and cultures of the Arab world reach back to the beginnings of his career with the publication in 1970 of "The Palestinian Experience" and "A Palestinian Voice".[35] Assessing Said's work in Middle Eastern Studies and political journalism over thirty-three years will take the research skills and background knowledge of scholars with qualifications in those fields, but even before such work is done American Studies scholars can learn much from Said's comparative studies of the U.S., Arab, and Israeli political and cultural contexts. In 1979, he wrote prophetically: "I do not recall a period in recent Arab history when there has been so widespread, so sustained, and so anguished an interest in the United States. Beneath all this interest there is of course the undisputed fact that America and American interests touch Arab lives with an intrusive immediacy".[36] A common criticism of the broadening of American Studies to include both the work of international scholars and considerations of the U.S. as a global power is that we cannot cover "everything" in our curricula and scholarly projects. Yet the assumption that the study of the U.S. in its connections with other nations, peoples and regions must somehow be done by each individual scholar or exclusively organized by American Studies programs and curricula is refuted by the work of many scholars responding to Said's provocations for a new understanding of our relations with the Arab world.

In the post-nationalist era we have already entered, characterized as much by neo-nationalist struggles as it is by a dizzying array of transnational dangers and hopes, the comparatism Edward Said exemplified in his public persona and his distinguished career should be the work of many different scholars, coming from many, increasingly overlapping disciplines such as American Studies, Middle Eastern Studies, Comparative Religions, History, Comparative Literature, Philosophy, Political Science, Anthropology, and Foreign Language departments. Their work ought to be diverse and contentious, but the goal should be certain intellectual coalitions essential for a new liberal education global in scope. Another goal should be the development of public policies that might confirm or challenge the knowledge of government sponsored experts on all sides. In short, we might work toward these difficult but imaginable collaborative ends as a way of replacing the singular celebrity of Edward Said with the more collective and diverse voices of professional intellectuals willing to take greater responsibility for the world in which they live. If we continue to work in the directions already suggested by Said's work and in the rich scholarship of Postcolonial Studies, Cultural Studies, and the new American Studies, we will remember Edward W. Said in the best way possible: as the teacher who encouraged us to go beyond his work.

In this spirit, I turn now to the development of an "American Orientalism" Said may have anticipated but did not live to witness in its current state, particularly manifest in the troubling Islamophobia evident in certain areas of contemporary U.S. society. The recent debates about the construction of an Islamic Center two blocks from "ground zero" in Manhattan, recently entangled with plans by a small-town preacher in Central Florida to burn Korans on 9/11 in protest against Islamic terrorists, are troubling examples of how polarized the U.S. and the Islamic world have become. My purpose is to suggest that Edward Said's contributions to American Studies are more than merely disciplinary and certainly more important than what he might have occasionally said about Henry James, Ernest Hemingway, and T. S. Eliot. Said's legacy for the new American Studies and its cultural politics must be understood as his elaboration of key ideas for our understanding of the U.S. as a global power deeply involved in the politics of the Middle East. By the same token, Said should not be treated as an omniscient prophet; American Orientalism is not merely an extension and elaboration of the European version Said interpreted so well in *Orientalism* and other scholarly and journalistic works. When Said died on September 25, 2003, the Second Gulf War had been officially declared over and our military "mission accomplished" in President George W. Bush's infamous speech on May 1, 2003, even though the U.S. military occupation of Iraq would last another seven years. Said certainly recognized Bush's military bravura and our unjustified invasion in the search for elusive "weapons of mass destruction" as the causes of the civil war that would break out in Iraq and the breakdown of civil society that would cause hundreds of thousands of Iraqis to die in sectarian violence and millions to flee the country. For Said, it was a familiar story in the history of Western imperialism in the region.

Said did predict how traditional U.S. imperialism would metamorphose into neo-imperialism from the First Gulf War to the Bush Administration's postulation of a "Great Middle East", balanced and secured by our disastrous invasion and occupation of Iraq in the Second Gulf War. This "new Orient" follows historically the paths of European colonialism in the Middle East, especially in the build-up and aftermath of colonial struggles in North Africa and the Middle East surrounding the construction of the Suez Canal, which opened in 1869, the balance-of-power European and Ottoman Empire politics negotiated in the region in the World War I era, and the first major foreign exploitation of Middle Eastern oil resources in the 1920s. Gun-boat diplomacy, spheres of political influence, such as the British Mandate in Palestine, commercial opportunism of first world nations disguised by the rhetoric of modern "development" and "free-trade" capitalism such as Standard Oil and British Petroleum relied upon, have merely been extended by the U.S. over the past two decades in typically "Orientalist" ways.

Said also understood how this imperial legacy shaped the current stalemate between the state of Israel and Palestine, as well as such immediate neighbors as Egypt, Lebanon, Jordan and Syria—a political stalemate virtually guaranteed by the territorial fractures that have made distinct national sovereignties in the region impossible to define, much less maintain. "Imperialism is finally about land," Said writes in *Culture and Impe-*

rialism, insisting upon an imperial bed-rock we are warned never to forget (*CI*, xii-xiii). A mere glance at a map of the distribution of Israeli and Arab communities in Israel and Palestine's divided territories makes clear how impossible any simple division of the region into Israel and Palestine would be, reminding us perhaps why Palestinian politicians in 1948 rejected the apparently common-sense solution of "partitioning" two distinct nations. Whatever successful solution is achieved will involve new conceptions of "national borders", changing notions of the self-containment and territorial autonomy of the nation-state.

But there are limits to the mere extension of the traditional imperialist model to the neo-imperialism of the contemporary U.S., which certainly dates from the Vietnam War (1965–1975). Said's insistence upon the irreducible "reality" of land as the object of imperialism's desire may also mark the limitation of his thoroughly *modern* conception of Orientalism as a key strategy of Western imperialism. In exposing how Orientalism disguised the basic land-grabs of European imperialists, Said imagined a relatively straightforward demystification of the Western discursive practices—scholarship, literature, visual arts, news media, et al.—that otherwise masked or disguised the real political situation in the Middle East. Feminized, marginalized, minoritized and above all linguistically and culturally excluded from this Western discourse, Arabic culture needed primarily to be reasserted in its venerable authority, both as it had informed and shaped the West and as it continued to represent itself in ways simply distorted and repressed in the willful misreadings of the West. Taking upon himself this task as cultural translator and demystifier, Said cast himself in the role of anti-imperialist critic of a West whose cultural protocols he understood at the professional level of a trained European Comparatist and Continental theorist.

Today, "covering Islam" has assumed some different modes not completely anticipated by Said that transform our understanding of what must be termed a "neo-Orientalism" manipulated by the U.S. State that draws only in part from traditional Western Orientalism, itself primarily the work of European imperialism. I will consider a few of these new modalities under a single, roughly formulated heading: the internalization of the traditional "Orient" within the U.S. nation. I prefer this description to "Americanization", itself an older form of cultural importation within the history of U.S. imperialism, because I think this process has some new features that differ from "Americanization" in the simplest sense, notably a complex and contradictory use of the "nation" by hegemonic powers that are themselves self-consciously transnational and global. Said certainly understood nineteenth-century European Orientalism to be a projection of Europe's own unconscious anxieties about the foreign, the feminine, the sexual, the racial and the irrational "other". Said objected to deconstruction and post-structuralism in general, but he himself "deconstructed" these "others" to expose the European psychosis, whose principal symptom must be its incurable, unsatisfiable imperialist desire.

But Said's criticism of Orientalism reaches its limit when confronted by such cultural productions as John Walker Lindh, "the American Taliban", and Azar Nafisi, the American Iranian; the former a convicted and imprisoned "enemy combatant" (legally, *not* a "terrorist," or else he would be in Guantanamo, probably untried, at this very moment), and the other a new "patriot" for both U.S. and Iran, perhaps even that inconceivable "transnational" entity, "American Iran". I consider both Lindh and Nafisi in their own terms in chapters five and six, respectively, but I want to use them here to exemplify the neo-Orientalism Said did not quite comprehend. Lindh draws the "new Orient" into the otherwise disparate field of "domestic terrorism", condensing David Koresh, Timothy McVeigh, Ruby Ridge (Idaho) secessionists with Middle Eastern, Islamic radicalism. Today, that relation has morphed to include Left politics' anti-imperialist struggle in the anti-Vietnam War movement and thus tacitly the anti-war movements against the immoral wars in Iraq and Afghanistan. Sarah Palin's resurrection of Barack Obama's association with William Ayres during the 2008 Presidential Campaign is symptomatic of how Obama's "criticism" of America and the Second Gulf War condenses the Weather Underground Ayres co-founded in the 1960s and the anti-Vietnam War politics it served with a more general anti-American "hatred" that improbably links critical positions as different as critical American Studies as a discipline, anti-Gulf War protests, such as MoveOn.org has sponsored, and neo-Nazi and radical Libertarian groups committed to American isolationism and racial purity. It would do no good to protest that such radical movements in the U.S., only some of which have been labeled "domestic terrorism", usually depend upon their profound patriotism, insisting that whatever criticism they advocate is necessary for a functional democracy.

Lindh posed a far greater threat to U.S. state authority because he refused that democratic and national universe of discourse. As a consequence, he had to be ideologically neutralized by infantilizing him and offering him a "lenient" sentence that further testified to his "adolescent" rebellion against Yuppie parents, Bay Area permissiveness, and other "symptoms" of a post-Vietnam generation that could not adequately parent because its members had themselves "never grown up". The familiar neo-conservative explanation of anti-Vietnam War protest, such as Paul Berman has claimed in *A Tale of Two Utopics* (1996) and its sequel *Power and the Idealists* (2005), dismisses strong criticism of foreign policy, imperialism, and unjustified warfare as "childish", out of touch with the "real world" and the presumed "Realpolitik" of U.S. military and economic policies around the globe. To be sure, the conflation of the "Orient" (Yemen and Afghanistan in the case of Lindh) with "infantilism" recalls sophisticated Hegelian theories of historical "development" from the "infant" East through the adolescence of Egypt to Greco-Roman young adults and the full maturity of German idealist philosophers, like Hegel himself. Lindh's domestication of Islamic radicalism turns on his adolescent rebellion against Western "modernity and development", a regressive gesture through which "he" displaces and incorporates Arabic, Afghani, Yemeni, and other "Oriental" social institutions and Islam, embodying this "new Orient" in the uncanny figure of the bearded Bay Area youth in the U.S. courtroom, once again confusing anti-Vietnam War hippies with radical Islam.

Another version of this misrecognition is the emigré Middle Eastern writer, Azar Nafisi, whose authority in *Reading Lolita in Tehran* (2003) is presumed to be that of a "native informant", familiar with the political and social history of Iran in the aftermath of the Shah's brutal rule. Nafisi is, of course, just one of numerous emigré writers who have capitalized on such eye-witness accounts, including the equally celebrated Khaled Hosseini, whose *The Kite Runner* (2003) is supposed to give us an insider's account of Afghanistan from the pre-Soviet era to the Taliban's rule. Of course, eye-witnesses are always to be judged skeptically, especially when we are considering politically conflicted societies irreducible to a single, representative perspective. Often enough the actual authority of the non-Western native is *Western*, threatening native credentials. Nafisi's authority is actually that of the Ph.D. in English literature she earned from the University of Oklahoma, not her ability to do the sort of social ethnography of modern Iran we identify with the new cultural geographers and anthropologists.

Traditional imperialism produces subalterns by shaping them in the mould of the cultural and social values of the metropolitan center of Empire. Nafisi and Hosseini carry this tradition further by adopting those values in active ways to construct a "representative" Iranian-American and Afghani-American, each of whom represents the utopian ideal of citizenship for Iran or Afghanistan *after* democratization. Of course, the political precondition for such democratization is military invasion and occupation, so that such utopian fantasies are always already predicated on U.S. imperial expansion. Nafisi and Hosseini represent traditional "assimilationist ideals", but neither author ever "forgets" his or her native culture as assimilated minorities are expected to do. Instead, these new subalterns actively construct fantastic Iranian and Afghani "cultures" *inside* the U.S., both in their English-language books (and among their primarily Anglo-American audiences) and in their special valorization of Iranian or Afghani refugee communities in the U.S. as models for those who will eventually "return" to their homelands.

A third version of this internalization of the Orient is the adaptation of mythic national narratives and archetypes to new foreign ventures in the Middle East, such as the various interpretations of Jessica Lynch in the context of Puritan captivity narratives and the condensation of domestic frontier conflicts with the Second Gulf War. To be sure, later developments, including Lynch's own repudiation of events and the melodrama of her heroic rescue by the U.S. military, have done much to challenge this national mythopoeia, but the speed with which Jessica Lynch was in fact adapted and adopted to domestic concerns is symptomatic of my general conception of the "U.S. nationalization of international crises" as means of containing and controlling those crises. The U.S. fascination with the fate of Patrick Daniel "Pat" Tillman (1976–2004), killed in Afghanistan by "friendly fire", may suggest that ideological complications, even contradictions, contribute to the new mythopoeia.[37] Both Jessica

Lynch and Pat Tillman remain figures of interest as long as they continue to represent the contradictions of the Second Gulf War and our ongoing war in Afghanistan, and they do so by bringing these wars "home" in all their unresolved political complications.

The broader cultural narrative is the Vietnam-Effect in both Gulf Wars and Afghanistan, whereby our ventures in one "Orient" (Southeast Asia) appears to condition our later policies in two other, very different "Orients" (Iraq and Afghanistan), confusing the three regions by mere nominal association. The "Vietnam-Effect" says it is all about us, not *them*, whether Iraqis, Afghanis, Vietnamese, Laotians, or Cambodians, so that we can readily transfer key terms, the operative metaphors of imperial poetics, from one domain to another without experiencing cognitive dissonance: quagmire (Vietnam and First Gulf War), dominoes (Southeast Asia and Afghanistan/ Pakistan), yellow ribbons (POW/ MIA and the VVA and Gulf vets), PTSD, Agent Orange and Gulf War Syndrome. Of course, these social psychological practices of projection and substitution are crucial to nineteenth-century European Orientalism, which began with its own fantasies of the exotic "East" and substituted such fictions for regions neither "eastern" nor "Oriental".

The difference of the new Orientalism is the self-conscious importation of these fantasies. In the nineteenth-century imaginary, distance was a crucial factor, which preserved the exoticism of distant lands and peoples, especially important when people from those lands had immigrated to the metropolitan centers of the empire. But today U.S. neo-imperialism depends upon rendering familiar the distant and exotic, especially their imaginary qualities, incorporating them into that powerful U.S. myth of assimilation. That old British fantasy of "the English world" in which everyone within the British Empire would speak English and behave according to the British standard of civil society has metamorphosed into the U.S. imaginary of an "end of history" when everyone will come to America to realize his or her destiny. And, of course, by implication "America" will be everywhere. In this dystopic view, we look inward to our domestic problems to work through foreign policy issues in anticipation of those "foreign" problems coming to us, as we know they will. It is this fantasy of "American universality", too often the model for new cosmopolitanism, including Said's own, that tells us U.S. neo-imperialism is not so much about land, natural resources, even global economic or military power, but primarily about a national identity we still cannot define.

The new Orientalisms are multiple, overlapping, and strategically confusing, enabling their authors to substitute foreign policy discussions for any genuine historical discussion of the Vietnamese, Iraqi, Israeli, Palestinian, Lebanese, Pakistani and Afghani peoples. The irony of these cultural processes of internalization, domestication and displacement is that they take place through a U.S. national model that has never been more fragile and fictional, irrelevant as it is to the global State power wielded by the Reagan-Bush administrations through transnational coalitions with the royal Saudi family, U.S. allies in the Greater Middle East, oil interests in the Black Sea neighborhoods of Afghanistan, and global capitalism's dependency on Chinese modernization and development. Barack Obama's administration has attempted to create an image of more cooperative international relations and a less militant foreign policy, even as the U.S. continues to wage two wars in the name of U.S. "national security". The Obama administration's new foreign policy and international image still depend upon a vigorous American exceptionalism. The U.S. is not just the "leader" of the "free world", but the democratic exemplar of religious, racial and ethnic, gender and sexual, economic, and political diversity and tolerance. The "Orient" is everywhere else, especially here at home.

CHAPTER 2

The "Vietnam Effect" in the Persian Gulf Wars

It's déjà vu all over again.

– Yogi Berra on witnessing Mantle and
Maris hit back-to-back home runs.

Prologue: 2010

In the previous chapter on "Edward Said and American Studies", I argued that the new Orientalism characteristic of U.S. neo-imperialism draws upon a "Vietnam Effect", in which foreign policy issues are incorporated into domestic U.S. issues in ways that distract us from the specific concerns of foreign peoples and states affected by our policies. The Vietnam War and thus the "Vietnam Effect" were consequences of Cold-War ideology. Although the Cold War focused attention on conflicts between the U.S. and the Soviet Union, the battles for global superiority were fought on the peripheries of Europe and North America, especially in the "Orient" that in the nineteenth-century European imaginary stretched from the Middle to the Near and Far East. U.S. fears that the "dominoes" would "fall" to Soviet and Chinese control in Southeast Asia if we did not assume the colonial legacy of the French in "Indochina" were based on the post-World War II foreign policy view that Asia was a principal battleground in the Cold War.

Christina Klein argues in *Cold War Orientalism: Asia in the Middlebrow Imagination, 1945–1961* that U.S. foreign policies and popular culture worked together to produce an imaginary Orient, which was both a projection of U.S. desires and a domestication of global problems, especially in Asia. What began as a U.S. dream of a "global imaginary of integration" is ironically shattered by the ideological production of Cold War Orientalism, so that "the foreign policies and middlebrow culture of the 1940s and 1950s culminated not only in the Vietnam War but also in John Woo".[38] We created the historical and transnational conditions that led not only to our disastrous foreign and military policies in Vietnam but also that produced a counter-narrative, exemplified for Klein in the career of John Woo, the Hong Kong film director who incorporates traditional Hollywood motifs in films like *Hard Boiled* (1992) and has influenced significantly U.S. films by such directors as Quentin Tarantino.[39] However fantastic its origins, U.S. Orientalism produced real effects that every day become more difficult to distinguish from our own national identity. In long historical terms, we should understand such U.S. Orientalism as shaped by globalization and Cold-War balance-of-power politics, but one of the clearest examples of how it works ideologically is what is known in popular culture as "the Vietnam Effect".

Popularized first in the late 1970s to refer to poor military and foreign policy decisions by the U.S. in the conduct of the War, the "Vietnam Effect", sometimes alternatively termed the "Vietnam Syndrome", referred to the defeatist mentality caused by our first loss in a major military conflict. Conservatives argued that Vietnam was a war we "won" on the "battlefield", but "lost" in the mass media, domestic politics, and the Paris Peace Talks. The "liberal media" supported the strong anti-war movement, crises in the Executive branch—the assassination of John F. Kennedy, Lyndon Johnson's decision not to run for re-election in 1968, Richard Nixon's Watergate Scandal in 1971—and concessions to the North Vietnamese in the Paris Peace talks had reversed our military successes. Other interpretations suggested that we were never close to "winning" our extension of the French colonial war against the Vietnamese, failing to understand the determination of the North Vietnamese Army and the insurrection by the National Liberation Front in South Vietnam. Even in strictly military terms, we had merely reacted to enemy actions, rarely taking initiative and never really "winning hearts and minds" of the Vietnamese civilians caught between warring adversaries. Traditional military tactics of territorial control failed and were replaced with equally unsuccessful "body counts" of enemy dead, which when broadcast on the evening news only fueled anti-war sentiments. From a conservative perspective, the "Vietnam Syndrome" was our defeatism in the aftermath

of losing the War; in the liberal view, the "Vietnam Effect" was a consequence of our Cold War-era neo-imperialism.

What follows is a historically specific interpretation of the "Vietnam Effect" first delivered on February 12, 1991 as a speech at an anti-war demonstration organized by the students and other activists at the University
of California, Irvine. "Why the War in the Persian Gulf Is Another Vietnam" was given less than a month after the U.S. aerial bombardment of
Iraqi military positions began the Persian Gulf War on January 16, 1991
and eleven days before U.S. ground forces would begin their military action in Kuwait on February 23, 1991. Much has changed in U.S. foreign
policy and cultural attitudes, especially toward the Middle East and Ar-
abs and Islamic peoples globally since 1991, but the historical aspect of
this essay remains important for two reasons. First, it was not intended
initially as a scholarly essay, but as part of political activism. Delivered to
a modest audience on a Saturday night in the Emerald Bay auditorium
of the University of California, Irvine Student Center, the talk was one
of several preceded by a recording of Gore Vidal criticizing President
George H. W. Bush for his decision to invade Iraq. Second, while I continued to participate in local anti-war demonstrations, I also urged my
colleagues on the national level to use our scholarly means to protest the
Persian Gulf War. As a member of the Editorial Collective of *Cultural Critique*, I urged Editor Donna Przbylowicz and Associate Editor Abdul Jan-
Mohamed to put together an emergency special issue, which they assembled on short notice as "The Economies of War" issue and published in
the Fall of 1991.[40] With a lead-off essay by Noam Chomsky and powerful
critiques both of the Persian Gulf and Vietnam wars by other recognized
scholars, this special issue declared its commitment to what I term in the
title of this book, "the cultural politics of the new American Studies".[41]

In what follows, I have made revisions only to clarify the historical contexts of President George H. W. Bush's administration (1989–1993) and
the First Persian Gulf War (August 1990–March 1991). Rather than draw
certain obvious connections with subsequent events, especially our disastrous invasion of Iraq on the false evidence of Saddam Hussein's "weapons of mass destruction", I have preferred to let this historical moment
speak for itself. Neither the anti-war activism in which I participated nor
the scholarship published in its cause, stopped the First Gulf War or pre-

vented our leaders from "finishing the job" in the Second Gulf War, with the disastrous results for the Iraqi people and the "Greater Middle East" we have witnessed since 2003. But the intellectual and political activities in real historical time to which my marching, speech, and published essay contributed in small ways finally "add up", if only because they offer the consistent rational critique of irrational policies, often bolstered by false patriotism, that is so necessary to a free society.

"The Vietnam Effect": 1991

Reporting to the Congress our military success in the Persian Gulf, President George H. W. Bush declared on March 3, 1991: "Thank God, we've kicked the Vietnam Syndrome once and for all."[42] Asked about the possibility of deploying U.S. troops to protect Kurdish refugees in northern Iraq, the President insisted in his April 14, 1991 press conference that we would not be drawn into another "quagmire" in Iraq. The words hardly needed to be uttered; from the beginning of our military involvement in the Persian Gulf, "Vietnam" has been a constant historical referent.[43] The slogan, "We support our troops," helped forge a patriotic consensus (85 % according to most opinion polls taken in the first week of the ground war) unmatched in U.S. history. That slogan referred explicitly to the Vietnam War and the cultural "memory" that the Anti-War Movement had systematically discouraged, even demoralized, U.S. combat troops in Vietnam. There is little in the actual history of the Anti-War Movement to support this "remembrance," which like most historical reconstructions conflates different historical moments. The slogan's implicit negative, "We did not support our troops in Vietnam," refers less to isolated incidents of anti-war demonstrators "spitting" on returning soldiers, chanting "Murderers!" or otherwise condemning military personnel for the conduct of U.S. foreign policy than it refers to the *aftermath* of the Vietnam War, in which veterans were ignored or considered "embarrassments" both by their government and the general population. The belated parades, monuments, and memorials often served only to remind veterans of the Vietnam War of the long silence that they met on their return.

That silence, however, was not merely a consequence of war-weariness, apathy, or even contempt for those who had served in Vietnam; it represented a genuine moral confusion on the part of most Americans. In many cases, embarrassment was entangled with *shame*—a sense of guilt regarding widespread support for a war whose purposes we did not understand. In short, our cultural shame had something to do with our unarticulated sense that patriotism had not been based on knowledge, reason, and justice. Slogans from the Vietnam era, such as "My country, right or wrong" and "America, love it or leave it," returned to haunt us not simply when we *lost* the war but when we began to recognize how misguided and misinformed our foreign policies had been. The lesson of Vietnam was simple: never again should sheer emotional support for our sons and daughters blind us to our patriotic responsibility to assess the reasons and motives for military action—that is, action that would put those very sons and daughters at risk.

The "Vietnam syndrome" meant for President George H. W. Bush a national sense of failure and powerlessness—a "habit" to be "kicked" as one would drugs or alcohol. Yet, the "drug" of the Vietnam era was the uncritical support for foreign policies we did not understand—the emotional enthusiasm for "victory" that cost 58,000 American and millions of Vietnamese lives. But this was precisely the drug that intoxicated us during the First Persian Gulf War, and our one-sided victory virtually guaranteed our repetition of the key mistakes of the Vietnam era. President Bush, Secretary of State Baker, Secretary of Defense Cheney, Vice President Quayle, and General Schwarzkopf have repeated ceaselessly: "Our action in the Persian Gulf will not be another Vietnam." The bombing of Iraq and Kuwait was designed to prevent just such a repetition of the military quagmire in Vietnam. The United Nations resolutions and its sanctioned military coalition were designed to protect the United States from criticism of neo-colonialism comparable to our policies of "winning hearts and minds" in Vietnam. Diplomatic negotiations with Iraq, despite obvious and enduring intransigence on both sides, were extensively covered in the press and on television, in part to demonstrate how we had exhausted all peaceful alternatives to military action.

For the American public, the political situation seemed convincingly different from that of the Vietnam era. Between November 2, 1990 and January 15, 1991, Tariq Aziz spoke almost nightly to the American television audience on *Nightline* and other news shows; Ho, General Giap, even Le Duc Tho (the North Vietnamese Foreign Minister interviewed frequently during the Paris Peace Talks) remained shadowy, elusive figures for the American public during the Vietnam War. Whereas Congress had waffled and equivocated during Vietnam, this time the televised congressional debates, often showcasing "eloquent" statements by congressmen both for and against military involvement, resulted in what was publicized as a clear mandate for our military presence in the Gulf. In fact, Congress merely delegated responsibility to the President, effectively mooting the long and important discussion since Vietnam regarding the issues of what assumed juridical form in the "War Powers' Act," by granting President George H. W. Bush even greater freedom to conduct war than Presidents Johnson or Nixon had during the "undeclared war" of Vietnam. Political scientists like Mark Petracca tried to remind Americans that the narrow but nonetheless decisive majority by which Congress delegated authority to the President constituted as significant an issue for protest as the threat of military conflict in the Gulf.

But the public discussion of such crucial issues of democratic governance depended to a large extent on *remembering* the continuing legacy of Vietnam. And it was precisely this sort of cultural memory that the decisive military victory in the Gulf helped to erase. The First Persian Gulf War was mercifully swift and relatively bloodless for the Coalition's forces. The "Vietnam without Trees" that some anti-war activists had predicted never came to pass in the desert along the Gulf. We have been encouraged to believe a "clean," "sanitary," and "smart" war was the result of the superior technology, organization, and justness of the Coalition's leaders, both in the field and Washington. As Kuwaiti coalition troops led the way into Kuwait City, to be met by resistance fighters, and as U.S. forces swept into southern Iraq, driving Iraqi troops across the Euphrates or into Basra, the fears of another Vietnam vanished. Anti-war organizations, put together with impressive speed and efficiency in the months leading up to the January 15, 1991 deadline the Coalition gave Iraq to withdraw from Kuwait, collapsed overnight. This time it was the tiny minority of stubborn protesters who were met with silence, if not outright censorship. The word on the streets was that protesters "had better shut up."[44] Public debate was over before it had begun, and patriotism had become an undisguised spectacle of cheering congressmen or replays of

Whitney Huston, tears streaming down her cheeks, passionately singing the "Star Spangled Banner" at Super Bowl XXV on January 27, 1991 in Tampa Stadium. On April 3, 1991, CBS-TV would broadcast its *All-Star Salute to the Troops*, which *TV Guide* described as a "patriotic orgy".[45]

From President George H. W. Bush's comparison of Iraq's invasion of Kuwait with Germany's invasion of Czechoslovakia to the ceaseless re-runs of World War II combat melodramas on TNT (as well as on many local channels) during the war, the improbable analogy with the Allies' efforts against Axis forces has been emphasized in several media. That analogy has had the rhetorical effect of underscoring the negative exam-ple of the Vietnam War. "Contained" between World War II and the Per-sian Gulf victory, Vietnam could be treated as an "anomaly," a unique case of failure whose mistakes might be "corrected" the next time. Contrived as this historical "containment" is in rational terms, its rhetoric helped strengthen revisionist historians' arguments that our failure in Vietnam had little to do with our general foreign policies (especially those framed in the so-called "Cold War" period) and much to do with Congressio-nal interference in the military conduct of the Vietnam war. In short, the rhetoric and spectacle of patriotic support for the Persian Gulf War was not the simple instrumentality of mass media propaganda, whether en-gineered or not by the government, but integral to the re-legitimation of foreign policies that since Vietnam and now in the aftermath of the Cold War have been subject to effective rational criticism.

Many opposed to the First Persian Gulf War argued that the "crisis" de-veloped conveniently at the moment when defense budget cuts seemed inevitable and advocates of a "peace dividend" for much-needed domes-tic programs were gaining popular support. This argument has led some to speculate that the bombing of Iraq was a sort of "showcase" for new U.S. military technology, both to support new and even larger defense spending and to provide a long-term economic rationale for military "research and development" in the export markets for such hardware as the Patriot Missile system. Although it is well worth considering that advocates of substantial defense budgets may recognize the need to use other arguments than "national defense" in the post-Cold War era, the general thesis that the First Gulf War was fought primarily for reasons of economic expediency or military self-interest is far too crudely materialist. Defense spending is simply one among many of the signs of political power; the grammar of such power remains U.S. foreign policy, which since Vietnam has relied on a strategic slippage from the purposes of "national defense" to the regulation of "international law and order."

In the Vietnam era, the war was often defended on the grounds that our containment of Communism was directly related to our national defense. Few arguments of this sort were offered by President George H. W. Bush, Secretary of State Baker, or Secretary of Defense Cheney in justification of the First Gulf War, although arguments connecting the global economy to the economic interests of the United States were made. In response to the anti-war slogan, "No Blood for Oil!," some followed Secretary of State Baker's claim that there was "nothing wrong with fighting for oil" and that we were in the Persian Gulf to "protect American jobs." Such arguments, however, seemed to have little influence on popular support for the war, and not simply because they could be so easily refuted. By contrast, the claim that "national security" was at stake in the Vietnam War was widely accepted, despite the difficulty of its demonstration. What made arguments regarding "national defense" ineffective, even half-hearted, in the justification of our military presence in the Persian Gulf was their incompatibility with the prevailing principle of U.S. foreign policy: the regulation of international law. Indeed, the success of this moral posture is evident in the public indifference to the fact that the United States conducted diplomatic negotiations with Iraq in the place of the United Nations. Once the U.N. resolutions and sanctions against Iraq had been approved, the United States was accepted as the *representative* of the U.N. both in the forging of a military coalition and in virtually all diplomatic negotiations with Iraq. Even after the First Gulf War was concluded with the Iraqi acceptance of the formal cease-fire of March 3, 1991, the United Nations debated new resolutions that supported the presence of Coalition forces in northern Iraq.

The First Persian Gulf War declared the United States to be the arbiter of international law; the United Nations, arguably the most appropriate organization for new power and authority in the "new global order," appears even less significant in the public's mind than during the Cold War. In this regard, the "Vietnam Effect" enabled President George H. W. Bush to reaffirm his authority as Commander-in-Chief by insisting that the

Pentagon would "not fight this war with one hand tied behind its back." Once again, George H. W. Bush's metaphors are significant, in this case implicitly judging debates in the Congress regarding the conduct of the Vietnam War—especially the debates leading to the reduction of funding for the War between 1971 and 1973—to be the *causes* for our failure. The rhetorical isolation of the Vietnam War had the effect of reaffirming the continuity, coherence, and justness of U.S. foreign policy from World War II to the Persian Gulf crisis. It follows the logic of what Robert Divine has termed the "Quagmire Thesis" argued by Arthur Schlesinger, Jr. and David Halberstam during the Vietnam War: "Schlesinger's quagmire thesis, while condemning American involvement, nevertheless excused American leaders of any real responsibility. It was all an accident, a tragic series of mistakes, but not one that called for a reconsideration of America's Cold War policies or for a searching reappraisal of men and decisions."[46]

During the First Persian Gulf War, the veterans of Vietnam, whose political grievances were about to be erased from the American agenda along with very name of "Vietnam," responded generally as if this were the "Welcome Home" they had been awaiting for more than fifteen years. With the exception of organizations like Vietnam Veterans against War (VVAW), the majority of Vietnam-era veterans organized and participated in pro-war demonstrations and helped the emotional slogan, "Support Our Troops," sweep the land and divide protesters. The Vietnam Veterans of America was first organized because of the exclusion of Vietnam veterans from Veterans of Foreign Wars and to serve as the means of sponsoring veterans' political and economic grievances, but during the First Persian Gulf War local chapters of the VVA became rallying points for pro-war demonstrations. Efforts to challenge the slogan itself were met with fierce opposition. Any attempt to remind people that many Vietnam-era veterans still suffered from PTSD (Post-Traumatic Stress Disorder) resulting from combat and shared by British veterans of the Falklands' War was flatly rejected. The elementary distinction between "support" for human beings and "opposition" to combat activities was considered "too intellectual" in a time when only emotion made *sense*. The term "Post-Traumatic Stress Disorder" was barely mentioned during the First Persian Gulf War (with the exception of a brief, midday special report on CNN, which included interviews with veterans from the Vietnam and Falkland Island wars). In effect, this serious disability suffered by many veterans of recent wars had been re-diagnosed. No longer referring to the psychological after-effects of combat, the "trauma" of Vietnam-era veterans in particular seemed to refer retrospectively to the American public's failure to "support the troops."

Amid such emotion, there were still implicit and recognizable "arguments" with respect to the meaning of Vietnam in U.S. culture. By virtue of their uncritical support for the troops in the Persian Gulf and their neglect of such crucial issues as PTSD, pro-war veterans implicitly argued that we had not fought to win in Vietnam but merely to maintain a symbolic presence in Southeast Asia against Soviet and Chinese challenges. In effect, they were favoring a version of the "Stalemate Thesis" best represented by Daniel Ellsberg (to be sure, an unlikely political ally for pro-war veterans), who blamed Presidents Truman, Eisenhower, and Kennedy for trying to juggle the contrary demands of not losing Vietnam to the Communists and not committing U.S. troops to an unwinnable land war in Vietnam.[47] Strong support of the First Persian Gulf War by veterans of the Vietnam War strengthened President George H. W. Bush in his resolve to avoid the historical trap, according to the Stalemate Thesis, that President Johnson had inherited from his predecessors' equivocal foreign policies in Vietnam. What the veterans of Vietnam seemed to have overlooked as they cheered the President and supported their fellow soldiers in the Gulf was that the Vietnam War and its consequences for so many veterans were being erased from the historical map of U.S. foreign policy. "Quagmire" or "stalemate," Vietnam had finally been "explained" in just the manner that the U.S. government had struggled unsuccessfully to do between 1968 (the Tet Offensive) and 1990. All along, what the government desired was an explanation that would allow us to isolate and then forget "Vietnam."

Under these conditions, the American people did not simply "forget" Vietnam, but like the President and other government officials repeatedly *denied* Vietnam in the manner of some collective repression. Such widespread denial helped the general public deny as well the carnage of this brief war. Few U.S. citizens have ever expressed much concern about the sketchy information about civilian and Iraqi troop casualties in the six-week war, even though those figures are two to three times greater than the American casualties suffered in the nine years of U.S. combat in Vietnam.[48] In all of this, dismissed by some as the inevitable euphoria of victory, but criticized by others as a dangerous symptom of long-term intolerance for political dissent in this country, the parallels between our foreign policy errors in Vietnam and our conduct in the First Persian Gulf War have been virtually ignored, despite the unavoidable "Vietnam Effect" of the official rhetoric, which has been mimed so well in the press and the general population.

We lost the war in Vietnam, because we had no plan for peace. We lost the war in Vietnam before we landed troops in Danang in 1965, because we utterly misunderstood the political situation in both South and North Vietnam. We lost the war in Vietnam in 1954 as decisively as the French lost the battle of Dienbienphu, because in that year we assumed authority for the political future of Vietnam and Southeast Asia. With the best intentions and noblest sentiments, we took over the colonial project the French had pursued for a century in Indochina. To be sure, our colonialism was different from that of Vietnam's many previous invaders. We did not want their latex or tin, as the French did, their hardwood or rice, as the Japanese did; we wanted to win hearts and minds. We wanted "a sphere of influence," which would "balance" the influences of the Soviet Union and China in Asia. We spoke loudly and tirelessly of political self-determination, economic self-reliance, and democratic institutions, but we viewed Vietnam and the rest of Southeast Asia as simply "dominoes" in an elaborate game of balance-of-power politics. We knew little of the Vietnamese, Cambodians, and Laotians whose governments and societies were destabilized by our larger ambitions. We didn't want to know much about them.

As we moved massive military force to the Persian Gulf in late 1990, we could not understand why demonstrators in Morocco, Jordan, Egypt, Malaysia, and other so-called "third world" countries both in the Middle East and other regions of the world should express such rage against our well-intentioned efforts to pursue a "just war," to "punish" and topple the dictator and aggressor, Saddam Hussein. Saddam Hussein is not a nationalist leader like Ho Chi Minh. Iraq's invasion of Kuwait on August 2, 1990 is not comparable to the Vietnamese people's struggle to rid their country of the French, the Japanese, the British, and the Americans. In these respects, President George H. W. Bush was right: this war was *not* another Vietnam. The war in the Persian Gulf was not waged as a neo-colonial effort against popular nationalist movements, like the National Liberation Front, the Provisional Revolutionary Government, and the Vietnamese Communist Party. And yet massive demonstrations against the presence of Coalition forces in the Gulf seemed united in their opposition to foreign intervention, especially by the U.S. and European forces represented in the Coalition.

A crucial part of the President's argument that military action in the Persian Gulf was not another instance of western imperialism was the strength of the military coalition. For many liberals, the fact that the Coalition "held together" is convincing evidence that our purpose in the Gulf is part of a larger policy of "collective security" by which nations join together to maintain international law. As Harold Meyerson argued during the First Persian Gulf War, the internal divisions of the American Left caused by the Vietnam War assumed new characteristics in the face of Saddam Hussein's expansionism: "Todd Gitlin calls this wing of the left 'the collective security gang'—pro- and anti-warriors who believe in some form of international action against Iraq, with a legitimate U.S. role, but who oppose the establishment of a new *Pax Americana*—as distinct from the 'anti-imperialist gang'—opponents of the war who elevate U.S. anti-interventionism to a universal principle."[49] The "collective security" argument, however, tends to confuse the procedures and, in this historical instance, resolutions of the United Nations with the decisions of a group of nations that have decided to "act" in the best interests of international law. The United Nations' resolutions did *not* authorize the bombing of Iraq or the occupation of southern Iraq. These military decisions were made by a coalition forged by the United States. From the very beginning, the "Coalition" was an obvious front for a *Pax Americana*.

We ought to have recognized the rhetorical slippage from "U.N." to "Coalition" to "U.S." as a kind of historical déjà vu. In 1954, Secretary of State John Foster Dulles and President Eisenhower formed a coalition that Dulles called at first "United Action" and later renamed the "Southeast Asian Treaty Organization." Both were designed to "guarantee the security of Southeast Asia." Neither proved very effective in the Vietnam

War. To be sure, some members of "United Action"—Australia and New Zealand—and some members of SEATO—South Korea, for example—sent token troops, advisors, and military support to the Army of the Republic of Vietnam (ARVN) and American forces fighting in Vietnam. But the "coalitions" were not politically effective; they were not strong organizations based on reasonable political and diplomatic solutions to the many problems left by European colonialism in Southeast Asia. They were symbolic coalitions patched together by the United States to justify its conduct in Vietnam.

There is a striking parallel between "United Action" and SEATO with the coalition forged to fight the First Persian Gulf War. Although the *number* of Middle Eastern countries participating in the Coalition Forces was impressive, a significant number of those countries are not democratic: Saudi Arabia, Qatar, the United Arab Emirates, for example. It is not just that we once again threw our lot together with repressive regimes in the "interests" of fighting another repressive regime—the "greater evil" of Saddam Hussein and Iraqi militarism; it is also that we mistook the support of these governments for the support of their peoples. Turkey's official support for our conduct in the Persian Gulf, for example, was not maintained by opinion polls of average Turkish citizens, most of whom opposed Turkish involvement in this war. What did we hear from the Egyptian on the streets of Cairo, the Syrian worker in Damascus? Precious little. Did they share the views of those "coalition" partners, Egypt and Syria, and their leaders, Hosni Mubarak and President Hassad? Without access to mass media, without effective means of voting against their governments' participation in our military coalition, people in these countries had only demonstration as their means of expressing their discontent. But President George H. W. Bush insisted he would not be "swayed" by these demonstrations and that they would have no "influence" on our national "resolve." One characteristic feature of more traditional western imperialism has been a refusal to listen to the interests of the people and treat instead exclusively with undemocratic rulers, who have notoriously found "foreign interests" to be in their self interest.

Just as we constructed something of a political "fiction" in the alliance of SEATO, so we manipulated the "consensus" of the United Nations, not in its condemnation of Iraq's invasion of Kuwait but in the U.N.'s deadline for Iraq's withdrawal from Kuwait and its tacit authorization of the United States' government as the United Nations' diplomatic representative. U.N. Secretary General Perez de Cuellar was treated as if he were a middle-level U.S. diplomat when he arrived in Baghdad at the eleventh hour to negotiate a peace settlement with Iraq. The Iraqi response to the U.N. Secretary General reflected accurately the secondary role he himself had assumed in the diplomatic negotiations.

In Geneva in 1954, while the French and Vietnamese ostensibly worked out the Geneva Accords, the United States was represented by Dulles and other high-ranking diplomats. Although claiming to be mere "observers," we were active participants in the drafting of the Geneva Accords, but we refused to sign them. Having refused to sign those Accords, we then proceeded to ignore their provisions, notably the mandate for free elections in Vietnam two years after the signing of those Accords. With the exception of the patently fraudulent elections of Diem, Khanh, Ky, and Thieu in the increasingly unstable political climate of South Vietnam between 1954 and 1973, no "free elections" were ever held in Vietnam after 1954. But why did we fail to encourage these South Vietnamese governments to conduct such elections, rather than wage an unwinnable war that only realized our worst nightmare: the destabilization of the entire region? Our arguments in the years leading up to the successful coup against Diem and his assassination were simple: the government of South Vietnam under Diem was not sufficiently stable. Hardly a translation was needed at the time for those paying any attention: the government of Diem was unpopular; Diem would have been voted out of office in any free election held in the South during his nine years of power.

Have we effectively overcome the mistakes of Vietnam in the sixteen years since the conclusion of that war in 1975? Despite official arguments supporting the Coalition as representative of Middle Eastern opposition to Saddam Hussein and support for foreign intervention, the Coalition was clearly the work of the United States. Even had the European and Middle Eastern members of the Coalition forces withdrawn or refused to cross the border between Saudi Arabia and Kuwait, U.S. troops were obviously sufficient to carry out our military purposes. Seventy percent of the combat troops were provided by the U.S. military; the vast majority of air sorties were flown by U.S. aircraft. The Coalition was quite obviously a thin disguise for U.S. military operations.

We sent troops to the Middle East to counter what appeared to be a political destabilization of the region comparable to the "collapse" of the "dominoes" in Southeast Asia. Yet, there is considerable evidence that we took such action without much knowledge of the political consequences. While diplomacy was still possible, President George H. W. Bush insisted tirelessly that there would be "no linkage" of the Palestinian question and Iraq's occupation of Kuwait. Yet even before the ground war had begun, the President announced in his "State of the Union" address in January 1991 that "some resolution" of the Palestinian issue would be a necessary part of the peace settlements following the war. Supporters of our policies might argue that we intended from the beginning to negotiate a peaceful solution to the Israeli-Palestinian controversy, but only when we could do so from a position of regional strength.

Yet President George H. W. Bush could have announced such an intention before the January 15th deadline expired, if only to strengthen the U.S. hand in diplomatic negotiations and win wider popular support among Arab peoples. Had we expressed clearly a plan for establishing a Palestinian homeland, guaranteeing their political and judicial rights in the region, and promptly entered into negotiations with the Palestinians and the Israelis, then we might have gained far more credibility in the region and diminished Saddam Hussein's effort to appropriate the Palestinian cause for his own purposes. In short, we could have used our influence in this crisis to initiate serious negotiations between the Israelis and Palestinians independent of Saddam Hussein's demands and the future of Kuwait. Our lack of a positive policy with respect to the Palestinian question is reflected both in our equivocation regarding the "relevance" of the Palestinian question to the stability of the Middle East and our postwar failure to do more than support a multinational Middle Eastern peace conference on the issue. Having just participated in a military action that has reorganized the political balance of power in the Middle East, we assumed in 1991 the position of having "no position" on the appropriate solution to what is arguably the most significant issue in the Middle East: the fate of the Palestinians. Such equivocation, if not outright foreign policy flimflam, recalls nothing so well as our indecision in Southeast Asia during the Vietnam War. If our government hoped to maintain a "symbolic" position by merely endorsing the "desirability" of a "peaceful solution" to the issue of a Palestinian homeland, then we may well understand why the next twenty years were marked by political stalemate in any solution to the Israeli-Palestinian question. History demonstrates in those two decades that we have indeed slipped into a "quagmire" in the Middle East no easier to escape than the political trap in which we threw ourselves during our two decades in Southeast Asia.

Since the conclusion of the Iran-Iraq War, our opposition to Saddam Hussein has grown from "concern" about his growing military power in the region to the outright demonization of the Saddam who appeared on posters during the War, complete with bulls-eye and the slogan, "Now, It's *Personal!*" As war fever spread in this country, debates concerning the "fate" or "future" of Saddam grew proportionately. With the war underway, there was ceaseless discussion about whether or not Saddam Hussein had been targeted by the U.S. military and whether or not he should be "terminated." Discussions of the "morality" and "legality" of murdering Saddam Hussein took center stage from the other, more reasonable question for the State Department and the U.S. public: what are the other political parties and who are the other viable political leaders in contemporary Iraq?

Anyone who recalls the years leading up to Diem's and his brother, Nhu's, assassinations must find some uncanny resemblances in this obsession with Saddam Hussein's "liquidation." Truong Nhu Tang, one of the founders of the National Liberation Front, complains in *A Viet Cong Memoir* that the U.S. government never familiarized itself with the many well-qualified leaders of various opposition parties that developed during Diem's rule in South Vietnam.[50] As he points out, we accepted Diem's and Nhu's caricatures of such opposition leaders and parties as "Communists," even though South Vietnam between 1954 and 1963 was alive with a wide variety of different political constituencies, despite Nhu's efforts to use his secret police to suppress every sign of political dissent. Even when the fall of Diem and Nhu's government was understood by Henry Cabot Lodge and others in the State Department to be inevitable, we did little to identify, much less encourage, opposition leaders. For Troung Nhu Tang, this failure on the part of U.S. foreign policy merely strengthened the coalition of political groups formed in opposition to Diem's government. In effect, our willful disregard of potentially popular political alternatives in South Vietnam helped turn the National Liberation Front into an effective political and ultimately successful military organization.

In a similar fashion, we seem to have ignored the possibility of any legitimate political opposition in Iraq to the dictatorial rule of Saddam Hussein. At the same time, we have encouraged the "people" to revolt and overthrow Saddam Hussein and the Ba'ath Party. Such conflicting messages have led to President George H. W. Bush's recent embarrassment regarding the plight of the Kurdish refugees, most of whom are fleeing the efforts of the Iraqi Army to suppress a rebellion tangibly encouraged by CIA radio broadcasts calling for open revolution against Saddam Hussein. Shi'ite Muslim rebellion in southern Iraq has received less attention, even though it has been just as ruthlessly suppressed by the Iraqi Army, but the U.S. administration's "policy" seems once again to reflect the equivocations of the Vietnam era. After all, "Shi'ite" simply means "Iranian" to the Bush Administration, and that argues for an even more dangerous "imbalance" of power in the region. Rather than identify leaders with popular support and plans for better government, we have concerned ourselves once again with the "caricatures" of foreign politics and issues that we learned to sketch during the Vietnam period.

During the War, the only hint of the United States' foreign policy in the Gulf in the postwar period was Secretary of State Baker's plans for a "Middle Eastern Bank" to finance the reconstruction of Iraq. Amid the jokes about such a plan as a clever solution for the crisis in American banking, the obvious implication was that this was the *only* idea that the State Department could formulate to meet the political crises after the war. Once again, the lessons of Vietnam seemed to have been forgotten. The enormous foreign economic assistance we gave President Diem to bolster his shaky government was largely wasted on hasty efforts to industrialize South Vietnam and "build" an army with equipment but without popular support. The enduring myth of U.S. economic aid to Vietnam from our last-minute economic assistance of the French to the evacuation of Saigon in 1975 is that such assistance was squandered by corrupt officials. Yet, the real waste of U.S. aid to South Vietnam resulted from our

68

misunderstanding of the needs of the Vietnamese economy and people. As George Herring points out in *America's Longest War: The United States and Vietnam: 1950–1975*, U.S. aid to South Vietnam between 1955 and 1960 initially helped stabilize the South Vietnamese government, but the disproportionate military aid and efforts to rapidly industrialize South Vietnam "did little to promote economic development or to improve living conditions in the villages where more than 90 percent of South Vietnam's population resided".[51] In our enthusiasm to strengthen the central, urban rule of Diem, in imitation of the developed nations, we ignored the rural infrastructure for both the economy and politics of Vietnam.

How will the funds of Baker's "Middle Eastern Bank" be distributed? In Vietnam, we confused buildings, factories, and consumer goods with what is vaguely designated by the word *culture*. Despite his militarism, his expansionist aims, and his tyrannical rule, Saddam Hussein enjoyed considerable popular support in the Middle East in the months *following* his invasion of Kuwait. President George H. W. Bush insisted that we would not be "swayed" by such popular demonstrations, as if they reflected merely some sort of "mass hysteria" symptomatic of our worst ethnocentric fantasies about the "Arab masses." Yet what seems so obvious in those demonstrations was the expression of protest against the inequitable distribution of wealth in the region, whether that wealth be measured in oil, jobs, land, or merely "voice"—that is, some recognition for the many social and political constituencies in the Middle East who are effectively unheard in the West.

Viewed in this way, can the poverty of so many Middle Eastern peoples, terrible when measured against the great wealth of the region, be relieved significantly by a "Middle Eastern Bank," however comprehensive its ambitions? Egypt, Saudi Arabia, the United Arab Emirates, Syria, and other Arab nations of the Coalition have already benefited economically from the First Persian Gulf War. It is quite clear, however, that Jordan is to be punished economically for its neutrality and King Hussein's protests against civilian casualties during the bombing of Iraq. Even in cases where popular sympathy has been elicited, such as for the plight of the Kurdish refugees, the economic future promises little more than infrastructure, even if we generously assume that such "reconstruction" would be done selflessly in the interests of the Iraqi people. Who will rebuild

Kuwait? For that work, no "Middle Eastern Bank" will be needed. One of the world's smallest nations, Kuwait is also one of the world's richest nations. Even before the end of the First Gulf War, fifty billion dollars' worth of contracts for reconstruction had been awarded by the Kuwaiti government-in-exile, virtually all to U.S. firms. The United States will rebuild Kuwait, and the United States will thus inevitably become the economic and military ruler of Kuwait. In this respect, we will succeed the British, who ruled Kuwait as a protectorate from 1914 to 1961, protected Kuwait from Iraqi territorial claims between 1961 and 1963, and worked out the agreements between the Kuwaiti royal family and British Petroleum, Getty Oil, and the Japanese owned "Arabian Oil Company" that shared Kuwait's oil wealth in the 1950s and 1960s. In light of the grotesque scandals surrounding the U.S. banking industry in the 1980s, it seems absurd that our government should propose taking the *initiative* in developing a "Middle Eastern Bank" that would "solve" the postwar problems of the region.

How will we protect this tiny country against Iraq, against future aggression in the Gulf region? Only by putting in power a puppet government in Iraq, one whose subservience or fidelity to U.S. interests are so clear that we can withdraw the majority of our troops from what certainly will be the postwar "Occupation Zone" of Iraq. Who will "save" the Iraqi people—17.5 million of them before the War, who are even now beginning to starve, to suffer the disease and pestilence that follow contaminated water supplies, whose doctors lack the most elementary medical supplies, who haven't the fuel to cook what little food they have or purify what water they can collect from fetid ponds and bomb craters? Needless to say, I am speaking only of the survivors, not of the corpses in the bombed out buildings, in the terrible heaps of rubble that the joint "censorship" of the Pentagon and Saddam Hussein have virtually erased from our minds. There are hints, of course, from refugees that the civilian casualties, even in the midst of the "smart bombs" and "non-civilian targets," will horrify us when their sheer numbers come finally, as they must, to light. I need hardly remind you that "collateral damage" means *people*.

Of course, the United States will assume responsibility for humanitarian aid, as well it should, but it will be a humanitarian effort that, for whatever good it may do, will nonetheless assure our political sphere of influence in Iraq for the foreseeable future. Like Diem, some well-intentioned but hardly popular Iraqi will be "selected" to restore his country to economic stability and bring the survivors back to "normal" life. And such a leader will depend, of course, on Western financial support; whatever his good intentions, he will be a bought man. But what of the countries neighboring Iraq and Kuwait? President George H. W. Bush refused to countenance what he termed "linkage" in the failed diplomatic negotiations with Iraq in the five months leading to this disastrous war. But how can the question of "linkage" be ignored when the war itself will command a new relation among the various states of the Middle East? The same questions were asked in the years following the landing of U.S. troops in Vietnam in 1965, when it became clear we were not just lending "advisors" but actively fighting the war for the South Vietnamese government. What would happen to Cambodia, to Laos, to Thailand? We know that we share considerable responsibility for the Khmer Rouge's military victory in Cambodia, following our bombing of NLF and PRG sanctuaries along the Cambodian border with Vietnam. We know that the genocide of 3 million Cambodians carried out by the Khmer Rouge government was a consequence of the "madness" of the war waged in Vietnam, spilling over into Cambodia.

Is it possible for a sophisticated world leader to refuse to countenance "political linkage" of Iraq's invasion of Kuwait with the other wars and territorial ambitions of the various countries in the region over the past fifty years, when in fact foreign policy cannot be understood as anything else than an effort to "link" different national interests? "Linkage" is now inevitable, and even in the specific case of what President George H. W. Bush considered the most unthinkable "linkage" five months ago: the "linkage" of the issue of Kuwait with the issue of Palestine and the 2.5 million homeless Palestinians. In his 1991 "State of the Union" address, the President suggested that some resolution of the Palestinian question will have to be part of the postwar peace settlement, if only for the pragmatic reason that no peace will be lasting in the region without addressing the question of Palestine and the Palestinian people. If this was so clear to President George H. W. Bush, then why was it an issue before he ordered military action to begin?

By refusing even to consider any "linkage" of the Palestinian question with Iraq's invasion of Kuwait, President George H. W. Bush initiated a military policy that made a wide range of "linkages" virtually unavoidable. Certainly Saddam Hussein's military policies depend upon such political "linkages," and they are likely to have disastrous military consequences for our coalition. After the air war began on January 16, 1991, Jordan's King Hussein protested angrily the military campaign and the growing civilian casualties. After the war began, Jordanians expressed strong support for the Iraqis and for Saddam Hussein. Our response was to threaten to cut foreign aid to Jordan and to trivialize the "military threat" of the Jordanian army and air force. In the meantime, Iraq has sent much of its remaining air force to bases in Iran, and we have trivialized the "military threat" of Iraqi planes in Iran. But the average Iranian citizen has expressed growing sympathy with the Iraqis and anger against the relentless bombing that continues unabated just beyond their western border. Should we simply fear the entrance of Jordan and Iran into this war on the side of Iraq? No, we should fear far more the lasting political consequences of the deep-seated resentment of the United States that our military policies have created among the peoples of Jordan and Iran. Even barring their entrance into the military conflict, can we be certain that their moderate leaders, King Hussein and President Rafsanjani, will survive politically the growing popular sentiments against U.S. actions in the Persian Gulf?

The terrible future that our military policies in this war may well be creating has clear parallels with what happened in Southeast Asia. If that future comes even close to what I have sketched—an Iraqi Diem, or worse, an Iranian Shah, propped up by U.S. economic aid and military support, then we already know the consequences. There will be no peace in the Middle East; there will be merely an acceleration of the wars that have troubled that region in the wake of French, British, and now U.S. colonialism. Or perhaps more terrible still than overt warfare, there may come to power even more of the unpublicized political terror we condemn in Saddam Hussein and yet supported in the Iran ruled with an iron fist by the Shah and his secret police, Savak, for more than a quarter of a century.

The Vietminh at Dienbienphu fought for a great military victory, which General Giap knew would serve primarily political ends. It was, of course, a very real battle with terrible casualties and acts of extraordinary heroism on both sides, but the Vietminh, Giap, and Ho knew that it was primarily a symbolic victory that strengthened their hand in Geneva. In a similar sense, the Tet Offensive of 1968 was a military disaster for the National Liberation Front as well as for the North Vietnamese Communists who supported it. It accomplished little, except for the atrocities in Hue and the destruction of that ancient city. The marines retook Hue with awful casualties, but they regained that ground. The U.S. combat troops in Vietnam were not zoned out, demoralized by anti-war protesters, and indecisive in military action. We won the battles, but we lost the war. Because we lost the peace before the war began.

In the First Gulf War, we also betrayed an utter ignorance of local politics—or perhaps it is simply a studied carelessness toward both regions and a lack of interest in their indigenous peoples and local politics. That, above all, seems to have been the cause of our failure in Vietnam. Our "Southeast Asian" experts were legion, scattered from the State Department to universities throughout the U.S. But none seemed to have the slightest understanding of the complex political divisions in Vietnam, the different local leaders, the ethnic and religious diversity. We poured foreign aid into industrialization and urbanization programs encouraged by Diem, an urban Catholic, who was also deeply nationalist. We ignored the agrarian traditions of Vietnam, especially important in the rich and fertile lands of South Vietnam. We dealt with European-educated intellectuals, often cosmopolitans with contradictory yearnings for western ways; we treated the village peasantry and their agriculture as "inconsequential." In terms of our global foreign policies, they hardly mattered, but in Vietnam they were keys to popular support as well as our own democratic values. We never won their "hearts and minds," because programs like the "Hamlet Resettlement Program" and the "Phoenix Program" treated their centuries' old traditions and values as the lingering traces of a "primitive" people in need of our enlightenment.

We repeated this pattern of arrogance in Iraq, Kuwait, Jordan, and the rest of the Middle East during and after the First Gulf War. Our allies, such as Saudi Arabia, Egypt, and the United Arab Emirates, suffered the consequences of their alliance with our imperial commitment to modern, technocratic "civilization" as a political solution to regional problems exacerbated by EuroAmerican imperialism.

Most Americans agreed in the early stages of the War that the censorship of the news imposed by our government was in the "best interests" of our nation. "Doesn't anyone remember the old adage from World War II: 'Zip the lip?'" a correspondent to the *Los Angeles Times* wrote shortly after the ground war began, complaining of CNN's coverage of military operations in the Gulf. I do not agree that we should accept such censorship, especially when it means keeping us in the dark regarding the casualties in Iraq and Kuwait. But even granting hypothetically such a need for military censorship, then can an equal case be made for the de facto "censorship" of our political plans for peace? If such plans are reasonable, especially when what we mean by "reasonable" takes into account the interests of the diverse peoples living in the Middle East, then shouldn't we publicize them broadly in the interests of gathering support from those who now seem to hate us more every day? Wouldn't a reasonable peace plan have helped bring the war to a more rapid conclusion, more convincingly encouraging the *coup d'état* that the U.S. government encouraged us would soon come to Iraq? Alas, it was the same in the Vietnam War. Our government encouraged us to believe that the "light at the end of the tunnel" would result from "internal" divisions of the Vietnamese Communists, disagreements between the North Vietnamese and Chinese, even the poor health and incipient death of Ho Chi Minh. Our hopes were as fantastic and as macabre as the CIA's infamous plot to poison the cigars and beard of Fidel Castro.

Or is it that, as usual, at the end of the First Gulf War the United States had no effective plan for peace, could not imagine any "linkage" that would transform military action into human and social action of lasting consequence? In the place of the terrible scenario for a nervous "peace" I have sketched above, I offer my own version. Acknowledge that the "new global order" is not merely an occasion for the United States to take advantage of problems in Russia and China to reassert the same old U.S. dominance in world affairs, but a genuine opportunity to create a "United Nations" that will govern by way of the human diversity it is intended to represent. Scrap the "Security Council." Cancel Veto-Power. Let every country admitted have one vote. Make consensus the aim for powerful and binding decisions regarding such matters as military aggression. Develop a genuinely multinational peace-keeping force, dividing the responsibility proportionately among the participating countries. Let this new United Nations negotiate settlements of issues of clear international consequence, and let this same United Nations delegate other issues of more local consequence to "subcommittees" composed of the nations in the region most immediately affected: in this case, a Middle Eastern Conference called by the United Nations and conducted according to general rules and guidelines established by the U.N. In effect, give the United Nations the powers to debate and finally *decide* legal, territorial, and economic issues of consequence to the world communities. In short, do not send James Baker III to Geneva to negotiate with Tariq Aziz in the "name" of the United Nations. After the Geneva Accords of 1954, who could believe in such a fiction? Why else did those last-minute diplomatic efforts collapse so quickly and so ludicrously?

Give the United Nations economic powers as well, so that this international body might impose long-term, effective economic sanctions against an aggressor-nation. All the arguments about how the League of Nations and then the United Nations have failed to bring about this new means of reaching global consensus and resolving legally and economically such disputes must for the moment be put aside. We have never before tried to forge such an international body for judgment beyond the logic of "balance-of-power" politics, outside the framework of European colonialism, or in the aftermath of the Cold War. We have such an opportunity now.[52]

If such a "peaceful solution" strikes you as naive, unworkable, or hopelessly unrealistic, I ask you to consider one more factor. Those who opposed this war were asked ceaselessly and rhetorically by other concerned citizens, "But what can we *do*?" The implied answer to this question is always the same: "We had no choice, but to pursue military action against Iraq." Of the many possible peaceful options available to us and the United Nations before military action began, none was given a reasonable chance to work.

We will not fight in the Persian Gulf with "one hand tied behind our backs," President George H. W. Bush insisted. And we would not lose our "resolve" to "finish the job" that according to this logic we "left unfinished" in Vietnam. But President George H. W. Bush was wrong on both accounts. To pit young men and women on both sides against smart bombs and missiles, Abrams tanks and land mines—in short, to pit the frail and precious human body against flying bits of sharpened metal—this is indeed to fight "with one hand tied behind our backs," the hand, in short, that extends a human touch, a certain sympathy, not for a dictator like Saddam Hussein but for the 17.5 million Iraqis who suffer most from this war and for the homeless, displaced, impoverished peoples of the Middle East, who in their desperation look to Saddam Hussein as a hero. To imagine that "war" is a "job to finish" only ignores utterly the lessons of the Vietnam War. For some, it was our ignoble retreat from Vietnam—from the rooftops of Saigon in 1975 or from the Paris Peace Talks in 1973—that led to the repressive regime in contemporary Vietnam. But it was our conduct in that War that caricatured the best minds and talents of the Vietnamese nationalist movements as vulgar Communists, as "enemies of the people," while we supported a succession of thugs, crooks, and megalomaniacs.

War is never a "job to finish," as the veterans of the Vietnam War will tell you. For those who fought and served in Vietnam, the war will never be over. For the 58,000 Americans who died there, for the 75,000 who committed suicide after they returned home, for the estimated 2 million Vietnamese who died in the war, for the families who have suffered, and for the veterans from all sides of our ugly war who still suffer Post-Traumatic Stress Disorder—for these and many other survivors of the Vietnam War, the parallels of this war, however "swift" and "surgical" it may have been conducted on the battlefield, are to Vietnam, the war we lost when we could not articulate the peace. The peace is made not when war is over, but before war has begun. The "just war," if such a notion is possible, depends not on arcane ethical debates, but on the promise of the peace that will come from such war, so that we may assess the cost of our brothers and sisters on both sides.

We have no plan for peace in the Middle East, no "policy" for the future of the region, unless it is a "secret" plan worked out in the offices of the Pentagon and the Executive branch of the government. Too often in our history, we have known how to make war but failed to imagine peace. 217 times we have fought in our brief history, only seven times with Congressionally approved declarations of war. It is not just the conduct of the war that we must protest; it is also our failure to pursue peace that we must protest. We should not be in the Persian Gulf to "win" the war we lost in Vietnam; we should be in the Persian Gulf to win the peace we never found in Vietnam.

During the First Gulf War, Harold Meyerson argued that the continuing crisis in the Middle East resembles neither World War II nor Vietnam, insisting that opponents of the First Gulf War "insist on a politics rooted in the present".[53] Meyerson wisely argues we should avoid historical comparisons that distract us from particular circumstances in global conflicts. Comparing Saddam Hussein to Adolf Hitler, the invasion of Kuwait to the Nazi invasion of Czechoslovakia, confuses by conflating different dictators, eras, regions, and peoples. By the same token, we should not rush to forget the lessons of the past, especially when they are hard lessons such as those learned in Vietnam. These are lessons to be studied by what Meyerson considers the "fractured" American left but also by all those who claimed a short-term victory in the six-week war in the Persian Gulf. Unless we articulate a detailed foreign policy, address the concerns of the politically and economically disempowered (both at home and abroad), and learn to deal with other *cultures* rather than with political celebrities, we shall be doomed to a "new global order"—the popular slogan of President George H. W. Bush's administration—of ceaseless little wars. Let us remember that opposition to the Vietnam War was not the *cause* of losing an unwinnable, immoral war; it was simply one expression of the dissent and debate that are the true signs of democracy and rational patriotism. Silence and forgetfulness have often enough been the heralds of history's most terrible epochs.

Afterword: 2010

It is chilling to read the previous pages after almost twenty years, a decade after 9/11, and realize how clear it was in 1991 that the unresolved problems in the Middle East, most of them resulting from the postcolonial effects of EuroAmerican colonial interference in the region, would only be exacerbated by the Coalition's military action in the First Gulf War. The emergence of al-Qaeda is not anticipated explicitly, but some organization of political and military resistance to the West seems nearly inevitable given our foreign policy myopia in treating Saddam Hussein as an isolable dictator, who could be controlled with sheer military force. The ceaseless "little wars" predicted in the final paragraph are now integral to our foreign policy and daily lives, affecting the lives of so many Americans and peoples in Iraq, Jordan, Syria, Gaza, Palestine, Lebanon, Israel, Egypt, Somalia, Afghanistan, Pakistan, India, the Philippines. These wars and their continuing after-effects are destroying our vaunted economy, even as some Americans have taken the oddly undemocratic tack of "celebrating" our neo-imperialism as a virtue or a sign of "success". Instead, we seem poised on the brink of those collapses that have resulted from almost every imperial power in world history committed to a succession of wars to maintain its ever-expanding empire. As I write these lines, President Barack Obama struggles to extricate the U.S. from two costly wars in Iraq and Afghanistan, his own executive authority and liberal identity threatened by what Bob Woodward has dubbed in a just published book, *Obama's Wars*.[54] Even before its release, the book was condemned by right-wing journalists for contributing to the defeatism originally associated with the "Vietnam Syndrome".[55]

CHAPTER 3

Covering Iraq in Our Time

Prologue: 2010

In the U.S. edition of *In Our Time* (1925), Ernest Hemingway included among the well-known stories brief vignettes or "interludes", many dealing with World War I and the unstable political situation in Europe before and during the war.[56] These prose vignettes had been published separately the year before in Paris as a modernist experiment in prose poetry, *in our time* (1924), by William Bird in his Three Mountains Press.[57] When hand setting the type for the Paris edition, Bird considered framing "each page with a border of newsprint, carefully selected to serve both as decoration and illustration ... fitting for a book by a young journalist".[58] When combined with the Nick Adams' and other stories of the Midwest in the U.S. edition, the vignettes were understood to suggest an oblique commentary, a sort of modernist palimpsest (perhaps recalling Pound's influence on the young Hemingway), relating the volatile politics to the apparent normality of everyday life in the U.S.

What follows then is inspired by Hemingway's interludes in *In Our Time*, as well as by his original idea that a collection of quasi-journalistic short pieces might be rendered as avant-garde prose-poems with the intention of shocking his readers into some sort of recognition of the horrors awaiting those living through the interwar years. William Bird may have been thinking of the newspaper headlines in James Joyce's *Ulysses* (1922) and John Dos Passos' *Manhattan Transfer*, even though the latter novel wasn't published until 1925. It is by now a commonplace that high modernism competed with journalism by incorporating its media (both text and image) in order to re-function the message.

Although I want to call attention to this modernist heritage in my own brief "news story" from the Second Gulf War, I also want to suggest a somewhat different role for the scholar in writing contemporary journalism as part of a progressive cultural politics. Hemingway, Dos Passos, and Joyce imagined that by changing the *form* in which journalistic prose appeared, the message might be more effective. People don't read newspapers carefully, Dos Passos argued implicitly in *Manhattan Transfer*, whose pages jumble together international and local news. What connects the global and the local is not clearly established, which is the task of the novelist. Yet the modernist assumption relied on *careful* readers, who would take the time to ponder what related such disparate events as the Greco-Turkish War, the subject of Hemingway's "On the Quai at Smyrna", and EuroAmerican and Native American relations in the U.S. Midwest in the story "Indian Camp", for example, or how life in Manhattan in the 1920s might be affected by the colonial struggle over Morocco included in Dos Passos's *Manhattan Transfer*.[59]

Yet writing for the thoughtful reader capable of understanding the impact of colonial instabilities in Northwest Africa or the consequences of the forced expulsion of Greeks from the city of Smyrna, renamed Ismailia by the Turks, in the Greco-Turkish War may not be a luxury the political activist can indulge. Today's media are too various and too rapid in their treatment of the news to allow such avant-garde interventions to have significant impact. Of course, scholars routinely write op-ed pieces in newspapers, are interviewed as experts on television and radio and Internet news, use their own web-sites and blogs to offer alternative news, and in many other ways realize the role of "public intellectual" I argued in Chapter 1 we all need to assume from time to time.

The activist scholar faces a number of problems as a public intellectual, including stereotypes of the scholar as left-wing, liberal, "politically correct", or tenured-radical. Popular assumptions about the scholar include clichés about disciplines, which are difficult to dispel. There is also a certain randomness to the ways mass media representatives consult scholarly experts. Ask a reporter how he or she "found" you and often the answer is through a departmental administrative assistant, a friend at another university hoping to dodge the assignment, or some hasty web-search. If scholar-activists are to make effective interventions in mass-media, then they must understand these variables and learn how to adapt to them.

I was asked to write the following 200-word response to a question posed by a reporter from the Long Island, New York newspaper, *Newsday*, one day after images of four Blackwater security "contractors'" burnt corpses were shown in news media around the world on April 1, 2004.[60] The event is by now a famous prelude to Coalition forces' military assaults on the Iraqi city of Fallujah in al Anbar Province between 2004 and 2006, resulting in the virtual destruction of much of the city and the displacement of most of the urban population. Scott Helvenson, Jerry (Jerko) Zovko, Wesley Batalona, and Michael Teague, employed by Blackwater Security, hired by the U.S. Department of Defense to provide various forms of security for support services in Iraq, were attacked by members of the Islamic Army of Iraq while driving their Blackwater SUV to guard transport of food catering services for the military in Fallujah. After their SUV was destroyed by a rocket-propelled grenade, the four dead contractors were dragged from the SUV and their corpses hung from a railroad bridge crossing the Euphrates River. Now informally called by Coalition forces the "Blackwater Bridge", the site with its burnt and grotesquely hanging bodies quickly became an image of the ongoing conflict in Iraq following the rapid and seemingly successful invasion by Coalition forces in March 2003.

Given the subsequent military events in Fallujah, including the abortive "Operation Vigilant Resolve", which began shortly after the global outrage concerning the images of the Blackwater contractors' burnt, hanging bodies, and the controversial Operation Phantom Fury, which began in November 2004 and resulted not only in widespread urban destruction and casualties but also lingering environmental damage, the question I was asked seems absurdly trivial in retrospect: "Is a picture worth a thousand words?"[61] There was more, of course, to this question. The editors of *Newsday* wanted to know if an "expert" on representations of warfare thought that this particular image would stir anti-war or pro-war responses in the U.S. They also wanted a response by the mid-day on April 1, so it could be revised and ready for publication on April 2.

This journalistic demand for immediate response leaves little time for reflection or research, which is why Joyce, Dos Passos, and Hemingway offered alternative literary responses to journalism. Yet with the Second Gulf War winding down in the imagination of the U.S. public, especially after President George W. Bush's infamous "Mission Accomplished" speech on October 29, 2003 on board the aircraft carrier, *U.S.S. Abraham Lincoln*, the *Newsday* assignment seemed a rare opportunity to call attention to the building problems in "postwar" Iraq. I entitled my one-page op-ed "Covering Iraq", alluding to Edward Said's *Covering Islam* (1981), especially its subtitle: *How the Media and Experts Determine How We See the Rest of the World.*[62] Said's main title is, of course, a pun on how the Western media stereotype Islam in ways consistent with the Western "Orientalism" Said famously analyzes and criticizes in *Orientalism* (1978).[63] In stressing the horrible consequences of military conflict on the four Blackwater Security "contractors", the news media had indeed "covered up" the ongoing violence against Iraqis in the Coalition's unjustified invasion of the sovereign nation of Iraq.

Not only did I attempt to change the subject from the clichéd question of whether or not a "picture is worth a thousand words" to the media's "coverage" of the ongoing war in Iraq, but I also attempted to call attention to the little-discussed use of independent "contractors" in the Second Gulf War. In 2004, this issue had hardly been discussed, and Blackwater Security was little known to the general public. Founded in 1997 by Erik Prince and Al Clark, Blackwater Security Consulting played an increasingly controversial role as a private security firm and militia in Iraq from 2003–2009, when the firm was expelled from Iraq by the Iraqi government. Struggling to refurbish its public image while doing little to change its paramilitary tactics, Blackwater changed its name in 2009 to "Xe Services", a strategy apparently designed to frustrate independent Internet searches of its personnel and corporate structure, and then on June 8, 2010 was put up for sale.[64] In 2004, long before public attention in the U.S. focused on "private contractors" in Iraq, I easily accessed the Blackwater Security Consulting site and was able to scroll through the names of employees, virtually all of whom were veterans of U.S., South African, and other national armies around the world. The impunity with which the U.S. Department of Defense was operating by employing such paramilitary organizations and thinly veiling their activities with the euphemism "private contractors" alarmed me, and I hoped in my brief op-ed to call attention to the issue, as the last line of the newspaper story does.

Did it "work"? No, it did not, if we judge merely from the fact that Blackwater Security operated successfully in Iraq for another five years and that in the meantime Erik Prince used the wealth generated by this firm to support anti-Islamic, fundamentalist Christian causes.[65] Resigning as CEO of Xe Services on March 2, 2009, Prince not only put up the firm for sale on June 8, 2010, but he moved to Abu Dhabi on August 18, 2010, because as some suspected the United Arab Emirates do not have an extradition treaty with the U.S.[66] My allusion to Said's *Covering Islam* was lost when the Editor retitled the one-page story, "Images from Fallujah Will Stir Debate, But…Won't Alter Policy", drawing a conclusion he had wanted but did not get. My message instead focused on Iraqi anger at U.S. imperialism, Blackwater Security's private role in the war, and the need for better information about casualties in the invasion and continuing violence.

In another, immeasurable sense, the 200-word newspaper story *does* work, because it asked such questions before they became routine topics of conversation and public debate. Blackwater Security has been expelled from Iraq and lost its credibility; no one is any longer fooled by the euphemistic term "private contractors"; few believe that the "civil war" in Iraq following our invasion was not directly related to our imperialism; information about casualties in the Second Gulf War and its aftermath is now provided by a variety of sources.

Covering Iraq: April 1–2, 2004

What should the news media *show* of the recent killing of four American civilians in Fallujah? Although debates revolve around what is proper to the victims and their families and how sensationalism should be avoided, the underlying concern is the political use of such imagery. Will the charred bodies of these four employees of Blackwater Security "intimidate" Americans and cause us to lose our "resolve"? Will we abandon our military and foreign policy missions in Iraq as the Clinton Administration was accused of withdrawing from Somalia in the now infamous aftermath of "Blackhawk Down"? Or will still and moving photographs of an angry mob exulting in its abuse of four American citizens strengthen a national consensus previously divided over the propriety of the Bush Administration's invasion of Iraq and its "war on terror"?

However powerful we think media images, they will do little in and of themselves to strengthen or challenge our military and foreign policies in Iraq. As anti-war activists discovered in the Vietnam era, the mere display of damaged bodies—the infamous photos of the VietCong suspect executed by the Saigon Police Chief and the naked, screaming child burned by Napalm—has not alone changed policy or opinion. In too many cases, such photographs have taken the place of serious historical and political discussion, substituting sentiment for reason. The mere exhibition of such human misery can at its worst take on a perverse allure, even aesthetic fascination, closer to the fetishistic use of human bodies in Fallujah than we care to consider. The fetish usually indicates a desire for power we do not have: our failure to comprehend the reason four more Americans died; the mob's inability to affect U.S. authority. If these deaths are not to be in vain, then we must look at what they tell us. The war in Iraq continues as a guerilla war against invaders, not a civil war. The rage of the mob in Fallujah is part of the anger felt by many in the Arab world toward the United States. The horrible deaths of four civilians call for better information about casualties to all combatants and noncombatants in this war. The role of private military companies in Iraq needs greater scrutiny.

CHAPTER 4

Areas of Concern

Area Studies and the New American Studies

The following chapter deals with the relationship between the micropolitics of academic disciplines and the macropolitics of nation-states. When neo-conservatives complain about the "politicizing" of education, often insisting that all forms of education remain "free" of political interference, they ignore the fact that educational curricula and pedagogies have always been deeply involved in specific political practices and positions. Insisting that we keep education free of political interests is simply unrealistic; students should learn instead how to negotiate specific political positions based on available information and defend their positions accordingly. It has often been argued that entire fields are shaped by specific epistemologies, which in turn represent particular political interests. The histories of both American Studies and various "area studies" are good examples, especially insofar as "area studies" have had close relations with state sponsorship, both intellectual and economic, since their beginnings. The following chapter treats the critical interpretation of these political interests of American Studies (both traditional and "new") and of various "area studies" as political practice, arguing that the activism of the new American Studies should not be restricted simply to macropolitical issues, such as those treated in the three preceding chapters.

American Studies has thus far avoided the heated debates concerning the restructuring of area studies prompted by dramatic changes in the geopolitical and economic maps as a consequence of globalization. In view of the U.S. role in the economic, political, and cultural changes produced by globalization, we might expect that American Studies would be as fiercely contested in its disciplinary borders as East Asian, Middle Eastern, Southeast Asian, Soviet, and Latin American Studies, to mention only a few of the areas established by post-World War II scholarship and facing dramatic challenges since the 1970s, especially in the aftermath of Soviet decolonization. Of course, the area studies model has defined primarily the social sciences—economics, political science, and sociology—and interdisciplinary conjunctures of history and the social sciences, including "historical sociology" and "social science history".[67] Given the centrality of cultural production, especially literature and the visual arts, and traditional history in the field of American Studies, it is not surprising that American Studies would be considered eccentric to the debates concerning the scholarly map of a new world order governed by new political, economic, and social forces. Whether treated as epiphenomenal or superstructural, the objects of study dominating post-World War II American Studies—"myths and symbols" to use a convenient tag—hardly warranted the attention of serious scholars dealing with urgent issues of global political instability, economic crisis, war, genocide, famine and drought, and the spread of infectious diseases.

In ancient Greece, geographers divided their field into three major continental areas: Europe, Asia, and Libya (Africa).[68] The sixteenth- to eighteenth-century voyages of European exploration and the consolidation of what Walter Mignolo terms the "modern/colonial world system" expanded the ancient continental model while relying on many of its basic assumptions regarding both the hierarchy of civilizations and the uniqueness of the peoples in these different regions.[69] The "seven-continent model of the modern elementary school classroom" led to refinements and subdivisions, most of them reflecting specific European colonial interests. As Martin Lewis and Kären Wigen have written: "[S]cholarly divisions of labor showed that the tripartite global model of the ancient Greeks was deeply entrenched. The West (North America and Europe) was conceptualized as the site for serious history and the social sciences; the East (stretching from Morocco to Japan), as the zone where Orientalists could ponder the cultural flowers of supposedly fossilized civilizations; and the rest of the world was the domain of anthropologists, who specialized in 'primitive' cultural and social systems" (163).

According to the "Best is the West" thesis, the U.S. and Canada shared the privileged status of Europe in the traditional area studies model that dominated the social sciences from their institutional inception in the nineteenth century through the formal reforms instituted by the Ethno-geographic Board commissioned by the U.S. government in 1942 (Lewis and Wigen, 163). Certainly the confusion of nationalist and racialist ideologies in the nineteenth and early twentieth century contributed to such myths as "the March of the Anglo-Saxon", whose "destiny" ranged from Northern Europe to England, Ireland, Scotland, and then across the Atlantic and the North American Continent in a "manifest destiny" that would civilize triumphantly the rest of the world. According to this familiar notion that the United States in particular (although Canada first as colony and then as member of the British Commonwealth also qualifies) is merely an extension of European Civilization, creating the "greater" Western Civilization also thoroughly challenged from the 1970s onward, it would seem that the United States and Canada (North America) and their prototypes in Europe would constitute the most important "area" for study and thus draw as much as possible on complementary fields such as American and Canadian Studies.

Yet this was obviously not the case when modern "area studies" operated under the shadow of the modern/colonial world system. Neither American nor European Studies existed in the period of nineteenth-century nationalism, the consolidation of European imperialism, and the emergence of U.S. imperial authority. The "serious history and social sciences" Lewis and Wigen contend were devoted to North America and Europe offered primarily a model to the rest of the world for "civilization", both in its contemporarily achieved and its ideal or destined forms. Walt Whitman's *Democratic Vistas* (1871/1876) is neither sociology nor history, but its incorporation of the rest of the emerging world into the "cosmic" destiny of U.S. democracy and individualism exemplifies this paradox that the privileged "areas" of Western Civilization—the U.S., Canada, Europe, and their Greco-Roman sources—are not "areas" at all, but conceptualizations or idealisms capable of thriving anywhere and everywhere, like the mind of God.[70] Neither North American nor European Studies were necessary to "study" such a historically and geographically specific suite of phenomena, because they were indeed the intellectual complements of the modern/colonial world system, hardly subject to the internal critique or metanarrative that might have resulted from taking "America" or "Europe" as "objects of study".

When at the beginning of World War II, the "U.S. government called upon the Smithsonian Institution, the American Council of Learned Societies, the National Research Council, and the Social Science Research Council to form a body known as the Ethnogeographic Board", the charge to create "a new system of global divisions" was hardly intended to do away with imperialist hierarchies of the older "area studies" and their commitment to "the West is the Best" (Lewis and Wigen, 163). The Ethnogeographic Board was formally established in June of 1942.[71] Carl E. Guthe, the anthropologist who chaired the new Board, characterizes it as "a non-governmental agency established in the name of the scientists and scholars of the country for the purpose of aiding the government" (Guthe, 189). This curious alliance of putatively independent foundations, scholars, and governmental institutions—a "state-scholarly complex"—continues to shape area studies to this day, even after the Cold-War era and funding have passed. What motivated the U.S. government was the need for more effective "language training" and "cultural fluency" to enable the U.S. and its allies to conduct "the war effort across large spans of the globe" (Lewis and Wigen, 163).

The work of the Board is characterized by Guthe as "interdisciplinary in scope, seeking to use the facilities and knowledge of the earth sciences, the biological sciences, the social sciences, and the humanities, in so far as these relate to regions outside of the continental United States" (Guthe, 189). Lewis and Wigen note that geography played a much smaller role on the Board than was initially imagined; Robert B. Hall is the only geographer on the original eight-scholar Board (Lewis and Wigen, 163). The Board membership in 1943 listed by Guthe includes two archaeologists (if you count Strong twice in this list), three anthropologists, a historian, a geographer, a biologist, a public health specialist, and an East Asian languages scholar.[72] Chaired by Guthe, the Board was directed by William Duncan Strong (1899–1962), the Columbia University archaeologist and anthropologist (1937–1962), who specialized in the indigenous peoples of North and South America, especially the Incas of Peru.[73] Thus Guthe's specific exclusion of areas within "the continental United States" clearly did not include "indigenous peoples and their cultures", reinforcing the notion that this "area studies" model was fully committed to the modernizaton and development processes. Archaeology and Anthropol-

ogy (especially if you count William Duncan Strong twice, as his expertise in both disciplines warrants) account for more than half of the disciplines represented on the Board (5 of 9). Only two of these scholars can
be considered vaguely connected with the "humanities"—the Sinologist
Mortimer Graves and historian Carter Goodrich.[74] Neither "American
Studies" nor "American Literature", indeed *any* literary or cultural specializations, other than those covered by the anthropologists and archaeologists, are represented on the Board.

The unmanageable "seven-continents" model and its "European colonial" subtext of the prewar era was replaced by the more specific "areas"
proposed by the Ethnogeographic Commission: East Asia, Southeast
Asia, South Asia, the Middle East, Africa, Latin America, North America,
Russia and Eastern Europe, Western Europe, and Oceania (Lewis and
Wigen, 163–164). The older colonial hierarchy was replaced by goals of
"modernization and development", whereby North America and Western Europe still retained their status as "superior civilizations" by virtue
of technological advances and claims to political innovations. The interdisciplinary alliance between the social sciences, the humanities, and geography was not realized. Lewis and Martin point out that although two
"prominent geographers, Isaiah Bowman and Robert Hall, were appoint-
ed" to the Ethnogeographic Board, "few geographers became involved in
the intellectual work of the board, and the task of delineating areas fell
primarily to anthropologists and other social scientists" (163).[75] Indeed,
"the anthropological imprint is evident in the use of the term area (derived from ethnological studies of 'culture areas'), rather than *region*", a
symptom to my mind of how such "area studies" were already motivated
by the "modernization and development" models isomorphic with neo-
imperialism, especially later versions of "free-trade imperialism", and
third-stage, postindustrial capitalism in its global form.

Interestingly, the work of the Ethnogeographic Board occurs contem-
poraneously with the emergence of American Studies as an "interdisciplinary field", however we might quibble over exact "origins", in the influential work of F. O. Matthiessen, whose *American Renaissance* is published
in 1941. And yet American Studies, especially in the Myth-and-Symbol
School so often traced back to Matthiessen, is by no means an "area studies" field as it was conceived by the anthropologists, geographers, biolo-

gists, and other scholars serving on the Ethnogeographic Board. If there is a connection, then it must be made through the cultural idealism of American Studies supporting, often unwittingly, the "modernization and development" ideology of the area studies developed by the Ethnogeographic Board in the early 1940s and fully institutionalized during the Cold War, especially with the "1958 National Defense Education Act, Title VI, [...] which supplied the funds to establish university area-studies centers" that by 1990 totaled "some 124 National Resource Centers,[...] each devoted to the interdisciplinary study of a particular world region" (Lewis and Wigen, 164). Of course, since Donald Pease published his pioneering "*Moby-Dick* and the Cold War" in 1985, much valuable work has been done on how American Studies participated in Cold War ideology, especially its articulation of an American Exceptionalism subsequently challenged by a "new" American Studies vigorously committed to transnational, postnational, postcolonial, indigenist, and multiethnic goals for understanding the "United States" in global contexts.[76]

Indeed, the critique of Cold-War area studies, initiated largely by left intellectuals in the 1970s, once again coincides historically with the criticism of first-generation American Studies (primarily the ideology of the Myth-and-Symbol School) directed by feminists, ethnic studies, postmodernists, gay studies, and other minoritized intellectuals at how their interests and rights were at worst neglected or at best "synthesized" in traditional American Studies. Lewis and Wigen attribute the "crisis" in area studies that begins in the 1970s to "the stalling out of the growth of U.S. universities in the 1970s", the "end of the Vietnam War" resulting in "a major loss of funding for Southeast Asian Studies programs", and extending to the more urgent crisis at the end of the 1980s "when the end of the cold war undercut the geopolitical rational for area studies expertise just as the demise of the Soviet Union and its sphere of influence rendered the postwar area-studies map outdated" (Lewis and Wigen, 164). The Gulbenkian Commission convened by Immaneul Wallerstein in the mid-1990s to propose alternatives to the area-studies model in its 1996 *Open the Social Sciences*, also cites "the challenge [...] from [...] 'cultural studies'" according to "three main themes": "the central importance of gender studies and all kinds of 'non-Eurocentric' studies to the study of historical social systems; second, the importance of local, very situated historical analysis, associated by many with a new 'hermeneutic turn'; third, the assessment of the values involved in technological achievements in relation to other values" (64, 65). Wallerstein's Gulbenkian Report considers these developments to promise new relationships among humanists (especially "among scholars in literary studies of all kinds"), anthropology, and "the new quasi-disciplines relating to the 'forgotten' peoples of modernity (those neglected by virtue of gender, race, class, etc.), for whom it provided a theoretical ('postmodern') framework for their elaborations of difference" (65).

But this promise to "open the social sciences" beyond the Cold-War area studies model to include developments familiar to scholars of the "new" American Studies does not sufficiently take into account the enormous institutional resistance of scholars trained in area studies, still committed to their specializations, and in some areas, notably "East Asian", "South Asian", "Middle Eastern", and "Latin American", benefiting, rather than suffering, from the collapse of "Southeast Asian Studies" and "Soviet Studies". Area Studies are alive and well, defending their territories with the determination of scholars whose very existences depend on this fight and have at their command an impressive arsenal of "common-sense" arguments opposing coalitions with "new" American Studies, Postcolonial Studies, Cultural Studies, and virtually any version of "postmodernism" and its assorted complements, "cosmopolitanism" and "post- or neo-Marxism". In these intellectual fights, there are lots of interesting figures at the vanguard; Walter Mignolo's "border thinking" and Juan Poblete's *Critical Latin American and Latino Studies* (2003) force area-studies scholars to defend explicitly intellectual boundaries that still retain their imperial legacies, buried for a time beneath a certain pseudo-scientific reliance on empirical data and disguised in part by a post-World War II U.S. provenance casting a vaguely "democratic" aura in which the "modernization and development" ideology is clearly announced.

Why should American Studies scholars engage in these fights, which are often staged in terms of national languages, local and regional histories, and institutional politics in which we are unevenly trained? And if we are committed, as I am, to the comparative study of Canada and the Americas, rather than merely U.S.-centric "American Studies", however diverse we may make it, then how do we respond to the familiar challenge from Latin American area specialists that our project is simply the next stage of U.S. imperialism stretching from the Monroe doctrine through the Spanish-American War to the Pan-Americanism of the Cold War era? Finally, is not this commitment to "hemispheric study" of Canada and the Americas merely a revival of the much older continental model for area studies, replacing contemporary problems with even more insidious difficulties haunting us from the European imperial past?

There are practical answers to each of these questions. American Studies must develop curricula that require foreign languages relevant to the different communities in Canada and the Americas, just as we should broaden our curricula to deal with local and regional histories beyond the United States. Of course, we must be attentive to the problems of linguistic, cultural, and epistemological imperialism, especially in a global era shaped by neo-imperialistic practices that work as much through cultural and intellectual means as through military, political, and economic tactics. But not all study of other societies is inevitably imperialist, especially when the method of scholarship is intended to investigate precisely the imperialist inclinations of knowledge to follow power. Comparative study of the different communities in the Western Hemisphere is intended to pay particularly close attention to the historical power dynamics that created hierarchies along the North-South axis as troubling as the imperial assumptions implicit in an earlier East-West divide (monumentalized in Hegel's ineluctable evolution of World-Historical Spirit from east to Western Civilization). Finally, the "Western Hemisphere" reproduces the older continental model of prewar area studies if we focus upon its "exceptional" status, either in its pre-Columbian, premodern indigeneity or in its extraordinary uniqueness as the "New World" that would realize the ideals of European imperialists. Understood as a particularly instructive instance of what Mignolo terms the "modern/colonial world system", the Western Hemisphere cannot be disengaged finally from the global processes in which it has been historically involved, including those that traversed it long before the arrival of European invaders. In this context, we must begin to think less in terms of the pertinent "rims"—Pacific, North Atlantic, mid-Atlantic, Caribbean—and more in terms of certain "flows" describing the terrestrial, maritime, modern avian, and postmodern transits of outer (military and communications' satellites) and inner (bodily prostheses and virtual realities) spaces.[77]

These answers are not really what many area studies specialists want to hear, because the threat posed to their disciplines also involves an internal critique already well underway in U.S.-centric American Studies and increasingly evident in Latin American Studies. Despite the very different European imperialisms and their historical modalities informing traditional studies of the "Americas", they have in common the Creole nationalisms that developed in rebellion against their imperial masters. Following Enrique Dussel's *The Invention of America*, Mignolo points out:

> "America", interestingly enough, is a name that became the territorial identification not for the Spanish crown, or for the Spanish in the Indias Occidentales, but for the Creole population and intellectuals, born in "America" from Spanish descent and leaders of the independence during the nineteenth century. It was also the Creole population and its intellectuals who initiated a process of self-definition as "Americans", with all its possible variations ("Spanish", "Indo", "Latin") [...]. The importance of the discourse of geocultural identity lies in the fact that it filled a space that was broken in the process of conquest and colonization. [130]

The "creoles" to whom Mignolo refers are the descendants of Spaniards or Portuguese born in the colonies, from whom "liberators" like Simón Bolívar and José de San Martín would emerge to lead the national revolutions of the early nineteenth century in what they themselves would come to term "Latin America".

Although we do not refer to the U.S. "founding fathers" or cultural nationalists, such as Emerson and Hawthorne and Whitman, as "Creoles", they fit Mignolo's conception of the anti-imperialist aura of national ideology in the Western Hemisphere.[78] Despite the enormous differences between Bolívar's struggle against Spanish imperial power in decline and Franklin and Adams's struggle against British imperialism, increasingly triumphant around the globe, South American and North American "Creole nationalisms" commonly "filled a space that was broken in the process of conquest and colonization" (130). Mignolo is referring to the massive destruction of indigenous societies by European conquest and colonization, and it is indeed remarkable how often U.S. and Latin American revolutionaries would invoke the imperial destruction of indigenous peoples as a justification for Creole revolution, despite the open hostility most Creoles displayed to their own indigenous populations. From American rebels disguised as native peoples their forefathers had slaughtered in the Pequot War and King Philip's War to the melodramatic outrage expressed by Bolívar regarding Spanish atrocities against Amerindians or José Martí's paternalism with regard to North American Indians with whom he claims a tenuous bond, the political writings of the Creole nationalists in North and South America are full of passionate commitments to the liberation of indigenous peoples from the slavery and exploitation of their common imperial masters.[79]

Despite very different national policies toward indigenous peoples throughout the Hemisphere, the "national" stage of the modern/colonial world system displays the perpetuation of colonial oppression under the guise of "national development" and "necessary modernization". And although these bourgeois, Creole nationalisms appear to have continued the policies of their imperial masters in ways that perpetuated the linguistic, ethnic, and cultural differences distinguishing Spanish, Portuguese, and British imperialisms (to deal with only the three most powerful between 1500 and 1800), they developed a certain strategic commonality that persists to this day and may well be one reason why Latin American area studies' scholars fight so vigorously against the hemispheric comparatism of the "new" American Studies. Mignolo is particularly clear on the development of an intriguing "commonality" of these diverse American "nations":

> [I]t is clear that between 1820 and 1830 the future historical paths of the two Americas, Anglo and Latin, were being decided. Before then, roughly from 1500 to 1800, the differences between the two Americas were the differences dictated between the Spanish and British empires in the modern/colonial world system. Language and race [...] were two crucial components in the articulation of the modern/colonial world system imaginary.

The commonality of the difference, however, lies in the way that, at the beginning of the nineteenth century, "America" was appropriated by intellectuals of the emerging states as different from Europe but still within the West. [...]. [P]olitical independence was accompanied by a symbolic independence in the geopolitical imagination. (134–135)

Mignolo identifies in this passage a nineteenth-century "American Exceptionalism" of hemispheric and transnational scope. We recognize immediately a host of possible examples ranging from the fierce struggle for "literary nationalism" in the antebellum U.S., which is haunted by European allusions and models, to comparable struggles of Latin American intellectuals to break free of European sources by adapting them to South American, Caribbean, or Meso-American human and natural environments. The latter project seems brilliantly represented and satirized in the Cuban novelist Alejo Carpentier's *Los pasos perdidos* (1953), often cited as one of the first works of the so-called "Latin American Boom".[80]

In the print-dominated era of nineteenth-century nationalism, literature played a crucial role in constructing and interpellating this national imaginary. The anti-imperialist rhetoric dominates not only the overtly "democratic" literature of the traditional "American Renaissance", but also includes many key Latin American literary texts of the period. *Jicoténcal*, the anti-imperial Mexican novel published anonymously in Philadelphia in 1826 and attributed by some scholars to the revolutionary Cuban priest, Félix Varela, occupies a celebrated position in the Latin American literary canon, in part because its stinging indictment of Cortès, his consort, Doña Marina (La Malinche), and the Catholic priests accompanying his military invasion appears written in support of the Mexican revolution against Spain, other revolutionary movements in Latin America, and the novel's vigorous defense of indigenous rights as equivalent to those of the Creole revolutionaries realizing three centuries later the failed democratic aspirations of the Tlaxcalan eponymous hero, Jicoténcal himself, and his long suffering lover and wife, Teutila.[81]

The "commonality of the difference" Mignolo finds in Creole nationalisms in the Western Hemisphere links these emancipatory movements with the imperialist agendas they transcoded from their imperialist masters: Spain, Portugal, Netherlands, England, and France. Although the

North-South divide in the Western Hemisphere has long been defined by the radical differences in public policies regarding ethnic and racial identities, there is also a "commonality of the difference" across this border when we consider how these same Creole nationalisms treated indigenous peoples and Creoles of color. At the height of nineteenth-century nationalist ferment in the hemisphere, Creole revolutionaries rarely invoked the Haitian slave rebellion, arguably the first successful slave revolt in history, and consistently incorporated indigenous issues into their own nationalist platforms while perpetuating, in many cases worsening, the social and human conditions under which indigenous peoples struggled to survive (Mignolo, 139). Immediately upon establishing "national" boundaries, most emerging nations also initiated vigorous campaigns of territorial expansion, entering into struggles with neighbors that in some cases last to the present day.

I repeat Mignolo's phrase "the commonality of the difference" in order to stress the point that a comparative study of the communities of the Western Hemisphere is not a question of identifying their deep-structural unity or their distinct "national exceptionalisms", as an older Comparative Literature did with its largely European models in the misnamed "World Literatures" project. The imperialist subtext I have interpreted as "common" to Creole nationalisms hardly leads to positive answers to such questions as posed by Gustavo Pérez Firmat's influential collection of 1990, *Do the Americas Have a Common Literature?*, or Mashall Eakin's more recent query, "Does Latin America Have a Common History?"[82] There are nevertheless points of contact and commonality that allow us to conduct such comparative work at crucial intersections or contact zones, rather than producing yet another testament to a monumental "exceptionalism" that is at root neo-imperialist. I will conclude by identifying and then discussing briefly some of the more important of these intersectional sites as ways of following out the logic of what Mignolo terms "border thinking".

National expansionist projects in contestation with other nationalist projects in the Hemisphere are particularly worthy of our attention. Mignolo focuses on 1848 and 1898 as crucial historical moments in "the early division between Anglo and Latin America" (136). The Treaty of Guadalupe-Hidalgo concluding the Mexican War (1846–1848) "was a conflict between new emerging nations", Mexico and the United States, and the open imperialism of the U.S. has often been cited as one reason the War has until recently played such a small role in U.S. cultural and social history.[83] Its significance in shifting the "border" between North and South, as well as incorporating in a very short span a significant "Latinidad" into the United States, cannot be ignored by the "new" American Studies. In most accounts, the focus is on victimized Mexico, just a quarter of a century free from Spanish imperial control and continuing to struggle with internal political and economic problems at the time of the War's outbreak. Lost in the course of most accounts, including literary and cultural histories, are the indigenous peoples, already systematically displaced, enslaved, and murdered during Spanish and subsequent Mexican colonization of Baja and Alta California, then subject to a host of new laws and rules imposed by postwar American officials and less formal, but accepted, practices of genocide practiced by U.S. citizens well into the twentieth century.

For Mignolo, 1898 also redraws the hemispheric map, ostensibly by asserting overtly the imperialist agenda of the United States in its invocation of the Monroe Doctrine and the collapse of Spanish imperial claims in the Hemisphere (136). I would add that U.S. negotiations with Great Britain for a Canal Treaty and during Secretary of State John Hay's "Open Door Policy" in Asia have to be considered, insofar as the result of these negotiations was that Great Britain agreed basically to U.S. hegemony in the Western Hemisphere in exchange for British dominance in Asia.[84] Too often forgotten in the invocation of 1898, however, is the U.S. co-optation of the republican struggles in Cuba and Puerto Rico, as well as in the Philippines. To study 1898, we must travel one of those strategic "rims" or follow one of those historical "flows" across the Pacific, recognizing that the U.S. suppression of Philippine nationalism in the Philippine-American War (1899–1902) followed out the foreign policy the U.S. applied in the Caribbean, especially to its current protectorate, Puerto Rico, and troublesome Cuba. The relationship between the U.S. and Spain in the Spanish-American War cannot be understood adequately without also examining the U.S. relationship to Cuban and Puerto Rican nationalisms. As scholars from Sundquist to Brickhouse have explained, the revolutionary ferment of Cuban nationalists in the nineteenth century is complexly entangled with different U.S. political and economic interests, including pro-slavery interests in controlling Cuba as a source of slaves after the banning of the transatlantic slave trade in 1808.[85]

Once again, the "border thinking" required to understand the historical development of these Creole nationalisms in contestation with each other must involve recognition of the forgotten populations on these islands. In Cuba and Puerto Rico, we cannot speak any longer in the nineteenth century of "indigenous" peoples, although Puerto Rican activists still refer to themselves as "Borricuans", in reference to the first inhabitants, because those indigenous populations were murdered by European imperialists. But in Cuba, Afro-Cubans and descendants of maroon communities must also be identified as the "forgotten" populations who historically demonstrate a repertoire of means to resist and evade imperial extinction and national incorporation. Once we think of the intersection among the different peoples and communities marginalized by European and then nationalist imperialisms, we begin to recognize how "border thinking" leads to the several versions of "mondialization" Mignolo invokes in his recent work. Non-European populations in the Western Hemisphere brought with them and elaborated differently over time and in specific sites their African, Asian, Oceanic, and Amerindian heritages, including non-European languages and religions and cultural practices. Sometimes these non-European influences were hybridized with EuroAmerican cultures, but there are many instances of what I would term "maroon" styles, forms, and practices surviving as resistant discursive practices that powerfully mark the "horizon" of the EuroAmerican imaginary.

The troublesome linguistic divisions of the Hemisphere seem to confirm the strict divisions of the "Anglo" North, the "Spanish" Southwest, and the "Portuguese" Southeast, with epiphenomenal traces of linguistic imperialism scattered here and there, especially in the polyglot Caribbean from Dutch Aruba through French Martinique. Yet when we take these linguistic divisions in the historical, cultural, and geographic contexts of the entire Hemisphere, we must recognize that we are following the tracks of European and Creole nationalist imperialisms, ignoring the massive destruction of Amerindian languages and their related cultures as well as the suppression of non-European languages occasioned by slavery's systematic detribalization and its customary ban on literary and other formal education for slaves.

Werner Sollors' and Marc Shell's wonderful *Multilingual Anthology of American Literature* (2000) gives us barely a hint of what a genuinely "multilingual" account of Canada and the Americas would be like, if we were to overcome what Mignolo terms the systematic imperial "denial of coevalness" between European and Amerindian semiotics.[86] Colonial semiosis depended crucially upon the destruction of the Amerindian archive of knowledge and the repression of that history, just as slavery depends on the systematic denial of African retentions, including languages, religions, and cultural practices. A similar colonial semiosis is structurally integral to Creole nationalisms, as even the casual tourist cannot help but notice in the plethora of signs that testify to various nations' presumed "rootedness" in their Amerindian histories, even as their policies toward indigenous peoples have been consistently genocidal. What would happen if we were to attempt "border thinking" that instead of "adding" Amerindian and diasporic semiotics to the variety of European-based languages would challenge the "commonality of the difference" in those imported languages and their epistemological protocols? In short, the traditional "problem" of different "languages" dividing the "areas" of the Western Hemisphere turns out to be even more complicated when we factor in the numerous languages (and semiotic systems) occluded by this apparent diversity of the imperial legacy.

The other "area" neglected both by "area studies" and by American Studies, new or old, also suggests how we might approach "Hemispheric Studies" from beyond the shadow cast by European power/knowledge. Mignolo's emphasis on colonial semiosis at times ignores the biological transit of imperialism and the literal destruction not merely of the "texts" of pre-Columbian peoples but of their *bodies* and biochemistries. Charles Mann's *1491: New Revelations of the Americas before Columbus* (2005) summarizes the new scientific evidence of the impact of European diseases on indigenous peoples throughout the Hemisphere.[87] Infectious diseases like smallpox, influenza, and measles had dramatic impacts on Amerindian populations between 1500 and 1900, and for many Europeans appeared to support claims to the "superiority" of European "civilization", even when crudely calculated according to a Social Darwinist standard of "survival of the fittest". Area studies following the ideology of "modernization and development" would in many ways reinforce just such an ideology, often manifested in the "conflictive encounters between Old World Europeans and pre-Columbian peoples of the Andes, Meso-american, and the Caribbean" in terms of a "dialectic of the filthy and the clean, the fetid and the fresh", even the "healthy" and the "sick" (Mignolo, 153). Indeed, the prevalence of public health programs and policies in the rhetoric of "modernization and development" is just one example of how this binary continues to do imperialist work, even with the most benevolent and humanitarian purposes.

We now know that the "immunities" Europeans acquired over the centuries against the infectious diseases they spread with such devastating consequences in the Western Hemisphere had much to do with the domestication of livestock they had learned from Middle Eastern agricultural practices they had followed and were thus hardly "inherent" to Europeans.[88] And the inoculation practices Europeans would adopt experimentally and unevenly in the eighteenth century were adapted from practices employed in China as early as 1100 to prevent the spread of smallpox. Add to all of this that the genetic differences between Amerindians and Europeans do not signal the superiority of one biology over the other, but simply human differences whose contact produced extraordinarily negative results for one group. Western "modernization and development" take on rather different ethical meanings when we are forced to conclude that in the case of the Western Hemisphere, such "progress" required the deaths of anywhere from 40 to 60 million Amerinidian people between 1500 and 1900.

"Border thinking" should deconstruct the "differences" between European imperial powers and Creole national powers, among European languages, and other manifest differences, such as those between the supposedly Catholic South and Protestant North, not only to expose the shared history of the "modern/colonial world system" worked out systematically for the first time in the Western Hemisphere. Such border thinking should also represent the histories and contemporary retentions of societies and communities that were overshadowed by the more imposing authority of their imperial masters. Adapting W. E. B. Du Bois's model of "double consciousness" to the study of the Western Hemisphere and drawing thus explicitly from minority discourses, Mignolo suggests that such a comparative approach to the Western Hemisphere might open us to a broader "worldly" thinking he projects doubly as "the future planetary epistemological and critical localism" (157).

I am happy to conclude that I am not certain what he means by what he also terms a "border gnosis" that would allow us to think differentially across the divides of those geopolitical, imperial, and semiotic "borders" that have been imposed upon us as scholars, as citizens, and as humans. What I do know is that Mignolo's challenging methodology enables us to achieve the sort of double-consciousness the "new" and "postnationalist" American Studies should welcome. With one consciousness, it enables us to understand the "conflicting homogeneous entities (Latin America, France, the United States, etc.) as […] part of the imaginary of the modern/colonial world system" (170). With another consciousness, we can understand that to "think 'Latin America' otherwise, in its heterogeneity rather than in its homogeneity, in the local histories of changing global designs is not to question a particular form of identification (e.g., that of 'Latin America') but all national/colonial forms of identification in the modern/colonial world system" (170–171). I would add that Mignolo's project, ostensibly the deconstruction of "Latin American" area studies, applies as well to North American Studies and "American Studies" as we know it in its modern and postmodern versions.[89]

I have focused on how the conflict between area studies and the new American Studies impedes the development of a comparative study of the many different communities in the Western Hemisphere, but Mignolo's "modern/colonial world system" is not restricted to this region. In the aftermath of 9/11, the ongoing U.S. occupation of Iraq, its central role in the war in Afghanistan, foreign policies that contribute significantly to the imperial subjugation of the Palestinian people, and growing Arabic immigrant communities in the U.S., "the Middle East" is a crucial field in the new American Studies. Yet the field itself is already defined by the area studies model I have traced back to the politically motivated work of the Ethnogeographic Board of the 1940s. Edward Said's criticism of nineteenth-century Western Orientalism needs to be updated to take into account more recent developments, and in that work the U.S. role in restructuring what George W. Bush termed "the Greater Middle

East" needs to be challenged in relationship to U.S. academic models for studying "the Middle East", global Islamic communities, Arabic cultures, and specific immigrant groups from these regions and communities now living outside their ancestral homelands as a consequence of diaspora or choice.

Paul Gilroy's *Black Atlantic: Modernity and Double Consciousness* (1993) fundamentally challenged "area studies" definitions of Caribbean, African American, and black British communities, directing us both literally and figuratively to the "Atlantic world" in which transnational flows of people, goods, and cultures moved incessantly and diversely.[90] David Lloyd and Peter D. O'Neill's *The Black and Green Atlantic* shows how the Black (African), Green (Irish), Red (Communist), and still other "Atlantics" have followed and broadened what we today understand as this oceanic complexity beyond the presumed stabilities of geopolitical states.[91] We need similarly flexible, transnational conceptions in the new American Studies that will work cooperatively with "critical area studies" of Latin America and the Middle East to respect the diverse communities we find in these regions and provide the critical terms for challenging their marginalization, even exclusion, by more powerful nation states.

In re-conceptualizing the global scope that American Studies must undertake to respond to U.S. neo-imperialism, we must remain vigilant regarding the specific ways knowledge and power have been coordinated historically. We would be naive to think that the production and circulation of knowledge in the late-modern research university can remain separate from the economic, political, and social interests of the states and industries that fund such work. Whether public or private, the research-1 university still functions as a representation of the nation in which it is permitted to exist, but such universities are also today pulled in a number of competitive directions by different state and corporate interests. We are already witnessing the globalization of the student, faculty, and research components of these educational institutions, and we must find the intellectual means to assure that such globalization works dialectically, offering those peoples rendered stateless, culture-less, and otherwise economically and politically disempowered the means of "decolonizing the mind", as the great Kenyan novelist and postcolonial theorist Ngũgĩ wa Thiongo, has put it.[92]

II

Cultural Practices

CHAPTER 5

Culture, U.S. Imperialism, and Globalization

The return of what was once termed gunboat diplomacy in the first decade of the twenty-first century as part of the "new global order" endorsed repeatedly and abstractly by George H. W. and then George W. Bush's regimes, could not have occurred without the prior work of culture. U.S. cultural production, the work of what Horkheimer and Adorno termed "the culture industry", conditioned American citizens to accept the undisguised militarism and jingoistic nationalism now driving U.S. foreign policy.[93] In its inevitably globalized forms, the U.S. culture industry continues to produce the deep divisions between local resistance and subaltern imitation so characteristic of colonial conflicts from the age of traditional imperialism to the neo-imperialisms of our postindustrial era. And the culture industry today does its work in ways that encompass a wide range of nominally different political positions, so that in many respects left, liberal, and conservative cultural works often achieve complementary, rather than contested, ends. In this respect, little has changed since Horkheimer and Adorno argued in 1944: "Even the aesthetic activities of political opposites are one in their enthusiastic obedience to the rhythm of the iron system".[94]

As the U.S. military raced toward Baghdad in the Spring of 2003, there was considerable criticism of the "embedded reporters" allowed to report the war under the special conditions imposed by the Pentagon and Department of Defense. Most of the criticism assumed that such reporting was biased or censored. When a *Newsweek* photographer was caught doctoring on his laptop a photograph of an encounter between Iraqi civilians and U.S. military personnel, his firing seemed to vindicate the news magazine of prejudice. Anti-war activists circulated two photographs of Iraqi demonstrators tearing down a monumental statue of Saddam Hussein in Firdos Square, Baghdad on April 9, 2003: the first was a familiar photograph in the news of demonstrators beating on the sculpture's foundation and then, with the help of an Abrams tank tow truck (equipped with a crane), toppling the hieratic image of the defeated dictator.

In the second photograph, not displayed in the popular press or evening news, the camera provides a wide-angle view of the scene at the square, where access roads have been blocked by the U.S. military and the "populist" demolition of the statue has been theatrically staged by U.S. forces. In a third photograph circulated on the Internet, the same Iraqis actively involved attacking the Baghdad statue are shown "one day earlier" in Basra, where they are preparing to board U.S. military aircraft for transport to Baghdad—identified in this photograph as members of the "Iraqi Free Forces".[95]

Peter Maass argues in "The Toppling: How the Media Inflated a Minor Moment in a Long War" that the event was not engineered by the U.S. State for propaganda purposes but was a consequence of foreign reporters staying at the Palestine Hotel on Firdos Square urging U.S. military officers to help Iraqis topple the statue. Relying on his authority as one of the reporters to witness the event, Maass contends that the primary purpose in staging the event was to produce a good news story.[96] Whether this "minor moment in a long war" was designed by the U.S. government or staged by journalists is not finally a crucial issue. Western journalism and the U.S. "coalition" cooperated from the beginning to represent the Second Gulf War as crucial in the global war on terror and Iraq as a strategic region in the building of a "Greater Middle East".

Such exposures of U.S. military or journalistic propaganda during the war have continued in news coverage of the putative "rebuilding" of the political and economic infrastructure in Iraq. The debate regarding who was actually responsible for the disinformation regarding "Weapons of Mass Destruction" used as the principal justification for the invasion of Iraq is the most obvious example of public concern regarding the federal government's veracity. For such propaganda to be successful, there must be a willing audience, already prepared for certain cultural semantics adaptable to new political circumstances and yet with sufficient "regional" relevance as to make possible the very widespread confusion between Saddam Hussein and Osama bin Laden, between a secular Iraqi state tyranny and an Islamic fundamentalist guerilla organization. How was it possible that such a preposterous war could be permitted by Congress and by the U.S. population? The answer is not simply that the Bush Administration ignored numerous international protests of the preparations for war and its eventual conduct. Nor is the answer simply that when the war began, the Bush Administration controlled the news and staged symbolic events to fool the public, although there is plenty of evidence to support these claims. The cultural preparations for a "just war" and for the U.S. as global "policeman" did not occur overnight; they are our cultural legacy from the Vietnam War and integral parts of our emergence as a neo-imperial nation since 1945. Central to this legacy is the conception of the United States as a discrete nation that nonetheless has a global identity and mission. Although traditional imperialism works by way of expansion from a national center, U.S. imperialism since Vietnam has worked steadily to "import" the world and to render global differences aspects of the U.S. nation—in short, to internalize and "hyper-nationalize" transnational issues. This "Vietnam-Effect" has taken on new features in U.S. neo-imperialism in the First and Second Gulf Wars and the ongoing war in Afghanistan, but the historical legacy of U.S. diplomacy and military strategy in Southeast Asia from 1955–1975 is both coherent and fundamental.

It is commonplace, of course, to criticize the United States as one of the several first-world nations to employ cultural media to market its products around the world. Neo-colonialism generally connotes some complicity between a "multinational corporation covertly supported by an imperialist power", to borrow Chalmers Johnson's definition, and thus implies some entanglement of economic, political, and military motives.[97] The globalization of consumer capitalism and the commodities of first-world economies (often manufactured elsewhere) are identified as specific targets by political movements as different as "Slow Food" in France, Earth First!, and al-Qaeda. Although the arcades and other defined shopping areas were developed in nineteenth-century Europe—Paris, Milan, Berlin, and other metropoles—the shopping mall is an American spinoff. With its emphasis on the "city-within-a-city", the linkage of entertainment and consumption, the faux cosmopolitanism of its "international" and regionally specific shops (Cartier, Mont Blanc, Nieman Marcus, Saks Fifth Avenue, "Texas Souvenirs") and its ubiquitous, often international "Food Courts", the American shopping mall was developed in the 1960s and refined over the past fifty years. Such mega-malls as Minneapolis' Mall of America, Houston's Galleria, and Southern California's South Coast Plaza have redefined the public sphere as the site of consumption and commodification both of products and consumers.

Whether directly exported by U.S. business interests or developed by multinational corporations to look like its U.S. prototypes, the international mall is often traceable back to U.S. funding, design, and marketing sources or models. A PBS *Frontline* report, "In Search of Al-Qaeda", which aired on November 21, 2002, includes footage of a shopping mall in Riyadh, Saudi Arabia, which is physically indistinguishable from European and American malls and includes many of the same stores.[98] Of course, the reporter calls attention to the presence of the Mu'tawah or religious police, who stroll through this mall looking for unveiled women or illicit liaisons between unmarried men and women. "In Search of Al-Qaeda" is a fine attempt by *Frontline* to explain the animosity felt by many different groups in the Arab world toward the United States. The mall in Riyadh represents quite clearly one common source of resentment: the rapid Americanization of Saudi Arabia and the tacit demand that everyday Muslim practices be adapted to the demands of the global market. From one perspective, the Mu'tawah operate comfortably within this typical mall, with its long, open corridors and the insistent appeal of its transnational commodities. In another view, the religious police seem already defeated by the cultural rhetoric of the mall, which encourages romance and consumption in the same free-wheeling space. As Anne Friedeberg has argued, the mall links consumer and psychic desires in ways that depend crucially on "the fluid subjectivity of the spectator-shopper".[99]

Commodities are neither passive nor politically innocent; they are perpetually active in the specific kinds of desires they produce in consumers and work by means of the social psychologies of commodity fetishism analyzed by Marx in *Capital* and reification elaborated by Lukács in *History and Class Consciousness*.[100] Specific consumer desires can also be traced back to hierarchies of specific kinds of capitalist labor. In modern, industrial economies, stores displaying high fashion and leisure-class products, such as designer clothing for women and luxury products for successful men, were central. The traditional display windows with their mannequins of elegantly dressed and sexually alluring women belong to the era of the large department stores and, while still a part of the postmodern mall, are challenged by stores displaying the most elaborate array of computerized bodily extensions and miniaturizations, labor-saving devices, and high-tech tools promising greater access to the primary source of wealth and power: the control and manipulation of information and its assorted hermeneutic and representational protocols. In the crush of the crowds defining the public space of the mall, the consumer is promised some individuality apart from just what forces him/her through the doors of his/her local "Best Buy". Such identity depends, of course, on its promise of communication, but not so much *with* other people, especially those who may be different from this consumer, but *apart* from others in the notable privacy of postmodern life. The new laptops, iPads, and smart phones are prized for allowing us to negotiate the crowd as we travel through it, but then saving from this mob our informational work, which can be stored, sifted, and processed in the privacy of our own homes. Of course, the peculiar desire for representational power and authority fetishized in computer hardware and software is rapidly displacing the public sphere created by the late-modern desire for more traditional commodities, such as fashion and luxury items. The mall is "morphing" into the Internet, an imaginary space so rapidly commercialized as to terrify even the most recalcitrant critic and sometime defender of consumer capitalism.

In spite of the admirable efforts of intellectuals to find emancipatory possibilities in the new technologies—alternatives to traditional social forms and practices certainly do exist today—the speed with which the Internet has been commercialized and hierarchized is symptomatic of the huge inequities dividing corporations that can afford access, individuals who merely use the technology (and are thereby used by it), and the majority of the world's population left entirely out of the new communicative practices. In *What's the Matter with the Internet?* (2001), Mark Poster recognizes most of these problems while stressing the "underdetermined" character of new digital technologies and thus their availability for new transnational politics: "The Internet affords an opportunity for a contribution to a new politics [and] [...] may play a significant role in diminishing the hierarchies prevalent in modern society and in clearing a path for new directions of cultural practice".[101] In *Ambient Television* (2001), Anna McCarthy acknowledges the ideological consequences of television's portability and publicity in achieving a culture of surveillance such as Foucault predicted, but she also imagines critical alternatives and interventions capable of disrupting and in some cases even transforming unidirectional television.[102] Such alternatives, however, are pushed increasingly to the margins of the Internet and television. Most television scholars agree that the "post-network era" has reconfigured the industry only by allowing more corporate giants to share the wealth of television programming. "Niche" television and "target audiences" have led to a wider variety of television only within certain limits of the liberal-to-conservative political spectrum. Radical television, such as Dee Dee Halleck's Paper Tiger Television, goes virtually unwatched, is financially marginal, and supported primarily by extramural grants. The networks long ago succeeded in defeating "public access cable" as a populist alternative to one-way television, and the short-term future of "interactive" television, especially when integrated with computers and the Internet, is likely to be little more than an extension of the enormously profitable video-game market.

Of course, blogs, personal websites and wikis, whether organized into "social networks" like Facebook or simply maintained by individuals, have offered inexpensive, multidirectional communications' systems as apparent alternatives to unidirectional technologies, such as television. What lures consumers to new digital technologies is the general promise of *social communication*, ironically just the ideal offered by Marx and Engels in *The German Ideology*, but it is a false promise that substitutes complex programming, technological innovation and software upgrades for socially meaningful communication.[103] Designed to serve business and commercial needs, predicated on the increasing privatization of the public sphere, whereby the illusion of sociability is simulated in the radical alienation and paradoxical exclusivity of the home office, commuter vehicle, or commercial airline's reserved seat, such devices produce specific desires structured by their ideological motivations. Watching urbanites rushing from place to place focused intently on smart-phone screens, often while navigating a car or bicycle, the postmodern flâneur cannot avoid the conclusion that digital technologies have further alienated us while promising the illusion of greater sociability. The imperial imaginary thrives upon these desires for what today is termed "connectivity", but which is little other than the venerable dream of social belonging. Cultural apologists for the "Americanization" of the globe, like Francis Fukuyama, imagine that such homogenization will take us to that "end of history" fantastically dreamt by Hegel and other proto-moderns, because such conditions will produce a political consensus.[104] Fukuyama is certainly right that one-way globalization is likely to result in an international consensus, even if it is one we can hardly condone, which we know will be not only excruciatingly tedious but finally "inhuman", and will require periods of incredible unpredictable violence.

Such criticism of what may generally be termed a "postmodern economy" focused on information, communications, and entertainment products, including their integrated research and development components, may seem strangely anachronistic when applied to the contemporary global situation. Today, we confront the revival of traditional imperialism as the United States towers over all other human communities and exerts its unchallenged power in the most flagrantly militaristic manner. Not since the British Empire ruled the world by force and fear in the late eighteenth and nineteenth centuries has there been such undisguised rule by military power. While recognizing important differences between contemporary U.S. global rule in the twenty-first century and that of the British in the nineteenth century, Chalmers Johnson traces a historical genealogy from British to U.S. imperial policies, especially in such critical regions as the Middle East and Southeast Asia (Johnson, 138–139, 217–218). In Somalia and most of Africa, Kosovo, Serbia, Cuba, Nicaragua, Panama, Salvador, Colombia, the Philippines, North and South Korea, Afghanistan, Pakistan, India, Israel and Palestine, Saudi Arabia and the Gulf states, Iraq, and Iran, the United States works by open military action or threats. Such situations hardly appear to have much to do with the postmodern economics analyzed by theorists of postindustrial or late capitalist practices, such as Ernest Mandel, Fredric Jameson, and David Harvey.

But there is an important relationship between the emergence of U.S. military power, along with the complementary threats of inequitable and repressive policies toward peoples (especially but not exclusively non-

U.S. citizens) at home and abroad, and the capitalization of "cultural exports" ranging from Hollywood entertainment and television programming to digital technologies and their protocols for communication, work, and social "networking". John Gallagher and Ronald Robinson's theory of "free-trade imperialism" is now half a century old and was formulated long before the postmodern economy came to dominate global relations by restructuring other forms of economic production and trade (especially devastating for the "industrialized" developing nations, now cast in the shadow of new, privileged forms of capitalization).[105] The thesis of "free-trade imperialism" still explains a good deal about how traditional imperial military power should emerge with such prominence and frequency as a "foreign policy" at the very moment when globalization seems the nearly inevitable consequence of U.S. economic triumphalism. Contemporary critics of U.S. foreign policy like Chalmers Johnson have also recognized that "free trade" is often used as a rationalization for the conduct of multinational corporations and for the U.S. government's development of "client states", like Israel and, until recently, South Korea (Johnson, 31).

Gallagher and Robinson refute traditional theories that imperialism—their principal example was British imperialism in Africa—proceeded historically from military conquest to consolidation of colonial rule only to be legitimated and transformed slowly through economic development. Gallagher and Robinson argue that "free-trade" policies generally *preceded* historically the militarization of colonies and that such military force was required only by the failure to negotiate trade agreements between metropolitan and colonial centers. Military force is thus held in reserve, not out of humane considerations of course but primarily for reasons of practicality and economy, while the imperial power promotes trade agreements—either for raw materials or finished products—with the appearance of favorable and equitable terms to colonizer and colonized. It is only when this illusion of "free-trade" is shattered that military force is required to re-impose imperial "order", when the appearance of free trade can be resumed, under whose guise what in fact usually occurs is demonstrably inequitable exploitation of natural or human resources of the colony. As they write: "[t]he usual summing up of the policy of the free trade empire as 'trade, not rule' should read 'trade with informal control if possible; trade with rule when necessary'" (Gallagher and Robinson, 25).

Is this not the situation we are witnessing today in the Gulf and in other strategic locations around the world? At present, the relationship between the United States and the Peoples Republic of China can be described accurately as one operating according to the logic of "free-trade imperialism" as China's economy booms in large part thanks to the exploited labor required to manufacture products for the U.S. export market.[106] One of the assumptions of Fukuyama's approach to globalization is that the "end of history" will bring an end of warfare and national struggle, that the "global village" and world peace are inextricably linked. From this perspective, whatever the cost of globalization in the mediocrity and uniformity of personal lives is more than compensated by the security achieved. In view of the everyday fear experienced by the majority of humankind, the sacrifices are well worth the enormous gains achieved by U.S. global hegemony. In his neo-liberal defense of the U.S. exercising power around the world in its own "defense", Robert Kagan reaches a similar conclusion, albeit one that involves his condemnation of both the European Union and the United Nations—the closest competitors for U.S. global hegemony at the present moment.[107]

Late capitalism thrives on fear, even employing fear as a principal marketing strategy. In the depressed U.S. economy of the past few years, one of the rare bright spots has been the booming market for self-defense goods, especially hi-tech gadgets, in response to 9/11 and the assorted xenophobic anxieties, such as the mailing of Anthrax, it prompted. In his documentary, *Bowling for Columbine* (2002), Michael Moore attributes violence in the U.S. primarily to a culture of fear propagated by the news media and federal government. If we accept the general outlines of his argument, then the globalization of U.S. cultural capital will involve the exportation of precisely this "culture of fear", a phenomenon we are witnessing as complementary with the increase in U.S. military actions as the Bush Administration took seriously its role as global policeman of the new world order. President George W. Bush left office insisting that his administration had made the U.S. more secure against terrorism, even at the expense of our civil liberties. Yet during the George W. Bush presidency, incidents of global terrorism in England, Spain, Indonesia, Pakistan, and India increased dramatically. The Obama administration has been criticized for not anticipating two abortive domestic terrorism "incidents"—the attempted bombing on December 25, 2009 of a Northwest Airlines flight from Amsterdam to Detroit, and the attempted car bombing on May 1, 2010 of Times Square—and still does not acknowledge the mass murder in the Fort Hood shooting on November 5, 2009 as an act of "domestic terrorism". Incidents of terrorism will continue to occur as long as the U.S. wages a global "war on terror", and such incidents, wherever they occur, will provide continuing support to foreign policies based on militant neo-imperialism. I want to propose then a dialectical relationship between cultural or free-trade imperialism and military imperialism that is mediated by way of a "culture of fear" that helps market late-capitalist products and encourages, rather than diminishes, military conflicts in the place of international diplomacy.

The history of this dialectic is understandably as long as that of modernity itself, especially if we trace modernity back to the voyages of exploration and conquest of the late fifteenth and early sixteenth centuries. Modernization begins not so much with the technologies used to achieve such conquests—no new technology was, in fact, invented just for the voyages of exploration—but with the imagining of other worlds and peoples. It is commonplace to speak of how easily the early explorers substituted one people for another, as Columbus mistook Caribs and Arawaks for "Indians" of the Far East (and the name continues to this day, albeit often contested by Native Americans and First Peoples). But there is a shorter history that tells us a good deal about this dialectic, especially in its present deployment in world politics, and that history begins with the military failure of the United States in Vietnam in the early 1970s. Beginning in that moment, U.S. culture attempted to explain and rationalize the war in a wide range of media and from virtually every possible political perspective. Sorting out these diverse outlooks on the Vietnam War remains crucial work for cultural and political critics, but the general impression this cultural work offers is that of the re-narrativization of a military and colonial failure into a foundation for subsequent military ventures in the Caribbean, Central America, the Persian Gulf, Africa, and the warring republics of former Yugoslavia.

What appeared in the mid- to late 1970s to be a series of critical interpretations of U.S. involvement in Vietnam—such films as *Coming Home* (1978), *The Deer Hunter* (1979), and *Apocalypse Now* (1980)—were replaced by films and television programs that appropriated the liberal rhetoric of these predecessors but incorporated it into compensatory narratives intent on imaginatively fighting the war again and winning. Sylvester Stallone's "Rambo" character is the locus classicus of just such heroic conventions. John Rambo fights the Vietnamese, the Russians, and other foreign enemies in the Rambo films, but he also combats *Americans* in ways that clearly anticipate the contemporary "nationalization" of global issues in U.S. mass media. The opening scene of the first film, Ted Kotcheff's *Rambo, First Blood* (1982), establishes John Rambo's motivation for fighting the local police department and eventually the National Guard called in to hunt him down. As the opening credits roll, John Rambo walks down a charming Northwest dirt road to a modest house on the edge of a lake. The African-American woman, who is hanging her wash on a clothes line and who centers a sublime prospect of natural beauty, is the mother of Rambo's best friend in Vietnam, Delmar Berry. In the opening dialogue of the film, Rambo learns from Delmar's mother that his friend has died of cancer, a victim of the Agent Orange sprayed as a defoliant in Vietnam. I have elsewhere interpreted how Rambo consequently appropriates the civil rights, anti-war, and countercultural movements of the late 1960s and early 1970s to legitimate the militarism he represents in *Rambo, First Blood*.[108]

In the second film, George P. Cosmatos's *Rambo, First Blood, Part II* (1985), Rambo's rage is directed at the CIA's reliance on high technology rather than human agency. In the concluding scene of the film, John Rambo fires the large automatic weapons he has used on his mission into Vietnam to destroy the computer command center of the CIA in Thailand, and then he releases a primal scream to accompany this ritualized destruction of the new automated warfare he clearly condemns as inhuman. Ironically, the Emersonian self-reliance and natural identity of John Rambo in both films is set in explicit contrast with the automated militarism employed by the Department of Defense and Pentagon in the first and second Gulf wars, which for many people were culturally justified by the revival of militaristic values exemplified by the character of John

Rambo. There is a direct line from the fictional John Rambo to Brigadier General Vincent Brooks, "the six-foot-plus, Hollywood-handsome African American spokesman for Central Command" during the Second Gulf war, who at Camp as-Sayliyah's state of the art, "$ 1.5 million, made-for-TV 'Coalition Media Center,' [...] gave hundreds of journalists his daily edited presentations" (Johnson, 249).

Never very precisely defined as a culture, geopolitical region, history, or people, "Vietnam" became a flexible term, so that the war refought in cultural fantasy could take place at home in such films as Louis Malle's *Alamo Bay* (1985) and Walter Hill's *Southern Comfort* (1981), or in other global hot spots, such as the Grenada in Clint Eastwood's *Heartbreak Ridge* (1986) or Central America in Mark Lester's *Commando* (1985) or Afghanistan in Peter McDonald's *Rambo III* (1988), where John Rambo fights valiantly with the Afghani *mujahideen* against the Soviets. Of course, the anti-colonial resistance movement in Afghanistan, supported by CIA advisors and U.S. funds and weapons, would in the mid-1990s align itself with the Taliban (Students of Islam), which in turn would host Osama bin Laden and al-Qaeda (Johnson, 177). Screening *Rambo III* today in the U.S. is a bizarre experience, as the viewer watches John Rambo learning and even participating in folk rituals, such as horse racing, of Afghani "freedom fighters" who by 2001 would be our unequivocal enemies.

Contemporary with these films and such fiction television programs as *China Beach* and *Miami Vice* or documentary series, such as HBO's *Soldiers in Hiding*, were military "tie-ins", which traded official sites as movie sets and insider information about military procedures for films that promoted military heroism and honor, such as *An Officer and a Gentleman* (1982), *Top Gun* (1986), and the many spinoffs, which have by now helped establish a cinematic and televisual genre, including CBS's long-running series, *JAG* [*Judge Adjutants' General*]). What came to be termed "the Vietnam-Effect" extended its aura to draw parasitically upon other wars, so that the revival in the 1990s of World War II as a topic in films, television docudramas, and print narratives (fiction, biography, and oral histories) had as much to do with the large-scale revision of the Vietnam War (and U.S. imperialism in Southeast Asia) as it did with such nominal historical markers as the 50th anniversary of D-Day or memorials for the end of World War II. Billed as "anti-war films", often because of their graphic and thus alienating violence, films like Steven Spielberg's *Saving Private Ryan* (1998), Terrence Malick's *Thin Red Line* (1998), and John Woo's *Wind Talkers* (2002) helped remilitarize the United States not only because they drew on the conventions of World War II heroism and military success but also because each in its own way borrowed liberal, often explicitly pacifist, sentiments for its purposes. Thus the Lieutenant (Tom Hanks) leading the soldiers assigned to rescue Private Ryan is a school teacher unwilling to risk human lives unnecessarily and obliged merely to do the unpleasant but necessary job of civilian soldier. Officers in *Thin Red Line* disobey orders from above when they put their troops at unreasonable risk, and the Navajo "wind talkers" in John Woo's film challenge the racism of their fellow soldiers. All end up fighting, however, thereby linking a "just war" thesis with liberal and anti-war sentiments. My point that combat films with radically different political perspectives often contribute equally to pro-military sentiments is confirmed by Anthony Swofford in his memoir of the First Gulf War, *Jarhead* (2003). Describing U.S. soldiers' fascination with antiwar films about the Vietnam War, Swofford concludes: "But actually Vietnam War films are all pro-war, no matter what the supposed message, what Kubrick or Coppola or Stone intended […]. The magic brutality of the films celebrates the terrible and despicable beauty of their fighting skills. Fight, rape, war, pillage, burn. Filmic images of death and carnage are pornography for the military man".[109]

In the years following the First Gulf War and before 9/11, mass media helped re-legitimate the U.S. military, reaffirmed "masculine" values (often in direct reaction to the women's rights movement), and defused the sort of anti-war dissent that did contribute significantly to ending the Vietnam War. Incorporated into domestic concerns or located historically or geographically elsewhere than in the Middle East, U.S. militarism and "warrior culture" were reborn in post-Vietnam guises. Populist media and documentary film-makers, including the surprisingly popular Michael Moore and less visible producers of "alternative" television, such as Paper Tiger Television's Dee Dee Halleck, rarely addressed the subtlety with which the mass media employed the rhetoric of its political opponents. In Moore's *Roger and Me* (1989), the CEO of General Motors is a classic capitalist hypocrite and thief; in *Bowling for Columbine* (2002), the President of the National Rifle Association is the senile, foolish, and contradictory Charlton Heston. Only demystify!

There were important exceptions, of course, in the aftermath of the First Gulf War and well before 9/11, such as Barry Levinson's *Wag the Dog* (1998) and David O. Russell's *Three Kings* (1997), both of which criticized the nationalist propaganda and media control that allowed the George H. W. Bush Administration to wage the First Gulf War with little public scrutiny and the illusion of an "international coalition" of allied forces. *Wag the Dog* is based on the premise that a "war" we are waging against Albania is entirely fabricated by a Washington spin-doctor (Conrad Bream, played by Robert De Niro) with the help of a Hollywood producer (Sidney Motss, played by Dustin Hoffman) to distract public attention from a sexual harassment charge against the incumbent President two weeks from his re-election. *Wag the Dog* brilliantly satirizes the increasing control the U.S. Federal Government has exercised over news reporting of its foreign military ventures. In many respects, *Wag the Dog* seems merely to elaborate in Hollywood film satire the claims made by Jean Baudrillard in his deliberately iconoclastic *La Guerre du Golfe n'a pas eu lieu* (1991).[110]

In a very different fashion, *Three Kings* attempted to peel away the mask of patriotic dedication in the Gulf War by exposing the greed of the U.S. soldiers for Kuwaiti gold looted by the invading Iraqi Army as a metaphor for U.S. self-interest in controlling the oil-rich Gulf. I admit that the pacifist and populist sentiments of *Three Kings* are noteworthy, especially in a period when Hollywood films were targeted increasingly at 12–17 year-old moviegoers, who still pay the most dollars per person on films and associated products of any age group in the U.S. The grisly scene in *Three Kings* of an M-16 bullet penetrating human intestines in slow motion and producing the green bile that will slowly and painfully kill the victim is far more effective than the slow-motion melodrama of U.S. troops dying on the beaches of Normandy during the D-Day invasion in *Saving Private Ryan*.

Nevertheless, both *Wag the Dog* and *Three Kings* rely on a narrative of Americanization that plays a significant role in the general public's understanding of globalization and anticipates how post-9/11 film and television would rely on similar processes of nationalizing international problems to "channel the nation back to normalcy—or at least [to] the normal flows of television and consumer culture", as Lynn Spigel puts it.[111] *Wag the Dog* does this cultural work in an obvious manner by locating all of the action of the film in the United States; the imprisoned soldier (Denis Leary), who is picked to simulate an actual U.S. soldier "downed" by hostile gunfire in Albania and miraculously "rescued", has to be picked up by the media team from his maximum-security military prison in Texas. The liberal politics of *Wag the Dog* make what I have termed "hypernationalization" an explicit theme in the film, so that we are expected to understand immediately the irony of the Hollywood producer Motss and the Washington insider Bream inventing an international crisis to cover a domestic sexual scandal. The film satirizes Americans' chronic ignorance of world events, thanks to news structured around entertainment and advertising, but it also reinforces the assumption that the United States is the center of the world and that even a fictional war can have meaning and value, as long as it is waged by the United States.

Carefully structured news stories about the Second Gulf war followed the example of *Wag the Dog*, despite its satiric and counter-cultural intentions. The "saving" of Jessica Lynch, the U.S. soldier wounded and captured by Iraqi troops on March 23, 2003 during the invasion, follows just such a narrative of Americanization, from her heroic rescue by U.S. Special Forces through her medical treatment and debriefing at a U.S. military based near Frankfurt to her triumphant return to her hometown in Palestine, West Virginia. Even more interesting and relevant are the subsequent events, in which Jessica Lynch denied the media's representation of her "heroism" and disputed the facts of her "rescue" by U.S. Special Forces. What is now considered a deliberate effort by the Pentagon to mount a propaganda campaign in support of the U.S.-led invasion resulted in a flurry of charges and counter-charges in news stories, books, television films, and news specials. As early as November 11, 2003, less than eight months after her capture and rescue, Lynch told Diane Sawyer in a CNN interview that the Pentagon "used me to symbolize all this stuff. It's wrong. I don't know why they filmed [my rescue] or say these things".[112] In her April 24, 2007 testimony before the U.S. House Committee on Oversight and Government Reform, Lynch referred specifically to how the Pentagon tried to turn her into the "Rambo from West

Virginia".[113] Susan Faludi reads Jessica Lynch's story as part of American paranoia and xenophobia traceable back to Colonial captivity narratives, and she is undoubtedly right that the Lynch story lent itself well to the conventions of American mythopoeia.[114] One characteristic of such national myth-making is incorporation of the foreign into the EuroAmerican symbology. Mohammed Odeh al-Rehaief, the Iraqi who first brought Jessica Lynch's captivity in a hospital in Nasiriyah to the attention of the U.S. military, not only was granted refugee status and allowed to emigrate to the U.S., but his book about his role in the rescue, *Because Each Life Is Precious* (2003), earned him a $ 300,000 advance.[115] Amid the proliferation of books, news stories, Congressional hearings, and television movies, "Jessica Lynch" helped transform the politically unjustified invasion of Iraq and its destabilization of the Middle East into a thoroughly American narrative.

More conventionally, *Three Kings* challenges self-interested U.S. militarism and foreign policy in the Gulf by condemning the command-structure of the U.S. military and countering it with the populist pacifism and humanitarianism of the "three kings", who finally live up to their Biblical titles by guiding dissident Iraqis and their families to their "promised land" across the border in Iran. The familiar imperial narrative of U.S. paternalism, of the "white-man's burden", plays itself out once again in terms almost identical with those criticized so thoroughly in nineteenth-century imperial narratives. The dissident Iraqis who save Archie Gates (George Clooney), Troy Barlow (Mark Wahlberg), Chief Elgin (Ice Cube), and Conrad Vig (Spike Jonze) from attack by the Republican Guard turn out to be primarily intent on "get[ting] rid of Saddam", in order to "live life and do business", as their leader Amir Abdullah (Cliff Curtis) says.

The film criticizes consumer capitalism and its globalization, but advocates on the other hand the value of small businesses. When Troy Barlow is captured and tortured by Republican Guards, he is made to drink crude oil poured into his mouth propped open with a CD case. The consumer goods stolen from Kuwait and heaped in poorly guarded Iraqi bunkers exemplify the meretriciousness of multinational globalization—tape and CD players in their unopened boxes, tangled skeins of jewelry, heaps of cell phones, and other consumer "junk" are visually effective, but the political dissidents these three kings will eventually save are committed to modest but meaningful businesses, such as hair-styling. Following a nearly schematic narrative of "education", the three remaining kings (Conrad Vig dies and is prepared for a Muslim burial) use the gold they have stolen from the Iraqis (who have stolen it from the Kuwaitis) to "buy" safe passage for the political dissidents into the relative safety of Iran. The final scene of the film in which the border crossing is enacted, replete with sentimental waves and sympathetic looks between the dissidents and the enlightened U.S. soldiers, is difficult to watch today as conservatives continue to call for the U.S. to extend its invasion and occupation of Iraq to include Iran.

The sympathy these U.S. soldiers establish with the Iraqi dissidents is certainly intended by David O. Russell to counter the Orientalist demonization of Arab peoples so common in U.S. mass culture since the nineteenth century, intensified as part of the build-up for the first Gulf war, and driven to near cultural hysteria in the months following the attacks on 9/11.[116] Yet the Iraqi dissidents are represented in what seem to be deliberately ambiguous regional, ethnic, and religious terms. The mercenary U.S. soldiers enter southern Iraq in quest of the stolen Kuwaiti gold, so the political dissidents they encounter in the aftermath of the First Gulf War would most likely be Shi'ite dissidents, similar to those who appealed to George H. W. Bush for military assistance and staged an unsuccessful rebellion against Saddam Hussein in the weeks following the conclusion of that war. Yet there is considerable cinematic evidence to conclude that the Iraqi dissidents are Kurds. Hair-dressing, for example, is traditionally a respected profession among the Kurds, so that one of the dissidents' plans to return to that profession hints at Kurdish affiliations, displaced of course from the main Kurdish population centers in northern Iraq to the film's setting in southern Iraq. Saddam Hussein's government did forcibly "resettle" Kurds in the South (including many who were murdered and buried in mass graves there) during the Anfal, the genocidal "ethnic cleansing" the Iraqi dictator conducted prior to the first Gulf war.[117]

The deliberate confusion of different dissident groups in Iraq seems intended not only to achieve cinematic economy, but also to make these dissidents more accessible to the four U.S. soldiers. These soldiers represented in the film offer a sample of U.S. multiculturalism: Chief Elgin is a devout Christian African American, Conrad Vig is an uneducated southern white racist, Archie Gates is a white career soldier taking early retirement, and Troy Barlow a model WASP. To be sure, the representativeness of this group is very narrow, but their respective sympathies with the Iraqi dissidents perform a narrative of cultural hybridity that unmistakably argues for greater understanding of other peoples as an alternative to unilateral globalization and to U.S. militarism. Chief Elgin appears to abandon Christianity for Islam, and he dons the traditional Arab male *kaffieyeh* ("head covering") to announce his conversion. Conrad Vig learns about Islamic burial practices, overcomes his racism toward Chief Elgin by way of their shared interest in Islam, and is eventually prepared for an Islamic burial of his own. In fact, when the dissidents cross the border into Iran, they are carrying his body with them for a proper burial on the other side. The protagonists learn to sympathize with and understand not historically and regionally specific groups of Iraqis, but generalized "Arab" and "Muslim" types. In this way, the four Americans act out liberal multiculturalism, which is often criticized for what Lisa Lowe terms its contribution to the "ideological representation of the liberal imperialist state".[118] Thus the cinematic experience of viewing in 2004 the concluding scene of Iraqi dissidents crossing the border into the relative freedom of Iran is not a prophecy from 1997 of how the Bush Administration would turn to military power again in 2003 because it failed to follow the humane and politically liberal advice of *Three Kings*. Instead, the liberal ideology, itself deeply invested in U.S. nationalism, helped produce the circumstances that would make the Bush Administration's invasion of Iraq a military and colonial reality and the "logical next step" of this foreign policy covert or military efforts at "regime change" in Iran.

What was particularly noteworthy in U.S. mass media since 9/11 and during the invasion and subsequent occupation of Iraq was a new twist on these old themes, but a turn that is compatible with them and readable as part of a history stretching from the Vietnam era to the present in the gradual, ineluctable control of the news and entertainment media by the U.S. government. Fiction and non-fiction television has understandably paid great attention to the related events of 9/11 and the justification of U.S. military intervention in Iraq and Afghanistan. Lynn Spigel describes in some detail how "traditional forms of entertainment" rein- vented "their place in U.S. life and culture" after 9/11, initially by reduc- ing the number of violent films released and replacing them on television with "family fare" (Spigel, 235). Spigel goes on to argue that very quickly after this period of self-censorship, Hollywood and television turned in- stead to familiar historical narratives to stabilize the myths of national cohesion and reaffirm a teleological narrative about the American experi- ence (Spigel, 240–241). Spigel's argument confirms my own sense that Hollywood and television quickly recycled old mythic narratives about America, rather than drawing the opposite conclusion: that the terrorist attacks of 9/11 indicate that Americans need to know far more about the world they are so intent upon "globalizing". As if in direct response to this promise of greater attention to the other peoples of the world, the media began to incorporate "terrorism" into the United States and strip it of its international threat. Like President George W. Bush's continuing efforts to link Iraq directly with al-Qaeda, the nationalizing of terror helped de- fuse its transnational, inchoate, and thus truly terrifying power. The con- tainment of terror on contemporary U.S. television follows the logic of the cultural imperialism I have been tracing thus far, but now with the claim that the best weapons against such "terror" are those of traditional U.S. democracy: the fairness of the law and the populism of an American people that exceeds party politics, even national boundaries.

From its debut on September 13, 1990 to its final episode on May 24, 2010, NBC's *Law and Order* was the longest-running serial in television history. Beginning with the debut in the Fall of 2010 (September 29, 2010) of *Law and Order Los Angeles*, the series will extend that record. The NBC legal-police melodrama has coincided with U.S. neo-imperi- alism in the Middle East since the First Gulf War and not surprisingly has often taken up issues related to our foreign policies in that region. Starring Sam Waterston as the lead prosecutor of the District Attorney's office in New York, the program makes moral claims specific to the me- dium of television and distinguishes itself thereby from other police and crime shows, which rely primarily on the urban public's anxieties about living in an increasingly dangerous America and world. The program is structured in two parts: in the first half-hour, police detectives investigate a crime, arrest a suspect, and present their case to the District Attorney's

Office; in the second half-hour, the Chief Prosecutor, Jack Mc Coy (Sam Waterston) and his attractive Assistant D. A., Serena, bring the case to trial and judgment. Although the detective and legal work do not always coincide, the errors in the system seem to confirm the overall checks and balances built into the police-judicial system, as it is referred to in the voice-over prologue to the program.

Here I want to digress for a moment to anticipate my larger argument. I disagree with Michael Moore's repeated claim in *Bowling for Columbine* that it is primarily the news media, rather than entertainment television and film, which have shaped the atmosphere of fear in the U.S. resulting in more than 11,000 gun deaths per year. Citing how other societies, like Canada and Japan, where gun deaths are less than 1,000 per year, still generate large audiences for violent films, television programs, and video games, Moore contends that in such societies even adolescent viewers can suspend their disbelief in fiction programs and understand the difference between fantasy and reality. But in the United States, there is a long tradition of confusing fiction and reality in the mass media, primarily for the purposes of maximizing the commercial advantages of each mode. We hardly need the examples of recent "reality television" to remind us that television thrives on what Baudrillard long ago defined as the "hyperreal", a phenomenon seemingly explained best by the way television gives us the illusion of heightened knowledge and authority over an otherwise baffling real. *Law and Order* certainly has this effect on its viewers, which may account for its huge success on network television otherwise challenged significantly by cable channels, such as "Lifetime" and "Oxygen", targeting specific market shares and trying to break up network hegemony in the so-called "post-network era".

I have argued elsewhere that the socially conscious television of the early 1970s, such as Norman Lear pioneered in *All in the Family*, was transformed in the 1980s into much more conventional "moral problem solving" within the existing legal and social boundaries of U.S. democracy (*NAS*, 170–71). *All in the Family* argued that racial and ethnic bigotry could not be overcome entirely by the law, but required changes in personal values. *Sanford and Son* joined that argument to claim that class and racial antipathies were inextricably bound together in psychological habits difficult but still possible to change. But *Law and Order* imagines that equality under the law, despite notable aberrations in U.S. legal history, is our best defense against injustices tied to class, race, ethnicity, gender, or sexuality. The cultural shift is clearly from television committed to political and social reform to television concerned with defending existing institutions, as indeed the title of the program—a slogan of conservative republican campaigns for the past forty years—suggests.

The episode of *Law and Order* I want to analyze focuses on the murder of a popular professor of Anthropology, Louise Murdoch, who is also the head of a community advocacy center for Muslim Women, and the eventual arrest and trial of a young American male, Greg Landen, who has converted to Islam. Of course, the most infamous American convert to Islam on October 2, 2002, the date this episode was first broadcast, was John Walker Lindh, the so-called "American Taliban", who had left his upper-middle-class home in Marin, California to study Arabic and thus the Qu'ran in Yemen and Pakistan and then to join the Taliban in Afghanistan. Two days after this episode aired, Lindh was sentenced to a twenty-year prison term in a "plea bargain" that reduced the charges against him to "one count of providing services to the Taliban and one count of carrying explosives during a felony".[119] In his sentencing hearing, Lindh was tearful and apologetic, denying he had any intention of taking up arms against the U.S., and his divorced parents stood by him throughout his arrest and trial.

Lindh is certainly the historical model on which the character of Greg Landen in *Law and Order* is based, but very important changes are made in his character and history. First, the young man in *Law and Order* despises his parents, the legal system, and America in general, so that his courtroom tirades as he takes over his own legal defense for purposes of political propaganda remind the viewer of news accounts of Zacarias Moussaoui, the accused "twentieth" hijacker in the 9/11 attacks, who also insisted on serving as his own legal counsel and used the courtroom as a "bully-pulpit". Testifying in his own defense, Landen makes some very reasonable connections between al-Qaeda's possible motivations and the historical motivations of oppressed minorities in the United States to resist domination:

"Since 1990, [the U.S.] has occupied our holy lands [...] America doesn't respect any culture but its own [...].Amer-

ica is a country that was born out of the mass murder of native Americans and built on the backs of Africans. If the native
Americans could have defended themselves by flying planes
into buildings, don't you think they would have? If the slaves
could have freed themselves by becoming martyrs, don't you
think they would have? And it wouldn't have been terrorism;
it would have been self-defense".

In Muslim male dress and beard, Greg Landen is exoticized and Orientalized, even though his testimony echoes reasonable arguments made by
many intellectuals in response to 9/11. In addition to his physical appearance, Landen is also alienated by his father, who is shown in the courtroom shaking his head from side to side and mouthing the unheard word,
"No", as his son testifies.

The young man's target in *Law and Order* is not the capitalist authority symbolized by the World Trade Towers in New York City or the military authority of the Pentagon, but a woman professor of anthropology,
who has devoted her life to liberal social change and exemplifies that
work in her diversification of the American university. Equating global
terrorist attacks, such as al-Qaeda's on the U.S. (or Israel, France, or Indonesia), with "domestic terrorism" within the United States, such as
Timothy McVeigh's bombing of the Murrah Building in Oklahoma City,
is a common response not only in the United States but in Islamic societies. But this episode of *Law and Order* constructs the plot in such a way
as to swerve widely from such a conclusion. Instead, we learn that the
young man believed his girlfriend, who worked at the professor's Center
for Muslim Women, was being drawn away from her responsibilities as a
submissive Islamic woman by her feminist work with the professor. In a
jealous, but also religiously motivated rage, he "smote" his enemy.

Cautious to protect itself against charges of insensitivity to Islamic
Americans, *Law and Order* carefully disengages the young man from
"true" Islam, but in much the same fashion al-Qaeda has been distinguished in the popular U.S. news from "true" Islam: by condemning the
"fundamentalist" irrationality of both, rather than making any substantive claims about the role of women in Islamic societies. In a decisive con-
sultation between the prosecutors and a woman psychologist whom the
prosecution will call as an "expert-witness", the psychologist concludes

that Landen's primary motivation for murder was his sexual insecurity, reinforced by his difficult relationship with his parents, and his desperate need to maintain absolute control over his girlfriend. I need hardly comment on how such a conclusion reduces to triviality all of the important ethical questions raised by this episode. To be sure, *Law and Order* does not argue that this young man represents all American Muslims, but it reinforces virtually every convention the West has used to distinguish its "civilization" from Islamic "barbarism" since Romantic Idealist philosophers, like Hegel.

The incorporation of left political dissent with Islamic fundamentalism has changed since 2002, gaining in rhetorical sophistication and working thereby to create further divisions among anti-war and other progressive groups in the United States and abroad. In an episode of *Law and Order* aired on February 18, 2004, sixteen months after the "John Lindh" episode discussed above, Kenneth Silva, an African American U.S. postal worker, who has himself immigrated to the U.S. from Brazil, is charged with the murder of Brian Teague, a Hudson University college student actively involved in anti-war and anti-WTO demonstrations in New York. It turns out that Silva is himself a decorated U.S. veteran of the First Gulf War who has recently lost his son to the Second Gulf War and considers Teague's "militant activism", as the defense attorney describes it, to have "desecrated" his son's memory. Silva is acquitted of the murder charge and the jury cannot decide on the "first degree manslaughter" charge, so a mistrial is declared. Although disappointed with the result, DA Jack McCoy accepts it, as his boss, the District Attorney (played by Fred Dalton Thompson), concludes that Silva escaped justice thanks to the "blue-collar workers" on the jury who sympathized with Silva's rage. Concluding that "those who avoid jury duty" are the "same ones who avoid active duty", McCoy's boss suggests that if legal justice has miscarried, then at least the immigrant, African-American Silva has been exonerated by his "working-class" allies. This conservative immigrant, dedicated worker for the federal government both at home and abroad, has effectively silenced dissent, marshalling racial identity to "support our troops" as they continue to die in a quixotic war.

U.S. media have moved quickly from the recognizable body of the "American Taliban" Greg Landen/John Walker Lindh in 2002 to thoroughly "Americanized" versions, usually identifiable with the misguided anti-war students and other dissenters. In a 2006 episode of *Crossing Jordan* (March 12, 2006), "Death Toll", two bombs explode on Boston subway trains during rush hour, killing and injuring many, including many school children.[120] Even before he is identified, the "domestic terrorist" is designated by one member of the Forensic Team as "worse than bin-Laden". Revealed in a climactic scene attempting to defuse the remaining bomb he has planted in a manner that combines both Madrid's 3/11 and London's 7/7 terrorist acts, the bomber turns out to be a "Harvard graduate student", whose wife was killed in the bombing of the London Underground (7/7) and who had planted three bombs in hopes of alerting Americans to the failures of our Homeland Security Administration.

Sadly, the naive graduate student failed to control his explosives (an allusion to the subsequent bombers in London whose main explosives failed to detonate), even though he himself had tried to stop the train by pulling the Emergency Stop cord. In his bumbling effort to defuse his own bomb, he saves others but is righteously killed in his heroic (but technically failed) attempt. Best to leave "terrorism" to the experts, whether they are from the Boston Coroner's Office or the Homeland Security Administration. The representation of this "domestic terrorist's" body is especially interesting in the final scene. Portrayed earlier as a pleasant, helpful, white, middle-class male, he is shown in the darkness of the tunnel as both a "shadowy" and "racialized" figure, much what the London Police must have "seen" as they gunned down a fleeing Brazilian electrician on July 8, 2005 as they looked for a scapegoat for 7/7.

I have focused on *Law and Order* and *Crossing Jordan*, rather than Fox's *24* (2001–2010), because the former television series do *not* take terrorism as their principal subject. Of course, Fox's *24* and its chief investigator, Jack Bauer (Kiefer Sutherland) have been the subject of countless interpretations of how U.S. popular culture and the mass media have represented terrorism, the U.S. role in the "war on terror", and the domestic consequences of the wars in Iraq and Afghanistan. Although eight seasons of Fox's *24* only confirm my arguments about the media's "hypernationalization" of foreign threats, especially terrorism, the series does so in terms of the overtly conservative politics, especially after 9/11, of the Fox network. Films like *Wag the Dog* and *Three Kings*, television series like *Law and Order* and *Crossing Jordan* are overtly liberal in their political affiliations. It is not just that their liberalism coincides with the neo-liberal strategies of U.S. conservatives in the post-9/11 era; such liberalism defines itself by way of U.S. national affiliations that make difficult, if not impossible, the transnational, global imaginary so desperately needed to address the social, economic, and political problems we face in the second decade of the twenty-first century.

Talal Asad has argued in *Genealogies of Religion* that the "West" begins with the "project of modernization (Westernization)" that is inherently colonial and "defines itself, in opposition to all non-Western cultures, by its modern historicity. Despite the disjunctions of modernity (its break with tradition), 'the West' therefore includes within itself its past as an organic continuity: from 'the Greeks and Romans' and 'the Hebrews and Early Christians,' through 'Latin Christendom,' 'the Renaissance,' and 'the Reformation,' to the 'universal civilization' of modern Europeans".[121] Western imperialism, then, is a story that is told in countless different ways, media, and genres, but with surprisingly few variations when looked at in this light, which allows "otherness" to be internalized and rationalized, historicized, and civilized.

It perhaps should not surprise or even shock us that popular American film and television contributes to this narrative teleology in such consistently reductive ways. "Islam" is for a young American, like John Walker Lindh or his fictional alter-ego, merely "acting out" childish rebellion, a confirmation of the "undeveloped" features of those "backward cultures", which like Hegel's Africa are "without history". In a similar fashion, conservative politicians and the general public accepted anti-war activism in the Vietnam War era as "college hi-jinks", "adolescent rebellion", a "rejection of their fathers' America". What the Vietnam War—and the ongoing inchoate "war on terrorism"—have in common is a desperate desire to reaffirm national values by repressing utterly the history and reality of supposed "enemies" in Southeast Asia and the Islamic world. Few today would disagree that the Vietnam War marked a historic moment in which the United States needed to change its foreign and domestic policies, its ties between government and corporation, its neglect of public opinion, and the changing political economies affecting these historical crises. If we are to learn the lesson of the Vietnam era, then we must learn to recognize, rather than repress, the complex, intertwined histories of Islam, its influence on the development of U.S. and other western societies, and our dependence on the economic means it has provided to "modernize" and thus "westernize", often at its own peril, the world. Before we can even begin to learn this lesson, however, we will have to read critically that other narrative of Western historicity Talal Asad has so cogently interpreted as dependent on a constant "assumption": "To make history, the agent must create the future, remake herself, and help others to do so, where the criteria of successful remaking are seen to be universal. Old universes must be subverted and a new universe created. To that extent, history can be made only on the back of a universal teleology. Actions seeking to maintain the 'local' status quo, or to follow local models of social life, do not qualify as history making. From the Cargo Cults of Melanesia to the Islamic Revolution in Iran, they merely attempt (hopelessly) 'to resist the future' or 'to turn back the clock of history'" (Asad, 19). It is time for us to think differently about how "history" is and has been made, to count the "local" as well as the "global", and to develop new institutions, not simply interpretive methods, to negotiate the inevitable conflicts of such histories. Without such critical knowledge, there is likely to be unending terror from all sides in a new era of global warfare only one stage of which is being enacted in the U.S. invasion of Iraq and its ongoing war in Afghanistan.

CHAPTER 6

Reading *Reading Lolita in Tehran* in Idaho

I do not consider myself Western, but rather modern.

> – Azar Nafisi, "Three Women, Two Worlds, One
> Issue", *SAIS Review* (Summer-Fall 2000), 37.

There is nothing political in American literature.

> – Laura Bush, *New York Times* (2001)

A neo-liberal cultural front opened quietly and effectively in conjunction with the George W. Bush Administration's military imperialism in Iraq and Afghanistan. It was supported by the many private think-tanks, foundations, and university foreign policy centers that have since the 1970s played significant roles in the success of political neo-conservatism. Although the election of President Barack Obama and the near collapse of late capitalism in 2008 seemed to indicate a change in political and economic directions, the popularity of Sarah Palin and the rise of the Tea Party and Tea Party Express in 2009–2010 indicate the strength of conservatism even in the face of such political and economic reversals. The strategic use of women in the new conservative movements deserves special attention, because of what it tells us about both neo-liberalism as a tool of neo-conservatives and about the changing social and political issues facing contemporary feminists. A good deal of attention has been paid since 9/11 to the ways the U.S. has used the issue of the international rights of women to bolster diplomatic and military interventions in Iraq, Afghanistan, Pakistan, Somalia, Morocco, Iran, and Turkey. Barack Obama's appointment of Hillary Clinton as Secretary of State seems to have extended the entanglement of U.S. neo-imperialism with international women's rights, although my focus in what follows is primarily on conservative uses of international women's rights, women émigré intellectuals, and EuroAmerican high culture during President George W. Bush's administration.

Azar Nafisi's *Reading Lolita in Tehran: A Memoir in Books* (2003) is an excellent example of how neo-liberal rhetoric is now being deployed by neo-conservatives and the importance they have placed on cultural issues.[122] For the past decade and especially in the critical period following 9/11, I have argued the importance of studying the long history of U.S. imperialism in order to understand the continuity of our current imperialist ventures abroad with traditional modes of political, economic, and cultural imperialism.[123] I have also consistently recognized the need to theorize and interpret new methods of cultural imperialism appropriate to the postmodern economic conditions fundamental to globalizing capitalism. Within these new transnational flows of goods, information, services, research and technology, cultural products, lifestyles, and political institutions, the U.S. nation continues to play a crucial role, despite the apparent "post-national" character of these phenomena. In the aftermath of 9/11, U.S. nationalism has taken on a peculiarly isolationist aura that is at the same time compounded by a deep investment in its own international deployment. The nearly hysterical patriotism legitimating the military build-up for the Second Gulf War and our continuing occupations of Iraq and Afghanistan are compounded by a rhetorical emphasis on the United States as the democratic model for the rest of the world.[124] Although this emerging mythology cannot be read with complete clarity at this moment, it has certain precedents in nineteenth-century Manifest Destiny, even its late nineteenth-century variant, "the March of the Anglo-Saxon", insofar as both depend upon a U.S. democratic utopianism built upon the heritage of Western Civilization.[125]

The defense of such Anglo-Saxonism has traditionally been conducted by white male politicians, intellectuals, and writers. Neo-conservatives have varied this pattern by supporting ethnic minorities who share their views and thus give legitimacy to the cultural diversity of their presumed meritocracy. George W. Bush Administration's Secretary of State Condoleeza Rice, Dartmouth graduate and American Enterprise Institute Fellow Dinesh D'Souza, Supreme Court Justice Clarence Thomas, and Judge Janice Rogers Brown, George W. Bush appointment to the U.S. Court of

Appeals for the District of Columbia, are familiar examples of ethnic minorities celebrated for their endorsement of this neo-conservative agenda. Azar Nafisi represents an important variation of these models, insofar
as her defense of literary culture, especially in the EuroAmerican examples she uses to organize her book, appeals powerfully to liberal cultural
values in ways specifically geared to attract intellectuals disaffected by the
so-called "culture wars" of the late 1980s and early 1990s. Liberal and
leftist intellectuals have readily dismissed Rice, D'Souza, Thomas, and
Brown as puppets of the neo-conservative agenda, but Nafisi represents
a more complex figure whose defense of the aesthetic critique of social
tyranny carefully imitates the rhetoric of classical liberalism.

In a 2006 article in the *Chronicle of Higher Education*, Richard Byrne describes the controversy surrounding Hamid Dabashi's article criticizing
Nafisi as a forerunner of U.S. plans to invade Iran.[126] Byrne cites several
scholars, who like Karimi-Hakkak of Maryland's Center for Persian Studies insist that Dabashi's criticism of Nafisi is too "shrill", especially in the
claim that Nafisi's literary criticism somehow prophesies "war" (Byrne,
A16). My own approach was developed well before the controversy surrounding Dabashi's article in "the Egyptian-language newspaper *Al-Ah-
ram*" appeared (Byrne, A12), and I will try to work out the scholarly and
historical terms that are often lacking in Dabashi's more strictly political
analysis. Nevertheless, even as I wish to distinguish my approach from
Dabashi's, I want to agree at the outset with his conclusions. Although I
do not think that there is a direct relationship between Nafisi's work and
U.S. plans for military action in Iran, I do think Nafisi's *Reading Lolita in
Tehran* represents the larger effort of neo-conservatives to build the cultural and political case against diplomatic negotiations with the present
government of Iran. Nafisi also brings together micropolitical academic
issues, such as the "new" aesthetics, and macropolitical questions, such as
the role of the U.S. in contemporary world affairs.

Drawing on the enthusiasm among some intellectuals for a "revival" of
the "aesthetic function", including its left-intellectual heritage of "negative dialectic" in Adorno's famous phrase, Nafisi appears to be following
the consensus forming around Elaine Scarry's *On Beauty and Being Just*
(1999) and other contributions to the "new aesthetics".[127] Scarry's arguments in favor of the aesthetic function as deeply involved in reformist

struggles for greater social justice are politically radical, however one might dispute her claims, and she has made her own politics explicit in other works, including *Dreaming by the Book* (1999) and *Who Defended the Country?* (2003).[128] Although Nafisi's work is easy to confuse with Scarry's or other figures among the "new aestheticists", Nafisi's political affiliations are indisputably neo-conservative. After leaving Iran in 1997, Nafisi found an "academic and intellectual home" at "the Paul H. Nitze School for Advanced International Studies (SAIS) at Johns Hopkins University", where she was able to complete *Reading Lolita in Tehran* and "pursue my projects at SAIS" with a "generous grant from the Smith Richardson Foundation" (346–347).

The Smith Richardson Foundation is based on the Vicks Vaporub fortune of H. Smith Richardson, and uses its $ 500 million in assets to make "nearly $ 25 million in grants a year", emphasizing work in political science, public policy, and international relations. The Foundation also "provides significant support to conservative think-tanks across the country", especially the American Enterprise Institute.[129] The Smith Richardson Foundation website traces its support of "conservative causes" to "1973 when R. Randolph Richardson became president" and "funded early 'supply-side' [economics] books of Jude Wanniski and George Gilder".[130] The Foundation's board includes some of the most influential neo-conservatives from government, the military, and higher education, including Zbigniew Brzezinski, Christopher DeMuth, Samuel Huntington, General Edward D. Meyer, Ben Wattenberg, and E. William Stetson.[131] Of course, the mere fact the Foundation supported Nafisi's work is by no means incontrovertible proof of her own neo-conservative politics; the Foundation's recent grantees have included Columbia University, the City University of New York, Boston University, and Cornell University, along with such neo-conservative groups as the American Enterprise Institute, the Hoover Institution, the History of Neo-conservatism, and Brigham Young University.[132]

Further circumstantial evidence for Nafisi's neo-conservative credentials is her association with Johns Hopkins University's The Paul H. Nitze School for Advanced International Studies, where she is Director of the Dialogue Project, "a multi-year initiative designed to promote—in a primarily cultural context—the development of democracy and human rights in the Muslim world". According to the Dialogue Project's website, the research group addresses topics "that have been the main targets of Islamists and, as a result, are the most significant impediments to the creation of open and pluralistic societies in the Muslim world, including culture and the myth of Western culture [sic] imperialism, women's issues, and human rights, among others".[133] Located on 1740 Massachusetts Ave., N.W., in downtown Washington, D. C., 200036–1983, independent of Johns Hopkins University's main Homewood campus in Baltimore, SAIS was founded to train members of the diplomatic corps and a variety of other government services, including positions in the intelligence communities. Former Deputy Secretary of Defense and President of the World Bank Paul Dundes Wolfowitz (b. December 22, 1943) taught at Yale University (1970–1973) and briefly at SAIS in 1980, just before heading the Policy-Planning Staff at the U.S. State Department (1981–1982) in the first term of President Reagan's Administration.[134]

SAIS is an unusual institution for a scholar with Dr. Azar Nafisi's credentials: a Ph.D. in English literature from the University of Oklahoma and previous positions as an Assistant Professor of English Literature at the University of Tehran (1979–1982), the Free Islamic University, seven years as an Associate Professor of English at the University of Allameh Tabatabai in Iran, and in 1994 as a Fellow at Oxford University who gave "tutorials on women and cultural change".[135] As far as I know, there is no connection between SAIS and Johns Hopkins University's English Department or other literature-based curricula, except for programs, such as the "3-2 year" program, which allow undergraduates at Johns Hopkins to move directly from their B.A. degrees to complete Masters' degrees (of several varieties) offered by SAIS. On the one hand, Azar Nafisi's professional identity as a "Professor at Johns Hopkins University" should raise no questions, except perhaps our admiration for the distinction of such a prestigious appointment. On the other hand, for a Ph.D. in English Literature to hold her appointment in SAIS, a school for the training of diplomats, certainly does pose a set of intriguing questions. In fact, Nafisi is listed by the SAIS website as "Research Associate" and her Department as "Instruction—Substantive", and in several other places on the Johns Hopkins University website she is listed as a "Visiting Research Associate".[136]

Of course, *Reading Lolita in Tehran* testifies to Nafisi's understanding of the complex political, social, and cultural realities of modern Iran from the fall of the Shah's regime through the Islamic Revolution and the rule of Ayatollah Khomeini to the status of that revolution under the current government of the Islamic Republic. After all, the purpose of Nafisi's book is to expose the extensive corruption of the ideals of the original revolution and the tyranny under which many people suffer in the current Islamic Republic. Given her credentials as an informed and native witness to social and political transformations in her home country, Nafisi would be an appropriate consultant to a school of international relations, like SAIS, but hardly eligible for a professorial appointment. Her specific professorial credentials have little to do with these questions and derive exclusively from the study of Anglo-American literature, supported by her two book-length studies: *Anti-Terra: A Critical Study of Vladimir Nabokov's Novels* (1994) and *Reading Lolita in Tehran* (2003).[137]

All of these factors are extrinsic to Nafisi's compelling narrative in *Reading Lolita in Tehran* and its interesting hybrid form, suggested in its subtitle, *A Memoir in Books*. Widely publicized, a # 1 *New York Times* bestseller in the year of its release, and winner of the 2004 Book Sense Book of the Year Award, *Reading Lolita in Tehran* has been praised by a wide spectrum of writers, intellectuals, and cultural commentators, ranging from politically identifiable leftists, like Susan Sontag and Margaret Atwood, to respected neo-liberal writers, like Cynthia Ozick.[138] Selected by countless reading groups as a title and used as "summer reading" for first-year college students at Mount Holyoke College, *Reading Lolita in Tehran* has quickly become a classic work, anthologized in the second edition of the popular college textbook, *The New Humanities Reader*.[139] As a consequence of her book's success, Nafisi has given numerous lectures, such as her appearance at the National Association of Independent Schools' annual conference in Denver, where she was promoted as "an educator and liberator".[140]

What accounts for the fascination and publicity stimulated by this book, which combines traditional literary criticism of four canonical western authors with an insider's commentary on the political failures and repression of the Islamic Revolution and Republic? In the aftermath of 9/11, many intellectuals have discussed the notorious lack of interest by the general public in the Middle East, Muslim religion, and related issues. I need hardly remind my readers who are professional literary critics how little interest there is today among the broad U.S. reading public in the hermeneutic problems of modern Anglo-American literature. The once thriving market for *belles lettres* has dwindled since the early 1960s to a professional niche market barely able to survive on substantial subsidies from major universities to their financially desperate presses. Even the brief public interest in the 1980s and early 1990s in "academic memoirs" and "autobiographies" by scholars as intellectually diverse as Frank Lentricchia, Edward Said, and Marianna Torgovnick hardly compares with the wide circulation and discussion of Nafisi's best-seller.[141]

Some scholars have suggested that the popularity of Nafisi's book has much to do with our interests in how literary and other cultural texts depend for their meanings on where they are read. Nabokov, Fitzgerald, James, and Austen may no longer be "radical" writers in the United States, but the enthusiastic responses Nafisi claims these authors attracted among her students in Tehran signal a culturally different reception history. In his analysis of *Reading Lolita in Tehran*, Steven Mailloux contends that "where you are *does* matter in reading Western classics, indeed, in reading anything".[142] Susan Friedman emphasizes how Nafisi's aesthetic values do very different political work in Tehran, where the U.S. and English novels Nafisi prizes are judged decadent, than in the United States or England, where their aesthetics are judged merely to be part of the cultural past.[143] The problem with this approach to the location of reading in the specific case of Nafisi's *Reading Lolita in Tehran* is that it reinforces Nafisi's own substitution of her reading group for "Iranian women" or even Iranians opposed to the policies of the Iranian state. Yet the intense privacy of Nafisi's reading group, according to her necessitated by state censorship, does virtually nothing to affect Iranian politics. Written by an Iranian immigrant educated and living in the United States and published only in English for Anglophone readers, *Reading Lolita in Tehran* relies primarily on its location within the United States.[144]

Nafisi's cultural politics in *Reading Lolita in Tehran* and in all of her journalism supports the "modernization" process we often identify with one-way globalization by the first-world nations, especially the United States. In *Reading Lolita in Tehran*, Nafisi makes only two brief references to the Shah's regime, leaving the reader with the overall impression that the Islamic Revolution occurred in a political vacuum and that its repressive rule was not motivated at least in part by the tyranny of the U.S.-backed Shah's regime and the brutality of its secret police, SAVAK.[145] In her journalism, Nafisi praises more clearly the Shah's era in terms of its advocacy of western-style modernization:

> Iran is interesting because during the Shah's time the laws passed in relation to women were very progressive, and one reason for that was that many among the Iranian women since the end of the nineteenth century had been fighting for women's rights, too, so there was a degree of consciousness among women. Also, the government wanted to be modern, so it accepted the modernity of Iranian women. But many in the traditional and religious families were opposed to this.[146]

Nafisi's phrasing "a degree of consciousness among women" is interesting, insofar as it recalls the second-wave feminist strategy of "consciousness raising" as a crucial stage in feminist activism. The "secret seminar" Nafisi organized for her students in her home in Tehran seems modeled on such "consciousness raising", which in the late 1960s and early 1970s in the United States often occurred by means of reading groups. She tells her readers in a matter-of-fact manner that, "It is said the personal is political. That is not true, of course", denying one of the basic tenets of second-wave feminism, but Nafisi nonetheless clearly emulates other second-wave feminist political practices in her university classes and the seminar she teaches in her Tehran home (273). This private seminar, organized after she left the University of Tehran in protest of its repressive practices, is composed exclusively of her women students. Nafisi argues that "to teach a mixed class in the privacy of my home was too risky, even if we were discussing harmless works of fiction", but she also permits "one persistent male student, although barred from our class, [...] [to] read the assigned material, and on special days [...] come to my house to talk about the books we were reading" (3).[147]

The success of *Reading Lolita in Tehran* is undoubtedly based in part on the book's appeal to many Western readers with feminist commitments, especially the feminist universalism that ignores the different historical and cultural situations of women around the world. Nafisi's reading group in her Tehran home differs only superficially from those held in the United States, despite Nafisi's bare gestures to give her class a regional flavor. Introducing her students at the beginning of the book, Nafisi portrays each woman in Islamic dress, which each student removes to reveal the Western clothes she wears in the safety and privacy of Nafisi's home (4–6). Mitra Rastegar notes how several reviewers of the book interpret this ritual of unveiling "as a process whereby the women 'emerge as individuals' [...], revealing 'vivid personalities' [...] and 'shedding their inhibitions, speaking openly' [...]".[148] Inspired by the Anglo-American novels they study with Nafisi, her students are effectively transformed into Western subjects, who are thus capable in Nafisi's view of recognizing and protesting the repressive policies of the Iranian government.

Many feminists around the world have criticized such feminist universalism as readily adaptable to Western cultural imperialist projects. Shortly after the United States invaded Afghanistan, Laura Bush justified our actions as opportunities to "liberate" Afghani women from the gender hierarchies of the Taliban. Lisa Yoneyama has argued that there is a long history of the U.S. government justifying its foreign policies and military actions in terms of "feminist emancipation", as the United States did during the occupation of Japan (1945–1952).[149] In his classic study of how cultural work helped legitimate U.S. policy during the Mexican-American War (1846–1848), Robert Johannsen interprets the "visions of romance and chivalry" in which U.S. forces "saved" Mexican women from barbarous Mexican men.[150] Less obviously, the "critical universalism" advocated by Martha Nussbaum as a measure of women's quality of life in different societies risks linking the ethics of human rights with economic developmental programs driven by first-world nations, especially the United States.[151]

In her analysis of the Anglophone reviews of *Reading Lolita in Tehran*, Mitra Rastegar observes that the book's popularity in the West has much to do with readers' desires to understand the authenticity of Iranian women: "Despite ambivalence about Nafisi's own 'authenticity' as 'representative' Iranian woman, her representation of *other* women and their interests and desires is read [by reviewers] as 'authentic,' as is her account of the appropriate solutions".[152] The tendency to transform per-

sonal memoirs, however idiosyncratic, into ethnographies of foreign
peoples has long been recognized as integral to cultural imperialism, especially in the history of the literature of exploration and travel. As Rastegar notes, Nafisi's autobiography is difficult to accept as "representative"
of a typical Iranian woman, but by stressing the diverse personalities of
the women students in her private reading group she offers the reader a
deceptive synecdoche for Iranian women. Within the reading group, Nafisi's students are quite equally committed to the aesthetic values of the
Anglo-American literary texts they read together, but Rastegar notes that
the "views of female students who actively supported the revolution are
never described".[153]

The popularity of *Reading Lolita in Tehran* among liberal feminists
committed to such western universalism is noteworthy, because Nafisi's
own views on women's rights are so inconsistent and at times contradictory. For example, she consistently criticizes second-wave feminists, like
Germaine Greer, often confusing them with "postmodern feminists",
whom she usually identifies as dogmatic and inflexible: "But what postmodern feminists deny us is the right to change".[154] Actually, postmodern
feminism, sometimes equated with "third-wave feminism", usually distinguishes itself from second-wave feminist values and strategies, especially
the tendency of the latter to universalize their own privileged situations
as white, middle-class, American women.[155] Nafisi not only confuses the
distinction between second-wave and postmodern feminist positions,
she also reverses the usual postcolonial critique of both feminisms for
their privileged *Western* perspectives by insisting that as an Iranian émigré
to the United States (her father was Mayor of Tehran during the Shah's regime) she is hardly privileged: "Now for the past twenty years I have not
been privileged at all. In Iran, my family, power, and money, if I had any,
was taken away from me. The right to dress, to act the way I wanted, all
of this was taken away from me".[156] This observation, valid in its reference
to Nafisi as an individual who has suffered in her diaspora from Iran the
consequences of the Islamic Revolution, leads her to an odd conclusion
regarding the postcolonial critique of Western civilization and values:
"Because *Western* is equal to *privileged*, not class, not power, just being
Western [...] I think that is such an insult to those societies".[157] Nafisi's
confusion of herself with the West is here quite significant, because it in-

dicates how amenable she is to serving as a non-Western representative of a renewed defense of Western civilization and its liberal promise, regardless of its historical failures to realize those ends.

We are familiar from the culture wars of the late 1980s and early 1990s with the neo-conservative confusion of such discrete political and intellectual positions as neo-Marxism, feminism, postcolonial theory, deconstruction, poststructuralism, and a loosely deployed "postmodernism". During the culture wars, many academics attempted to sort out this confusion, assuming that once neo-conservative "mistakes" were identified the terms of the cultural and political debates might be more effectively conducted. But it now appears that the confusion of different positions and their respective terms may have been a well managed rhetorical and cultural strategy from the beginning, much as other propaganda campaigns have worked to combine different groups into a single "enemy". Something of this sort seems evident in the particular uses to which Azar Nafisi's own political and cultural values have been put in the period of her association with SAIS.

In *Power and the Idealists* (2005), Paul Berman uses Nafisi's career and book to exemplify the shift within Muslim political radicalism to "liberal antitotalitarianism".[158] Berman focuses on Nafisi in the first half of his chapter on "The Muslim World and the American Left", another installment in his larger argument that the "New Left" has warped into a new "liberal and anti-totalitarian thinking", which has abandoned the "radicalism" of its past. Crucial to Berman's argument in this book, which he considers "a freestanding sequel" to his 1996 *A Tale of Two Utopias: The Political Journey of the Generation of 1968*, is his contention that the "idealism" of the New Left survives in "liberal antitotalitarianism", whereas the American Left's failed bid for power lingers only in the political correctness of tenured radicals.[159] Berman considers *Reading Lolita in Tehran* a "classic in this particular genre" of books that recount the "evolution" "from the revolutionary leftism of the student movement [...] to a moral or philosophical crisis, to a new stage of antitotalitarian liberalism in adult life" (152). He also judges the book "doubly dramatic, not just because of the revolutionary past that it recounts, but because of its date of publication, which was March 2003: the very moment when the invasion of Iraq was getting underway" (152).

Berman has very little to say about Nafisi's literary analyses or aesthetics, except to endorse the general liberal values represented by the Anglo-
American authors she discusses. Berman is far more interested in Nafisi's
conversion from "radical" leftist at the University of Oklahoma, where
she wrote her doctoral dissertation on Mike Gold, to the neo-liberalism
Berman advocates: "Here, then, in Nafisi's *Reading Lolita in Tehran*, is the
story of someone who enlisted in the leftism of circa '68, and went on
to discover moral and political failures in the left-wing movement, and
came to adopt a different attitude altogether—an attitude of respect for
the individual imagination. A liberal attitude" (165–166).[160]

Just why Berman considers it important for Nafisi's book to have appeared at the same time as the U.S. invasion of Iraq is clear enough:
"antitotalitarian liberalism", Berman's neo-liberalism, finds the same totalitarianism represented by Saddam Hussein as it does by the Ayatollah Khomeini and his heirs to the Islamic Republic of Iran. Like George
Bush's infamous reduction of Iraq, Iran, the PLO, and North Korea into
related parts of an "Axis of Evil", Berman's liberalism creates a simple binary between liberal democracy, represented best by the United States,
and totalitarian regimes around the world. Dismissing arguments that
Islamic fundamentalism is very different from the modern fascist states
ruled by Mussolini, Hitler, and Franco, Berman equates Iraq, Iran, Franco's Spain, Hitler's Germany, Mussolini's Italy, Soviet Communism, and
Maoist China: "The political scientists, some of them, may go on waving their European check-lists and objecting that Khomeini's Islamism
cannot possibly be a modern totalitarianism. But I think that readers of
literature, who judge by smell and feel, will sense at once that Nafisi is
speaking of familiar experiences" (170).

Yet what does this curious adaptation of neo-liberal discourse by neo-
conservative political interests have to do with the cultural values Nafisi
defends with such passion in *Reading Lolita in Tehran*, especially when we
consider how her enthusiasm for aesthetic "radicalism" accounts in part
for the success of this book in the United States? Nafisi's literary examples
constitute a short history of Anglo-American literary modernism and
thus constitute a spirited defense of its internal critique of modernization
we have often identified with positions as various as classical liberalism
and the Frankfurt School's cautious defense of an "aesthetic function",

either in Adorno's "negative dialectic" or Brecht's *"Verfremdungseffekt"*.[161] Nafisi's cultural history is arranged in her narrative in a chronologically reversed order, beginning with Nabokov's *Lolita* (1955 in Paris; 1958 in US) and followed by F. Scott Fitzgerald's *The Great Gatsby* (1925), Henry James's *Daisy Miller* (1878) and *Washington Square* (1881), and Jane Austen's *Pride and Prejudice* (1813) and *Mansfield Park* (1814). Nafisi's regressive literary history interestingly culminates with a sort of intertextual reading of Austen and Saul Bellow (1915–2005), the contemporary U.S. novelist and neo-conservative intellectual who figures prominently in "Part IV: Austen".[162]

One of the powerful appeals of Nafisi's uses of these canonical Western authors must be the possibility that they do new political work in the radically different cultural context of the repressive regime of the Islamic Republic. Such aesthetic and political *re-functioning* has often been praised by liberal and left intellectuals as one means of challenging the hegemony of Western Civilization and its cultural colonialism. There are, of course, many circumstances in which we can interpret just this sort of effective ideological critique in even the most traditional literary and aesthetic works. Indeed, I will try to suggest some of the ways in which alternative interpretations might bring forth this potential in the Western literary examples Nafisi offers us, even as I argue that Nafisi's own literary interpretations work to re-legitimate the broadly defined Anglo-American modernization process. In developing this dialectical argument, I do not presume to know the appropriate terms for an effective criticism of the Islamic Republic of Iran. Indeed, I confess my ignorance of the internal workings of that state's political institutions and its social habitus, simply as a statement of fact that I am incapable of challenging Nafisi's account of the repressive conditions under which she and many others lived (and many died) from her return to Tehran in 1980 (at the age of 30) to her departure in 1996. In my confession of ignorance, I also do not mean to turn a blind eye upon the conditions Nafisi describes in Iran. Those conditions may well be as terrifying and terroristic, especially toward women, minorities, and political opponents of the state as Nafisi claims. My concern is with her proposed alternative: the cultural, economic, and political "modernization" offered by liberal western democracies, especially as they are exemplified in the liberal idealism of what she judges our "best" literature.

A full study of how scholarly studies of Nabokov, Fitzgerald, James, and Austen have changed under the influences of deconstruction, feminism, New Historicism, postcolonial studies, and cultural studies of the past twenty years would be very long and complicated. There is very little mention of these professional studies in Nafisi's book. In the few places she comments on the general status of "critical theory" in literary study, she follows the neo-conservative tendency to dismiss many different competing approaches as "postmodern" or "relativist". Nafisi's colleague Mina, a specialist in Henry James, who loses her university position, complains that critical studies like Leon Edel's *The Modern Psychological Novel* and Ian Watt's *The Rise of the Novel* "aren't so fashionable these days", because "everyone has gone postmodern. They can't even read the text in the original—they're so dependent on some pseudo-philosopher to tell them what it says" (236). One of Nafisi's students, Nassrin, who has fallen in love, complains that "girls like me, [...] who talk about Derrida and Barthes and the world situation [...] know nothing, *nothing* about the relation between a man and a woman, about what it means to go out with a man" (297). Of course, Nafisi's book is aimed at a non-professional audience, but her literary interpretations come from a much older generation of professional criticism. For Nafisi, "a novel is not an allegory" and the best novels, like *The Great Gatsby*, are "non-political" (111, 129). Novels offer us "the sensual experience of another world", which requires us to suspend our disbelief and enter them with the "empathy [that] is at the heart of the novel" (111). Several different formalist approaches to literature from the late 1930s to the early 1960s advocated similar values, including Anglo-American New Criticism (Murray Krieger), the "literary phenomenology" of the Geneva School (Georges Poulet and J. Hillis Miller), and the "reader-response" theories of Wolfgang Iser, David Bleich, Jane Tompkins, and Steven Mailloux in the 1970s and 1980s.[163]

Such critical approaches rejected overt political intentions in literature and made sharp distinctions among propaganda, mass culture, popular culture, and literature—the last term reserved for a special discourse that transcended its historical circumstances and appealed to audiences beyond the time and place of the literary work's production. Much scholarly work has been devoted to the ways American New Criticism in particular reacted to the presumably "failed" project of the 1930s Left and the unsuccessful "cultural fronts" announced at various times by the CPUSA.[164] In "Part II: Gatsby", Nafisi contrasts Fitzgerald's novel with Mike Gold's orthodox Marxism. Both authors "had written about the same subject: dreams or, more specifically, the American dream", but "what Gold had only dreamed of had been realized in this faraway country, now with an alien name, the Islamic Republic of Iran. 'The old ideals must die[...]' he wrote. 'Let us fling all we are into the cauldron of the Revolution. For out of our death shall arise glories.' Such sentences could have come out of any newspaper in Iran. The revolution Gold had desired was a Marxist one and ours was Islamic, but they had a great deal in common, in that they were both ideological and totalitarian" (109).

Fitzgerald imagines instead "the American Dream", which is what makes *The Great Gatsby* "an American classic, in many ways the quintessential American novel", alongside of which Nafisi considers some of the "other contenders: *The Adventures of Huckleberry Finn, Moby-Dick, The Scarlet Letter*" (109). Her desire to identify *the* "Great American Novel" recalls a nearly forgotten era in American literary criticism, satirized effectively by Philip Roth's *The Great American Novel* (1973), when critics struggled to identify the novel most representative of the "American Experience".[165] A significant number of scholarly studies between roughly 1950 and 1970 focused on the elusive "American Dream", with its promise of an ideal democracy characterized by the individual's capacity to realize his promise and as a consequence the civic virtue of the self-reliant, self-conscious citizen. Myth critics in this same period often keyed their own specific studies of Manifest Destiny, the Brooklyn Bridge, the Mississippi River, and Pastoralism to an Ur-myth, such as R. W. B. Lewis's *American Adam*.[166] Circulating through both of the main American literary critical discourses of the post-World War II era, the New Criticism and the Myth-and-Symbol School, the "American Dream" was firmly grounded in the liberal tradition, especially identifiable with Emersonian self-reliance and Walt Whitman's expansive "democratic vistas". What I have criticized elsewhere as the "Emersonianism" that urges "aesthetic dissent" in the place of political activism and genuine social reform is yet another way to describe the liberal tradition informing the myth of the American Dream.[167]

In her classroom at the University of Tehran, Nafisi finds that Fitzgerald's novel provokes such widely divergent responses from her students that she proposes the students stage a mock-trial of the novel. Condemned by Islamic fundamentalists as an "immoral" novel for romanticizing the adulterous relationship between Gatsby and Daisy Buchanan and as "decadent" by the Communist students for its idealized portrayal of Gatsby's aristocratic pretensions and corrupt accumulation of wealth, the novel is vigorously defended by a handful of Nafisi's women students and Nafisi herself, who has the last word in this trial: "'You don't read *Gatsby*', I said, "to learn whether adultery is good or bad but to learn about how complicated issues such as adultery and fidelity and marriage are. A great novel heightens your senses and sensitivity to the complexities of life and of individuals, and prevents you from the self-righteousness that sees morality in fixed formulas about good and evil...'" (133). Of course, Gatsby's deep conflict between crass materialism and lofty idealism has long distinguished Fitzgerald's novel as an eloquent defense of liberal individualism. Zarrin, a woman student who defends the novel, points out that Nick Carraway's strict insistence on "honesty" as the moral standard against we should judge all of the characters, including Gatsby, reinforces this myth of American individualism, distinguishing its ideal form from mere selfishness.

Professional readers of *The Great Gatsby* know there are profound ironies in both Gatsby's idealism and Nick's standard of "honesty". Claiming descent from "the Dukes of Buccleuch", an English aristocratic line "invented" by King James II to secure his power after the Restoration, noting that other family members had sent paid "replacements" to the Civil War, Nick hardly comes from an "honest" family.[168] Indignant that Jordan Baker cheats at golf and is a reckless driver, Nick is himself a bond broker in the highly speculative economy of the roaring 1920s and obviously enjoys rubbing shoulders with the rich and famous at Gatsby's elaborate parties. Long after Gatsby's funeral, when Nick leaves Long Island and the "big shore places", closed for the season, he makes a final visit to Gatsby's shuttered mansion. He finds "some boy with a piece of brick" has scrawled "an obscene word" on the steps, which he erases with his shoe to preserve Gatsby's "Platonic conception of himself", rather than tell Fitzgerald's story of Gatsby's personal and public corruptions.[169] Interestingly, both the Islamic fundamentalist and Leftist condemnations of Gatsby's immorality are easily readable in Fitzgerald's novel, but Nafisi allows both groups only the most dogmatic rants in her classroom trial, noting explicitly how little they cared to *read* the novel, enjoying instead their own tendentious speeches about religious or political proprieties.

Quite predictably, Nafisi urges careful attention to the literary text—close reading—as our only way to access the "magical" aesthetic experience offered by the novel. Equally important for her is how a great novel "disturbs us", recalling the Russian Formalists' emphasis on the aesthetic function of *ostranenie*, strategic "estrangement", as an integral part of literature's ability to subvert the automatizing processes of modernization (129).[170] To be sure, her repeated claims that we must *read* the novels she assigns (either in her classes or her book) are irrefutable, but the sleight-of-hand comes when she argues that the Islamic and Leftist students *refuse to read*. There is a rhetorical slippage between her suggestion that these students are simply bad students for not doing their homework or they are not reading *according to Nafisi's hermeneutic protocols*. Such debates over "close reading" should remind us of similar disputes within the academy during the culture wars when the entrenched method of literary *explication de texte* was under considerable pressure and its academic defenders fought back by claiming that other approaches "failed" to "read the text".[171]

Nafisi recalls her "radical" past as a college protestor against the U.S. involvement in Vietnam and later as a graduate student participant in the Islamic Students Confederation at the University of Oklahoma, citing her research on Mike Gold's leftist fiction and journalism. Like other recent "converts" to more moderate, even conservative, political positions, Nafisi attributes her early enthusiasm for leftist politics to a naive idealism. She credits her students at the University of Tehran, especially the young women repressed under the religious patriarchy of the Islamic Republic, for reviving her own passions for Western canonical writers identifiable with "what we generally label as culture [...] one domain where ideology played a relatively small part" (39). These Iranian women students had "a genuine curiosity, a real thirst for the works of great writers, those condemned to obscure shadows by both the regime and the revolutionary intellectuals, most of their books banned and forbidden. Unlike in pre-revolutionary times, now the 'non-Revolutionary writers,' the bearers of the canon, were the ones celebrated by the young: James, Nabokov, Woolf, Bellow, Austen and Joyce were revered names, emissaries of that forbidden world which we would turn into something more pure and golden than it ever was or will be" (39).

These sentiments sound like thinly disguised warnings to U.S. readers that neglect of our "great writers", the "bearers of the canon", by the advocates of "political correctness" may well result in a totalitarianism in the U.S. analogous to what Nafisi finds in the Islamic Republic. "Be careful what you wish for", Nafisi frequently reminds her leftist and Islamic fundamentalist students, and that monitory tone seems directed as well to U.S. readers, who given the English-language text and its publication by Random House constitute the largest percentage of Nafisi's readers. *Reading Lolita in Tehran* can be read productively with John Ellis's attack on cultural studies and assorted other "new" approaches in his *Literature Lost: Social Agendas and the Corruption of the Humanities* (1998).[172] What makes Nafisi's approach more appealing and less obviously reactionary than Ellis's denunciation of anti-literary approaches is her neo-liberal feminism, which she positions carefully apart from the radical "postmodernist feminism" she consistently condemns in her journalism.

Not only do her women students in Tehran find radical potential in these non-ideological writers of the Western canon, but the canonical texts themselves are read with a keen eye for the emancipatory possibilities offered their women characters. Thus Humbert Humbert projects onto Lolita all of his aesthetic passions, his love of beauty, and the high cultural, European ethos he finds so absent in meretricious America. Yet Humbert is, like the immoral characters in Fitzgerald's *The Great Gatsby*, "careless" with other people, treating them with a "cruelty" that includes the murder of Lolita's mother and his kidnapping and rape of Lolita herself (43). Responding to recent criticism of Nabokov's *Lolita* as a narrative that verges on and for some participates in a culture of pedophilia, Nafisi defends Nabokov by condemning Humbert's misguided aesthetic sense and reading within the novel a subtle "sympathy for Humbert's victims", especially the victimized "child", Lolita (42, 43). *Lolita* thus becomes a rather improbable proto-feminist narrative, which Nafisi subtly links with the situations of her young Iranian women students, each of whom as young as nine years' old "would have been [...] ripe for marriage to men older than Humbert" under the laws of the Islamic Republic (43). Although we are warned repeatedly not to confuse Humbert Humbert with the Ayatollah Khomeini or other representatives of the Islamic state, Nafisi draws exactly this analogy on repeated occasions. Nafisi's conclusion is that Nabokov motivates our compassion for Humbert's victims (and our condemnation of Humbert's misuse of his considerable aesthetic powers) in order to teach us "the first lesson in democracy: all individuals, no matter how contemptible, have a right to life, liberty and the pursuit of happiness" (42). Of course, Nafisi's claim about Nabokov's moral purpose is profoundly political, even if we agree with it, and it is recognizably part of the "classical liberalism" often touted by neo-conservatives. It is no coincidence that the Bush Administration's foreign policy of "regime change" and military occupation was legitimated in Bush's second inaugural address with his appeal for the U.S. to "take up the cause of liberty [...] to seek and support the growth of democratic movements in every nation and culture, with the ultimate goal of ending tyranny in our world".[173]

Nafisi interprets her two other canonical authors, Henry James (Part III) and Jane Austen (Part IV), in much the same fashion as she reads Nabokov and Fitzgerald as champions of liberal individualism and its democratic protections. James and Austen have been traditionally read from a wide variety of feminist perspectives, unlike Nabokov and Fitzgerald, so the narrative order gives the reader the impression that the feminist themes of Parts I (*Lolita*) and II (*Gatsby*) are becoming more explicit, even working out a *progressive* sequence, even though we are moving *backwards* historically. It is also interesting that Nafisi begins her book with two sections devoted to novels whose protagonists—Lolita and Gatsby—exemplify their authors' liberal ideals, whereas the last two sections deal with *authors*—Henry James and Jane Austen—who embody Nafisi's models for liberal individualism.[174]

James's Daisy Miller and Catherine Sloper and Austen's Elizabeth Bennet have long attracted interesting, divergent scholarly interpretations of what each character tells us about changing gender and sexual relations in nineteenth-century America and England. Although she cites very little recent scholarship on James and Austen, Nafisi claims to have selected these particular heroines to demonstrate how "the novel, as a new narrative form, radically transformed basic concepts about the essential relationships between individuals, thereby changing traditional attitudes towards people's relationship to society, their tasks and duties" (194). Nafisi's theoretical claim about the novel is profoundly *political*, insofar as she claims for the genre the power for social change. Although she mentions Ian Watt's influential *Rise of the Novel* (1963), she does not draw on his argument that the novel helped legitimate middle-class socioeconomic authority, especially by placing special emphasis on bourgeois individualism (236). Instead of analyzing bourgeois individualism in the novel, as Watt does, Nafisi stresses how Daisy, Catherine, and Elizabeth "come from a long line of defiant heroines", who "create the main complications of the plot, through their refusal to comply" (194–195). Tempting as it would be to suggest that this genealogy of "defiant heroines" extends from Daisy Miller to modern feminists, like Gertrude Stein and Virginia Woolf, to the radical artists and intellectuals of second- and third-wave feminisms, Nafisi explicitly rejects this heritage by claiming these protagonists are "more complicated than the later, more obviously revolutionary heroines of the twentieth century, because they make no claims to be radical" (195).

Nafisi's disavowal of virtually the entire tradition of twentieth-century women's writing and political activism is not as bizarre as it seems when we recall how vigorously she rejects "postmodernist feminism" in her journalism. For Nafisi, Daisy Miller, Catherine Sloper, and Eliza Bennet are not feminists, but rather courageous *individuals* who defy social conventions through their imaginations and thus empathy for different people (333). Daisy Miller can flirt with both Winterbourne and Giovanelli, relying on her sexuality, rather than avoiding it, as Nafisi suggests both western-style feminists and the repressive Islamic Republic require, even if Daisy's iconoclasm means her ultimate social exclusion, even symbolic death. Catherine Sloper rebels against the hypocrisy of her suitor, Morris Townsend, the sneakiness of her Aunt Penniman, and the tyranny of her father, Dr. Sloper, affirming in her truculent spinsterhood her moral rigor and honesty (225). Eliza Bennet insists upon courtship and marriage on her own terms, rather than those dictated by her class, her family, or the broader standards of social respectability. Each character individuates herself in the course of the narrative, achieving the specific sort of identity that liberal democracy at its best makes possible for everyone, regardless of race, class, gender, or sexual identifications.

It is this "ideal democracy", especially as it is embodied in idiosyncratic and thus individual characters, that Nafisi argues the greatest novels offer us. Interestingly, Nafisi's male confidante, her "magician", delivers this message toward the end of *Reading Lolita in Tehran*, but only to remind Nafisi of her own words.[175] It is a strange ventriloquism:

> "You used to preach to us all that [Jane Austen] ignored politics, not because she didn't know any better but because she didn't allow her work, her imagination, to be swallowed up by the society around her. At a time when the world was engulfed in the Napoleonic Wars, she created her own independent world, a world that you, two centuries later, in the Islamic Republic of Iran, teach as the fictional ideal of democracy. Remember all that talk of yours about how the first lesson in fighting tyranny is to do your own thing and satisfy your own conscience? [...]. You keep talking about democratic spaces, about the need for personal and creative spaces. Well, go and create them, woman! Stop nagging and focusing your energy on what the Islamic Republic does or says and start focusing on your Austen". (282)

These sentiments express clearly liberal "aesthetic dissent" by stressing the "revolutionary" power of the imagination to preserve "the personal" and the "private" from contamination by the "political" (237). When Mr. Nahvi, one of her Islamic fundamentalist students, criticizes Austen as a "colonial writer", noting that "*Mansfield Park* was a book that condoned slavery", she is at first dumb-founded, because "I was almost certain Mr. Nahvi had not read *Mansfield Park*" (289). What her student has been reading, she claims to learn on a subsequent trip to the U.S., is the "revolutionary" work of "Edward Said's *Culture and Imperialism*", reminding her readers once again how dangerous it is when students don't "read the text in the original", instead relying "on some pseudo-philosopher to tell them what it says" (236). Sad, indeed, Nafisi opines that "reactionary elements in Iran had come to identify with and co-opt" Said's radicalism, and her moral for the U.S. reader seems quite clear (290). Yes, right and left do meet in their extremes—another truth that must be universally acknowledged.

What Nafisi values in these literary texts is their ability to transcend politics and offer social and personal ideals uncontaminated by ideology. And yet there is plentiful evidence from the authors she has chosen how their own and other literary works are deeply invested in the political and ideological conditions of their production. Nafisi is following Daniel Bell's conservative argument that liberal democracy is "beyond ideology" and Francis Fukuyama's contested claim that laissez-faire capitalism in its global stage has taken us to the "end of history".[176] What Nafisi adds to these neo-conservative arguments is her claim that "great" literature provides us with the role models—either the authors or their heroes and heroines—that will lead us beyond the impasses of political conflicts resolved usually by force and violence. It is, after all, the imagination which Nabokov's Cincinnatus employs so skillfully at the end of *Invitation to a Beheading*, thus causing by verbal magic "the scaffold and all the sham world around him, along with his executioner, [to] disintegrate" (77). Nafisi makes passing reference to other writers who might approach this same literary "greatness"—Langston Hughes and Zora Neale Hurston from African American culture, a handful of Persian titles, including *A Thousand and One Nights*, Iraj Pezeshkzad's *My Uncle Napoleon*, and Marjane Satrapi's *Persepolis*—but the overall impression of her book is that Western Civilization, especially in its British and U.S. variants, has provided the largest number of aesthetically triumphant testaments to this universal model for democratic individualism.[177]

Is Azar Nafisi part of a neo-conservative conspiracy to co-opt neo-liberal rhetoric for its own purposes, including the manipulation of "culture" as a weapon in the ongoing war for the "hearts and minds" of Americans and the citizens of those states we hope to convert to our forms of democracy? The extrinsic evidence of her position as Director of the Dialogue Project at SAIS, her support from the Smith Richardson Foundation, and her participation in the public relations' campaigns of SAIS to promote the United States as the "protector" of the Free World is compelling. The intrinsic evidence of *Reading Lolita in Tehran* is even more convincing, suggesting not that Nafasi has fallen into the conservative "traps" readied these days for unwitting liberals, but that she actively participates in the agenda of an overtly "depoliticized" cultural study that is in fact profoundly *political*. My purpose is not to pose as a cultural "whistle-blower", some policeman for Political Correctness. Nafisi is free to write what she wishes and advocate whatever retrograde and fallacious aesthetic ideas she chooses.

Nafisi's second memoir, *Things I Have Been Silent About: Memories of a Prodigal Daughter* (2008), relies primarily on Persian and Middle Eastern literary texts in its account of Nafisi's family life and education in Iran, as the "Suggested Reading List" at the end of the book indicates.[178] Three of the four part divisions of the book use epigraphs from Emily Dickinson's poetry (the fourth is a quotation from the émigré writer, Joseph Brodsky) and there are frequent references in this memoir to the importance of Western literature in Nafisi's life and work, especially after the 1979 Revolution. She briefly recounts why she "started writing about Vladimir Nabokov partly because of my students' enthusiasm for his works", as well as her own sympathy with Nabokov's "preoccupation with exile, a firm belief in the portable world of the imagination, and the subversive power of the imagination" (*Things*, 289). Although she details her personal and political activities at the University of Oklahoma, Norman while an undergraduate and then graduate student, including her participation in anti-Vietnam War demonstrations and membership in the Confederation of Iranian Students, opposed to the Shah, Nafisi only refers in passing to her doctoral dissertation on Mike Gold's fiction and the 1930s Left. Nevertheless, she tacitly links her participation in anti-government, anti-Shah demonstrations in the U.S. with her work on her doctoral dissertation: "I turned the living room of our rented apartment [in Washington, D. C.] into my office, and as soon as I woke up and showered I would take my coffee back to bed and read the news about Iran. One corner of our bedroom was soon filled with old coffee-stained copies of *The Washington Post* and *The New York Times*. Some mornings I would go to the Library of Congress, where I spent delicious hours looking through old microfilms of *The Masses*, *The New Masses*, and other publications from the thirties for my dissertation" (*Things*, 212–213).

Things I Have Been Silent About ends with her departure with her husband, Bijan, from Tehran for Washington, D. C. in 1997, although the last two chapters (30 and 31) deal with her mother's death in 2003 and her father's death in 2005. Little mention is made of her two-year "fellowship [...] at Johns Hopkins University's School of Advanced International Studies" (*Things*, 294). In short, she *remains* silent about the ways in which she came to be associated with SAIS, the terms of the fellowship, the faculty at SAIS (or elsewhere) who supported her application, and her professional reasons, beyond simply her husband, Bijan's work in Washington, D. C., for doing research at an institution designed to train diplomats and intelligence officers. *Things I Have Been Silent About* does not answer questions about how a scholar with a Ph.D. in English literature, as well as experience teaching Persian and world literatures in Iran, should be of interest and herself interested in the School of Advanced International Studies.

Things I Have Been Silent About does address in great detail her father Ahmad Nafisi's political career, culminating in his position as Mayor of Tehran, his arrest and imprisonment by the Shah, and his eventual exoneration and release by the Iranian court. Nafisi also recounts in detail the personal difficulties between her mother, Nezhat, and father, as well as Nezhat's position in the Iranian Parliament until she was forced to resign after the 1979 Revolution. Nafisi's account of her family history is indeed a fascinating story of how upper-class, politically moderate Iranians, like the Nafisis, found themselves historically tossed between the extreme regimes of the Shah and the Ayatollah Khomeini. It makes perfect sense to me that Azar Nafisi would want to write about the complexities of this history, especially as it is represented in a single family, in order to explain the human consequences of both regimes.

Yet such family and macropolitical histories are not the center of her best-seller, *Reading Lolita in Tehran*, the book she tells us she was completing when on January 2, 2003, her mother died in Tehran (*Things*, 304). By then, Nafisi's "two-year fellowship" at SAIS had evolved into an appointment as "visiting professor", then into "director of the Dialogue Project at the Foreign Policy Institute of Johns Hopkins University" (*Things*, endpaper). *Things I Have Been Silent About* is another volume in the melancholia experienced by families and individuals caught between colonial and postcolonial societies. *Reading Lolita in Tehran* is a narrative of recolonization, in which the exiled subject embraces new conquerors. The larger issue is the extent to which "culture" has undergone a paradigm shift from the "property" controlled by those Spirow Agnew, Richard Nixon's Vice President, dubbed "effete intellectuals" or the "tool" of those "tenured radicals" (Roger Kimball) and "feminazis" (Rush Limbaugh) attacked by conservatives in the heyday of the culture wars to a resource of the new imperialism. Some time after Nixon's disgrace in the Watergate Scandal and his voluntary resignation to avoid Impeachment and likely conviction on those charges, neo-conservatives in the United States organized to retake the "liberal media", not just by creating competitive, alternative media but by co-opting the idea of "liberalism" itself and along with it the very concept of "cultural critique". Azar Nafisi's *Reading Lolita in Tehran* re-legitimates Western cultural texts as forerunners of the political revolution and regime change in Iran that the George W. Bush Administration openly advocated, especially in its identification of the Islamic Republic of Iran as part of a global "Axis of Evil".

Although Barack Obama's Administration has softened the diplomatic rhetoric, military action against Iran remains an "option", especially in response to Iran's growing nuclear threat. President Obama's repeated invocation of the "American Dream" and the uniqueness of the "American experience" helped him achieve wide popularity with the electorate, but such nationalism also helps sustain the illusion that the "West is the Best". The conservative Tea Party movement has flourished in part as a consequence of the Obama Administration's determination to chart a middle course. The greatness of America is its tolerance of everything and anything. In view of the conservatives' strategic battle for cultural power I have analyzed in this chapter, I am not confident that the Obama Administration's meliorism and nationalism are capable of responding effectively to the cultural politics of neo-conservatives.

I first began reading Nafisi's *Reading Lolita in Tehran* in Idaho, where Kristin and I spend most of our vacations. High in the Rocky Mountains, in the tri-state border region of Idaho, Montana, and Wyoming, we are often told by our neighbors that we are in "God's country". Fiercely independent ranchers fight the hated Bureau of Land Management, National Forest Service, and National Park Service, imagining that these federal agencies are determined to erode the ranchers' freedoms. In stores and restaurants, bearded frontiersmen, or at least their late modern simulations, pay cash for everything, drive pick-up trucks outfitted for any possible emergency, and pride themselves on their abilities to field strip and rebuild anything from an agricultural pump to a handgun and to hunt and "dress" in the woods a grizzly bear, elk, or moose—all of which can still be hunted in that region. Suspicious of strangers, especially California "tree-huggers", the locals tend to be profoundly religious, openly racist, and incurably sexist. To be sure, Idaho is hardly a match for the repressive regime of the Islamic Republic of Iran, but "God's country" is certainly as fanatically political and ideological in its fantastic commitment to its version of "liberal individualism". Reading *Reading Lolita in Tehran* in Idaho is an object lesson to the attentive cultural critic that we face our own dangers in the U.S. of a growing intolerance and political extremism that have more similarities with the extremism Nafisi criticizes in the recent politics of Iran than most Americans are willing to recognize. It is even more troubling that such political extremism openly employs cultural materials and academic disciplines to achieve its ends.

CHAPTER 7

The Death of Francis Scott Key and Other Dirges
Music and the New American Studies

*I think it's a despicable thing that someone is going into our society
from another country and [...] changing our national anthem.*

– Charles Key, great-great-grandson of Francis Scott Key

*The first verse of 'The Star-Spangled Banner' should
be kept in English, but the other verses should be
given to whoever wants them, because those are the
verses Americans don't want or won't sing.*

– Jon Stewart, comedian

September, 1964, 150 years to the month after Francis Scott Key composed his famous poem, "The Defense of Fort McHenry", while witnessing the bombardment of Fort McHenry from a British Man-of-War, I reclined at my ease on one of the grassy embankments separating the outer fortifications from the inner Fort McHenry on Baltimore Harbor. Three months shy of my nineteenth year, I was killing time before the Fall Semester began at Johns Hopkins, where I would begin my sophomore year. A naive Californian in Baltimore, ignorant of history and yet determined to major in that discipline, I rationalized my idleness as "study". Not quite the Grand Tour, my little tourism in Baltimore followed the high-cultural path my parents and teachers had beaten for me. Visit museums, look at paintings, read the "best that has been thought and written", become a leader in "... *Hey, you! What are you doing there?*" I was hustled to the Commandant's Office—Fort McHenry was still administered in those days by a quasi-military command—and brought immediately to the Commandant himself.

Gaping and dawdling, dreaming of the misty grandeur of an American past about which I knew very little and such knowledge a passel of schoolboy's clichés, I had missed the official closing of the Fort and been caught "after hours", like some burglar trapped in the central vault by the Bank of England's time lock or a cat burglar cornered by searchlights on the parapet of the Monte Carlo Casino. What they feared even then in the innocent early 1960s must have been some sort of "terrorist" act, which in those days went by the more modest names of "vandalism" and "vagrancy", each with its imperial heritage. Somehow, I talked my way out of my tight spot, avoiding arrest with a quick rhetorical flourish. I don't quite know what I said, but somehow it worked. All I know is that from that day forward I hated Francis Scott Key.

Behind the patriotic sentiments of Key's lyrics and his venerated captivity on board that British naval ship, the familiar song that would become our National Anthem directly derives from our global ambitions in the early years of the nation. Michael Oren notes that the lyrics of "The Star Spangled Banner" were first "composed for [William] Bainbridge and [Stephen] Decatur in 1805 and set to an old English drinking tune", in response to Bainbridge's and Decatur's roles in America's Barbary Wars. The anthem that celebrates our defense of the young nation against the British originated in response to our naval victories over North African leaders, whose "'turbaned heads bowed' to the 'brow of the brave' and 'the star-spangled flag or our nation.'"[179] Although Francis Scott Key would revise the lyrics "after the Battle of Fort McHenry in the War of 1812", the echo remains of the Barbary Wars, arguably the U.S. nation's first adventure in foreign warfare. As Oren argues, America's involvement in the Middle East has a history that stretches from the Revolution to our contemporary military occupation of Iraq (Oren, 596). Although Oren's purpose is to show that on balance this history displays America's "beneficence" more than its "avarice" toward the Middle East, he also demonstrates our consistent imperial designs on the region as part of our larger imperial ambitions for global power (Oren, 603). The origins of Francis Scott Key's "Star-Spangled Banner" in the celebration of American victory over the Barbary states is by no means the exception in the cultural history of U.S. patriotism: patriotism functions culturally by way of constructing enemies, thus working out an imperial logic.

It should not be necessary to criticize the rhetoric of patriotism, but it is a sign of our desperate times that American patriotism must be challenged and replaced with something that will bond our affections and our thoughts in less deadly ways. During the George W. Bush Administration's pursuit of its "war on terror" in utter disregard of public opinion, signs emerged of a "new" expatriotism of intellectuals intent on reaffirming the promise of U.S. democracy by criticizing the Bush Administration's imperial "democracy".[180] What the Bush Administration accomplished has lasting results, as well as deep historical roots. It is clear that President Obama has chosen not to abandon the use of patriotic rhetoric that reinforces American Exceptionalism, despite the broad international support for his presidency. His foreign policies in the continuing occupation of Iraq, the ongoing war in Afghanistan, and political instability in Pakistan depend upon his repeated affirmation of U.S. moral superiority and the relevance of U.S. democracy and capitalism to the far corners of the globe.

I still respect our customary intellectual means to criticize social and political practices in conflict with our understanding of justice, equality, and humane behavior, and these include scholarly discourses of the most sophisticated kind, high-cultural work in which imaginative solutions are considered and worked through, popular cultural resistance to inequitable social norms, and everyday political practices from legal to performative activism. We have long known, of course, that none of these activities will in itself be sufficient to bring about social and political change, but each requires the complement of other practices and all of them depend upon propitious, contingent historical circumstances. The Berlin Wall did not fall, the Marcoses did not flee, Havel did not suddenly rise to popular power, slavery did not end, and women did not win the vote merely because people acted courageously and in concert. History happened, too, often well beyond such human agencies.

I do not want to mystify (or even capitalize) "H"istory in this regard. What exceeds our active reach and we call for want of a better term "history"—paradoxically, I think, because we are referring to everything that is in fact *not* historical—may refer in part to what occurs beyond our rational powers at the affective level of individual responses, multiplied vastly, to social and political conditions that eventually become unbearable and must be overcome. American popular disgust with the Vietnam War developed in this manner, I think, aided significantly but not comprehensively by a vigorous and multifaceted anti-war movement in the U.S. and around the world. Emotional transformation is crucial in bringing about necessary social and political changes, because it affects the truculently unconverted and unconvinced, those citizens who otherwise find every provocation from activists to bind them more firmly to their own positions and the reasons they have given for discrimination, war, genocide.

Most American Studies scholars, whatever their specific disciplines, are students of literature and know how its rhetoric works both rationally and affectively to shape readers into what Étienne Balibar has termed "citizen-subjects". And, of course, music is a crucial part of American Studies, but I think it has remained until quite recently marginalized as a "specialization", not enjoying the centrality we have reserved for historical and literary texts as agents of social and political change. This chapter is thus an effort to re-conceive popular music as central to the new American Studies and to political activism, in short as an integral part of the cultural politics of the new American Studies.

U.S. popular music can employ emotionally appealing lyrics and music for extremely effective ideological purposes. The Congressional adoption in 1931 of Francis Scott Key's "The Star Spangled Banner" as the National Anthem is itself an excellent illustration of this ideological purpose. Music is a crucial component of U.S. nationalism. For this very reason, the use of popular music for the purposes of challenging U.S. nationalism and patriotism ought to be a crucial part of any activist agenda, especially in those historical periods when the distribution and reproduction of music makes it one of the fastest communicative media. The hegemonic and counter-hegemonic functions of music are well known both within and outside scholarly discussions, and it is this very political malleability that poses a third part of this thesis: because critical music often relies on familiar musical melodies and motifs, it is especially susceptible to conservative re-functioning. Bruce Springsteen's famous "Born in the U.S.A." was intended to criticize the collusion of U.S. domestic and foreign policies during the Vietnam War to exploit American workers and colonial subalterns. With the greatest ease, of course, President Ronald Reagan turned "Born in the U.S.A." from an ironic commentary on U.S. citizenship into a patriotic theme song for his re-election campaign.

Since the First Gulf War, conservative political interests in the United States have co-opted "American patriotism" for their own purposes, relegating the traditional role of the self-conscious, skeptical, and questioning citizen to the social and political margins and sometimes into effective exile. "Support our troops" was a popular slogan in the First Gulf War, which in the invasion and occupation of Iraq has become a nearly hysterical mantra to silence dissent and control a large but still minority anti-war movement in the United States. Displayed proudly on the windows of cars and trucks, the doors of businesses, even on T-shirts and jackets and dresses, the twisted "ribbon" used first to represent the solidarity of those people committed to fighting the pandemic of HIV/AIDS, then adopted as the symbol of those contributing to the fight against breast and other cancers, is now the national symbol for those who "support our troops" in Iraq.

The twisted ribbon as a sticker or decal derives in part from the "yellow ribbons" tied around trees during the Iran Hostage Crisis in 1980–1981 in both the Carter and Reagan Administrations to show support for the release of the 52 Americans held hostage by students in the U.S. Embassy in Tehran. When those hostages were finally released by the Iranian government on January 21, 1981, Tony Orlando and Dawn's 1973 popular hit, "Tie a Yellow Ribbon Round the Old Oak Tree", was played as a joyous homecoming theme. During the First Gulf War in 1991, the George H. W. Bush Administration urged Americans to "display" yellow ribbons outside their homes to "support the troops" by expressing our desires to "welcome them home", combining thereby the original populist and ostensibly anti-war sentiments in the Iran Hostage Crisis to "bring the hostages safely home" with the tacit conservative criticism of how veterans returning from the Vietnam War had been mistreated by anti-war demonstrators.[181]

Tony Orlando and Dawn's song was based on an actual incident on board a southern bus heading for Miami, Florida. One of the passengers told the driver that he had just been released from prison, where he had served three years for passing bad checks. While in prison, the man wrote his wife to tell her she did not have to wait for him to serve his sentence, but if she was still interested she should let him know by tying a yellow ribbon around the only oak tree in the city square of White Oak, Georgia. When the bus passed through town, the driver slowed down and to the convict's tearful relief the wife had tied a yellow ribbon around the town's central oak tree. The driver phoned this story to the wire services, which spread it all over the country. Songwriters Irwin Levine and L. Russell Brown read it in the newspaper, then composed their million-selling song, which was released by Bell Records in February 1973 and by the week of April 23, 1973, was the number one popular song in the United States.

Although Saigon did not fall to the North Vietnamese and the U.S. did not hastily evacuate military and diplomatic personnel until 1975, 1973 is the year of the negotiated peace accords between the U.S. and North Vietnam. Tony Orlando and Dawn's popular song certainly owes its success not only to its reliance on the conventions of country pop music, a hybrid musical genre of growing popularity in the early 1970s, but to the optimism in the United States that the Vietnam War was finally over and at that date had been concluded "honorably". The prisoner returning home to his devoted wife was a figure for the POW, many of whom like today's Senator John McCain, had been tortured in the "Hanoi Hilton" in explicit violation of the protections of prisoners-of-war guaranteed by the Geneva Convention. Of course, insofar as the Vietnam War remained to the very end an "undeclared war", claims to violations of the Geneva Convention's protections of combat troops could not be legally maintained.

In the aftermath of the Vietnam War, the "yellow ribbon" originally representing public relief at the end of an unpopular war and personal hopes for family members to come home safely, has come to represent an unequivocal patriotic zeal that substitutes "troops" metonymically for "our foreign policies". The "yellow ribbon" has now taken on numerous different color combinations, the most popular of which is the red, white, and blue ribbon arranged to combine the American flag with the ribbon's multiple connotations.

We know from Benedict Anderson that patriotism is an elaborate fiction sustained by countless cultural and symbolic acts, but we still find ourselves "stirred" and "moved" as flags wave, anthems play, and foot-

ballers score points.[182] It is still difficult to understand how such patriotism motivates individuals to die for a foreign policy toward a distant and
relatively powerless nation—Vietnam, Iraq, Afghanistan—posing no immediate threat to those individuals before they enter combat. How is it
possible that large numbers of people from many different backgrounds,
most of whom will never meet each other or, if they did, would find they
have nothing in common, will embrace and sing together as "their" flag
is displayed and "anthem" is played? Although this is the typical "patriotic scene of instruction", it is rarely performed with much enthusiasm or
even consensus. In a televised broadcast on Memorial Day (2006), President George W. Bush praised the sacrifices of the military in a speech at
Arlington National Cemetery, and he was joined by Secretary of Defense
Donald Rumsfeld and others in singing the National Anthem. Like some
distracted fan at a sporting event, Rumsfeld clearly had difficulty with the
lyrics, lip-synching at times and others remaining silent. "Patriotism" is
thus not performed simply as the repetition of certain symbolic acts, like
the singing of the National Anthem or the recitation of the "Pledge of Al-
legiance". Patriotism depends on a much wider culture industry, whose
products are generically and temporally diverse. Without "new" productions, patriotism would simply fail. Much of its vitality depends, then,
on a ceaseless re-functioning of older cultural myths adapted to new
circumstances.

Since the First Gulf War, patriotic rhetoric has relied on the substitution of military personnel, often individualized or collectively represented through fictive individuals, for embattled political leaders and institutions. In the County-and-Western hit, "Arlington", Trace Adkins sings
in the voice of a dead veteran of the Second Gulf War, who has recently
been buried at National Arlington Cemetery, "a thousand stones" away
from his "grandad", who died fighting in World War II.[183]

The veteran's reward for service to his country is "this plot of land [...]
for a job well done", just below "a big white house sits on a hill just up the
road". The "white house" is, of course, the Custis-Lee Mansion, the original estate on which National Arlington Cemetery was built when Brigadier General Montgomery C. Meigs appropriated the house and established a cemetery for the Union war dead on June 15, 1864. But Adkins's
"white house" also refers to the Executive branch of the government, thus

aligning the dead veteran's sacrifice and patriotism with unquestioning support of the Bush Administration's foreign policy in the Middle East. Adkins's lyrics pun on the veteran's "hometown" and his ultimate coming "home" to Arlington National Cemetery, glossing the "big white house [...] on a hill" as the proper destination for "the chosen ones" who have made such a sacrifice. The cemetery is "this peaceful piece of property", which is "sacred ground" where the young man can "rest in peace". Playing on the promises of the Bush Administration to protect Americans against "terrorism" and guarantee their "homeland security", Adkins suggests that such policies represent a national consensus: "We're thankful for those thankful for the things we've done,/We can rest in peace, 'cause we are the chosen ones,/We made it to Arlington, yea dust to dust,/Don't cry for us, we made it to Arlington". Of course, the Biblical reference links the Bush Administration's foreign policies with the civil religion, just as allusions to the "city" (in this case, "a white house") on "a hill" and the "chosen ones" recall the Puritan doctrine of supralapsarian Election.

Some neo-conservatives have attempted to equate "civic virtue" and "good citizenship" with "patriotism", effectively "rationalizing" patriotism (that is, giving it the aura of "reason"). In *Who Are We? The Challenges to America's National Identity*, Samuel Huntington complains that "elements of America's business and intellectual elites [identify] more with the world as a whole and [define] themselves as 'global citizens' [...]".[184] Huntington takes a populist stance in the book, lumping liberal academic and multinational corporate "elites" together in an improbable conspiracy to denationalize the United States with immigrants, who in their refusal to accept the American consensus end up working out the "cosmopolitan" agenda of their allies in the university and corporations. Fixing on immigrants with legal or de facto dual citizenship and tagging them "ampersands", Huntington fuels the recent rage against undocumented workers in the United States by insisting: "Previous immigrants maintained an ethnic identity as a subcomponent of their American national identity. Ampersands, in contrast, have two national identities. They eat their cake and have it too, combining the opportunity, wealth, and liberty of America with the culture, language, family ties, traditions, and social networks of their birth country".[185] What links together these unlikely forces is finally their unpatriotic, anti-national, and perversely destructive impulses. We are saved only by the grass-roots Americans who constitute what Huntington terms the nation's "'patriotic public", which is "foremost among peoples in their patriotism and their commitment to their country".[186] As rational or historically accurate argument, *Who Are We?* makes no more sense than the shifting symbolism of those "yellow ribbons", but in both cases a vague rhetoric of "patriotism" as necessary "consensus" holds both symbolically in place.

Samuel Huntington is a frequent target of liberal criticism, of course, because his arguments rely so centrally on neo-conservative rhetoric, especially by linking "values", "faith", and "nationalism". Yet even more sophisticated and less obviously politically interested criticism has been directed in recent years at the new "cosmopolitanism" or what Robbins and Cheah have positively formulated as "cosmopolitics".[187] The new "world or global literatures", "post-nationalist" and "transnational" cultural and political projects, "traveling theory", and "postcolonial theory" have been criticized for their totalizing impulses, their impracticality, and their tacit acceptance of (or at least failure to distinguish themselves from) unilateral, first-world globalization. Although Alan Wolfe's notorious review of the so-called "Anti-American Studies" in *The New Republic* is an extreme example of this tendency, there are many more "reasonable" arguments against the "internationalizing" of American Studies, especially if this requires us to study comparatively the polylingual, ethnically diverse communities of the Western Hemisphere and their pertinent rims or "contact zones".

In *Cosmopolitanism*, Kwame Anthony Appiah argues eloquently for the transnational ethics of the cosmopolitan, who takes "seriously the value not just of human life but of particular human lives, which means taking an interest in the practices and beliefs that lend them significance. People are different, the cosmopolitan knows, and there is much to learn from our differences".[188] Appiah's approach respects human differences, including those established by national boundaries and customs, but in doing so tries to develop an ethics that is not restricted to nation-specific knowledge and morality. As Appiah acknowledges, it is difficult for us to acknowledge the cosmopolitan ideal "that we have obligations to strangers", but even the smallest "nation" is composed primarily of strangers.[189] What allows us to identify with "fellow Americans" (or Swiss or Ugan-

166

dans) whom we do not know personally and not make the same connection with other human beings? The problem is in part the result of
nation-specific knowledge, especially in the disciplines associated with
culture and history. Whatever critical and educational purposes these
disciplines may serve in the interpretation of the nation, they have done
considerable work toward the legitimation of nations as discrete "objects"
of study.[190]

Cultural, economic, and political globalization makes patriotism and
nationalism appear increasingly naive and irrational. At the same time
that U.S. popular music reinforces sentimental patriotism in work like
Trace Adkins' "Arlington", it also calls attention to an ineluctable global
awareness critical of the provincialism of the nation. The cross-over Folk-
Country musician Steve Earle explains in the liner notes for his disc, *The
Revolution Starts Now*, that he felt a special urgency when composing this
album to "weigh in" on "the most important presidential election in our
lifetime", the 2004 Presidential election that would occur seven months
after the album's release in May 2004.[191] The Country-and-Western melodies sound much like those employed by Adkins in patriotic songs, like
"Arlington", but Earle's message is distinctly radical—in the spirit of what
he terms the "radical [U.S.] revolution"—and global in perspective. The
music lyrics in "Home to Houston" recall countless Country songs celebrating the hard work of truckers, but Earle's driver is making the run
from Basra to Baghdad "with a bulletproof screen on the hood of my
truck/And a Bradley on my backdoor". The trucker's refrain—"God get
me back to Houston alive/and I won't drive a truck anymore"—repudiates the conventional celebration of the trucker's hard but honorable life,
as well as the freedom of the open road.[192]

Earle's trucker may want to get back to Houston as quickly as possible,
recognizing his mistake in participating in a war so far from home, but
Earle makes it clear that one lesson of the Second Gulf War is that working people share common bonds that reach beyond national borders. In
"Rich Man's War", Earle argues that U.S. grunts, like Bobby, are fooled
by patriotism—"Bobby had an eagle and a flag tattooed on his arm/Red
white and blue to the bone when he landed in Kandahar"—in order to
fight "a rich man's war", leaving at home "a stack of overdue bills" while
"the finance company took his car". In the same song, the Palestinian

"Ali", "the second son of a second son,/Grew up in Gaza throwing bottles and rocks when the tanks would come/Ain't nothin' else to do around here just a game children play/Somethin' 'bout livin' in fear all your life makes you hard that way".

Both Bobby and Ali answer the same call of "rich men", who manipulate their workers as if they were children. When Ali gets "the call", he "Wrapped himself in death and praised Allah/A fat man in a new Mercedes drove him to the door/Just another poor boy off to fight a rich man's war".[193]

Customarily represented as religious fanatics in the U.S. media, Palestinian suicide-bombers are identified by Earle as sharing a transnational cause with U.S. troops in Iraq and Afghanistan.

Cheah, Robbins, Appiah, and Earle are working out a new cosmopolitanism that should guide our efforts to "internationalize" American Studies. The curious hybrid term "international American Studies", which in its very name appears to combine incompatible categories of world and nation, offers us an excellent opportunity to offer a sustained criticism of nationalism and its emotional complement "patriotism" from perspectives both transnational and "rational". The first task in this work is, then, profoundly theoretical: how can we disarticulate "reason" and "knowledge" from specific national or state interests? *Denationalizing* knowledge complements the work of *decolonizing* knowledge advocated by the postcolonial theorist Walter Mignolo, especially if we understand the historical relationship between the nation-state and colonial expansion.[194] And can we do so in ways that will escape the totalizing universals of the past, especially noticeable in the Enlightenment heritage of modernity? In my concluding remarks, I want to suggest that popular music offers one possibility of moving in these directions beyond the nation, beyond universal reason, and against neo-imperialist versions of globalization.

Liberalism within the nation-state is no longer a possible alternative to a "neo-liberal ideology" that is profoundly conservative in its politics and yet rhetorically liberal. The ease with which a well-intentioned intellectual or artist can be captured by such neo-liberal rhetoric is exemplified by Richard Rorty's *Saving Our Country* and by Neil Young's recent album, *Living with War*. Young's long career is an interesting mixture of his Canadian backgrounds, musically documented in *Prairie Wind*, the album (and documentary film) released just prior to *Living with War*, his countercultural identification with the anti-Vietnam War generation when he was part of Crosby, Stills, Nash, and Young, who performed memorably at Woodstock, and his appeal to libertarian political positions in the Country Folk songs he produced in the late 1970s and through the 1980s, after leaving the instrumental Blue Grass group to become an independent composer and performer. Often referred to as libertarian "anthems", songs like "Long May She Run" tap into the individualist, anti-government values of political conservatives while his continuing critiques of U.S. imperialism, such as "Pocahontas" and "Powder Finger", even the feminist sentiments of "A Man Needs a Maid" (*Harvest*) appeal to various elements of the New Left.

Although Young often turns to his rural Canadian roots to explain his criticism of U.S. policies, he also resembles New Left intellectuals who often insisted on liberal "nationalism" as an alternative to the corrupt "patriotic propaganda" of the government. Young concludes *Living with War* with a brief and deliberately fractured verse of "America the Beautiful", having criticized the U.S. for its reliance on religion ("After the Garden"), consumerism ("The Restless Consumer"), and militarism ("Shock and Awe"). But Young tries to work through U.S. ideology by offering alternative national values, including the pacifism in "Living with War", which uses lyrics from "The Star Spangled Banner" in conjunction with the pacifist values of many anti-war demonstrators: "I take a holy vow/To never kill again/Try to remember Peace/The rocket's red glare/Bombs bursting in air/Give proof through the night/That our flag is still there".[195]

Like Bill Clinton trying to counter the "family values" rhetoric of George H. W. Bush's campaign, Young tries to offer an alternative set of "family values" in "Families" as he tacitly calls for the troops to come home: "I'm goin' back to the USA/I just got my ticket today/I can't wait to see you again in the/USA". In "Flags of Freedom", patriotism cuts both ways, the American flag flying ostensibly in the parade on "the day our younger son/is going off to war", but also "blowin' in the wind" are "the flags of freedom flyin'" that Young identifies with "Bob Dylan singin' in 1963", presumably Dylan's composition for Peter, Paul, and Mary's hit from that year, "Blowin' in the Wind", which celebrated not only the heroism of the Civil Rights Movement but also the beginnings of the anti-war movement. Young's album focuses on such noble tasks as "Let's Impeach the President" and "Lookin' for a Leader", but both are integral to the U.S. nationalist agenda of the album. Of course, this is not the only reason *Living with War* bombed on its release. In a hurry to release an album critical of the war, Young relies on melodies, especially those with driving downbeats, long equated with his musical style and somewhat clichéd as a result. We might add to such criticism, which was prevalent in the popular reviews of the album, that those same musical motifs have been associated with so many conflicting political positions in his music as to muddle their musical import.

Steve Earle's efforts to transnationalize the otherwise deeply patriotic styles of Country music might find their political, even musical, allies in the long history of music by U.S. ethnic minorities intent on getting a "hearing" from audiences deeply resistant to their values, even identities. From W. E. B. Du Bois's pioneering work on African-American "Sorrow Songs" in *The Souls of Black Folk* (1903), arguably the first scholarly treatment of the cultural, social, and political significance of African-American spirituals to Americo Paredes' work on Mexican-American *corridos*, there is a long tradition of popular minority music whose central purpose has been to challenge the geopolitical and cultural boundaries of the United States and citizenship. Du Bois rediscovers the international meaning of his "grandfather's grandmother"'s "heathen melody", which she sang "to the child between her knees" somewhere "in the valleys of the Hudson and Housatonic".[196] As Du Bois points out, for "two hundred years" the song "travelled down to us and we sing it to our children, knowing as little as our fathers what its words may mean, but knowing well the meaning of its music" (Du Bois, 207). By "music", Du Bois clearly means not just the melody, even though the notes are transcribed in his text, but also the spirit of rebellion which the African words—"Do bana coba, gene me, gene me!"—express for the diasporic African American under slavery or racial discrimination in North America (207). The foreignness of the language to the African-American child's ear is for Du Bois itself a sign of the transnational alliance that challenges the bondage of the U.S. nation and the textual literacy of the EuroAmerican tradition from which the slave was specifically excluded.

"Nuestro Himno", aired first on Hispanic radio stations on April 28, 2006 to anticipate the May Day demonstrations against HR 4437 and the general anti-immigration temper in the U.S., draws on the traditions of the Mexican *corridos* to challenge U.S. imperial domination in the "borderlands", but what Ariel Dorfman terms "the Star-Spanglish Banner" also suggests that "la frontera" is now in the midst of the U.S. nation, not just at its geopolitical edges.[197] As Dorfman points out, politicians as different as "the conservative Lamar Alexander and the liberal Edward M. Kennedy [...] declared that 'The Star-Spangled Banner' should be sung exclusively in English", as did Charles Key, "great-great-grandson of Francis Scott Key", who "'finds the Spanish version unpatriotic and is adamant that it should be sung only in English'" (Dorfman).

Dorfman reminds us that in the 1860s, more than 70 years before "The Star-Spangled Banner" was made the national anthem, there were Yiddish and Latin translations of the song (Dorfman). There was also a German translation in 1861, and it has been translated into French by Cajuns. "The website of the U.S. State Department also has been providing multiple Spanish versions of the anthem".[198] Giacomo Puccini uses musical motifs from "The Star-Spangled Banner" to identify B. F. Pinkerton, the U.S. Navy Lieutenant who betrays Madame Butterfly in the opera (1904), even structuring the duet between Pinkerton and Sharpless (U.S. Consul at Nagasaki) in Act II in terms of the song's music. The American opera historian Gustave Kobbé felt compelled to comment in 1919 that "the use of the *Star Spangled Banner* motif as a personal theme for Pinkerton always has had a disagreeable effect upon me, and from now on should be objected to by all Americans".[199] The Earl of Harewood, who revised Kobbé's reference text in the 1970s, notes that Puccini's use of the anthem's music never had the "disagreeable effect" on American audiences and "seems now to cause no comment after some seventy years of repeated hearings" (1181).

But Puccini's early twentieth-century Italian libretto and the previous translations hardly pose the same threat to U.S. nationalism and patriotism as "Nuestro Himno", which complements the symbolic power of the many Mexican, Salvadoran, Nicaraguan, and other Latin American national flags displayed in the May 1, 2006 and 2007 pro-immigration demonstrations across the U.S. Conceived by British music executive Adam

Kidron, performed by Haitian-American singer Wyclef Jean, Cuban-American rapper Pitbull, and Puerto Rican singers Carlos Once and Olga Tañón, "Nuestro Himno" is a genuinely transnational work that calls attention to the increasingly limited horizons of the nation-state for understanding and governing our economic, political, cultural, and human relations. "Nuestro Himno" departs strategically from the original English.

The second verse stanza claims U.S. equality for non-English singers, insisting "Sus estrellas, sus franjas, la libertad, somos iguales./Somos hermanos, es nuestro himno" ("Its stars, its stripes, liberty, we are equal./ We are brothers, it is our anthem"), and casting the original anti-colonial struggle against Great Britain as a new revolution against U.S. economic imperialism: "En el fiero combate, en señal de victoria,/fulgor de lucha ... (Mi gente sigue luchando.)/... al paso de la libertad (!Ya es tiempo de romper las cadenas!)" ("In the fierce combat, as a sign of victory,/The brilliance of battle ... (My people keep fighting.)/... in step with freedom, (Now is the time to break the chains!)".[200]

"Nuestro Himno" draws on traditions of polylingual U.S. culture, the challenges to assimilationship norms of the borderland *corridos*, and the more general oral traditions through which minoritized peoples have often communicated and built political and cultural solidarity. Dorfman claims that "Nuestro Himno" has provoked such extreme responses because it has "inadvertently announced something many Americans have dreaded for years: that their country is on its way to becoming a bilingual nation" (Dorfman). The reality of multilingual America has, however, long been accepted, even if begrudgingly, by most Americans, and previous English-Only movements have failed primarily because of their impracticality. What threatens many Americans in "Nuestro Himno" is the reality that the fiction of the U.S. national border can no longer be maintained, in part as a consequence of our own need for economic and now political globalization and in part as the result of new political formations, ranging from such formal organizations as the European Union to emerging alliances among migrant workers to the indefinite threats of "global terrorists".

Adam Kidron produced "Nuestro Himno" to demonstrate international solidarity with Hispanic immigrants to the United States, and the song is featured on the album *Somos Americanos*, a part of whose proceeds were donated to the National Capital Immigration Coalition in Washington, D. C. (*Wikipedia*). Kidron's activism within the U.S. originates outside its geopolitical borders, as does the labor of 12 million undocumented laborers working *inside* the U.S. Under slavery, African Americans were not citizens; until well into the twentieth century, native Americans were not citizens; under the Chinese Exclusion Acts, Chinese Americans were not citizens. The U.S. has maintained its national identity thanks to the labor of countless people who have not been entitled to citizenship.

Popular music freely crosses borders in car radios, iPODs, CD players, traveling bands, and pedestrians, with or without documents, singing along to their favorite tunes. Lyrics signify, of course, as I have argued in this essay, but they also depend on their beats and melodies, so that a "foreign" lyric, like Du Bois's ancestral "Do bana coba", can still signify, even when the specific words may not be understood. People listen privately to music, but they also dance to it, swaying to its rhythms with others who know or at least know how to fake the appropriate steps. Music can bind us to flags and wars, of course, as military personnel listen to their iPODs while racing into battle, but music can also take us apart, move us across borders, and link us with surprising communities with little more than the twist of a dial or that wonder of technology, a human voice. Mobile, inexpensive, adaptive, and politically possible, popular music is one means of creating the transnational coalitions that will take us beyond the prison-house of the nation.

CHAPTER 8

Visualizing Barack Obama

Prologue: 2010

I include here another "interlude", in the manner of chapter 3 in the first part of this book, to suggest that cultural politics also depends on scholarship quickly produced in response to new circumstances and published in a wide range of journals now available for such rapid interpretation. Marquard Smith and the Editorial Group of the *Journal of Visual Culture* distributed by email a questionnaire on Barack Obama and visual culture to a wide variety of "scholars, educators, curators, activists and artists working in academia across the Arts, Humanities and Social Sciences, in cultural institutions and in the public sphere".[201] The questions from the questionnaire are included in their "Editorial" to the special issue, but the editors decided not to repeat the questions in the twenty-three different responses they chose to publish.[202] Published ten months after Obama's election, the special issue was not intended to affect the election or public opinion, but what the editors termed the "time-sensitive nature of the subject-matter" was certainly related to the evanescence of visual semiotics in political campaigns.

Today, two years after "The Obama Issue" of the *Journal of Visual Culture* was published, most of the images reproduced and analyzed in this issue have vanished from public view. To be sure, the Shepard Fairey "Hope" poster of Obama, contested over its originality, and Tina Fey's comic impersonation of Sarah Palin on *Saturday Night Live* continue to shape visually the Obama Administration and its most vigorous opponents, especially among the Tea Party and Tea Party Express, whose members have chosen Sarah Palin as a symbolic leader. Just what happens to the other, more fleeting images in major political events is an interesting question, which would require me to analyze in greater depth the visual narrativity that develops from both manifest and latent contents of the highly visual cultures that rely on electronic and digital media.

In terms of "cultural politics", however, my purpose in including this already dated bit of scholarly journalism is to stress the importance of scholars responding with some speed to culturally and politically imme-diate events. Careful scholarship takes time, of course, and should not be replaced with rapidly produced interpretations. The bathos of so much discussion of serious issues on personal blogs and wikis, telegraphed on Twitter, and personalized on Facebook reminds us that carefully re-searched scholarship, refereed by experts, and published in reliable schol-arly sources continues to play a crucial role in the public sphere as well as for its intrinsic value as knowledge. Traditional scholarship is time-con-suming work, even if the time for its dissemination has shortened con-siderably. Scholars should not be primarily focused on affecting public policies, but not because of some fantastic commitment to the "apoliti-cal" nature of scholarship. Scholarly knowledge is always political in one way or another, and it is best for scholars and the public to understand this ineluctable fact in order to judge scholarship according to its diverse political interests. But the relative slowness that so much lasting scholar-ship requires does not lend it to direct public policy recommendations, even if the longer history provided by substantial scholarship can and of-ten is employed in making successful decisions affecting public policies.

The conventional wisdom is that scholars should remain focused on their archives, sharing their conclusions with colleagues and students in several pedagogical contexts (conferences, classrooms, research centers), venturing occasionally into the public sphere by way of opinion-editorials (such as I included in chapter 3), museum exhibitions and other public performances, and as consultants to mass media or expert-witnesses in legal cases. Although all of these untraditional activities might be includ-ed in a faculty member's annual personnel review, few have much value in the overall judgment of a professor's "work". Exhibition catalogues are not "books"; op-eds and responses to questionnaires are not "essays". Be-cause they don't "count" significantly in the usual judgment of scholarly capital, professors tend not to choose them as projects, reinforcing the separation between the "ivory tower" and the "marketplace". Younger, untenured professors are under intense pressure by their colleagues *not* to produce work that has relatively little scholarly "value" and "impact", the latter word designating the distinction of the scholarly venue and the number of citations within its disciplinary community. Such terms as capital, value, and impact are obviously drawn from a capitalist economy, and it is worth noting that public complaints regarding the "politicizing" of knowledge far outnumber those challenging the commercialization of scholarship.

What, then, should be the criteria for valuing "The Obama Issue" of the *Journal of Visual Culture*? The editors' idea for this issue returns me to a quixotic plan I once proposed to colleagues at the University of California, Irvine for a regular television program, in which scholars would comment on popular and mass culture, recent politics, and other news requiring historical, analytical, and theoretical perspectives unavailable on traditional news and talk-shows. To be sure, public television, alternative news, National Public Radio, and a host of other media have drawn increasingly on scholarly "experts" in the preparation of programs and documentaries that have vastly increased the public's options for news and reporting with the waning of the major broadcast networks' dominance. But with the exception of brief cameo appearances, scholars remain "consultants" rather than interpreters and analysts in most of this alternative news and history.

What follows, then, is simply one small example of how the "cultural politics of the new American Studies" should function as ongoing commentary on "current events". In an era when both our economic and political lives are structured by highly mediated cultural productions, we need more than ever rapidly deployed intellectual analyses to accompany the more reflective, research-intensive scholarship that explains and clarifies the emergence of certain phenomena, narratives, formations, and identities that assume social reality for so many. Whereas some people will insist that such intellectual work should be value-neutral and thus apolitical, I would argue that these interpretations should be primarily free from economic entanglement or interest. Whereas the evening news and the Internet are penetrated by advertising no longer easily distinguishable from information and knowledge, scholars should provide their own "freedom of information", in which what they offer in this manner has only the most tenuous connection to their salaries, royalties, or other sources of remuneration.

Visualizing Barack Obama: 2009

The Obama presidential campaign certainly used the Internet, including its visual imaging and streaming video capabilities, to great effect in the recent primaries and successful presidential campaign. The "Obama Is Hope" image was also extremely effective in advertising Obama's commitment to cultural diversity and the effort to overcome racial and ethnic divisions in the United States. In his first "100 days" as President, Obama created a one-way "Facebook" page, retained his private Blackberry amid much publicity regarding possible breaches of its security, and otherwise announced himself as the most technologically sophisticated U.S. president. The "visibility" of Barack Obama is not entirely a consequence of new digital, internet technologies; it relies on many traditional media, including the theatricality of political speeches, the body language (especially facial expressions) he employed in the Presidential Debates, his self-deprecating humor (such as he employed while giving the Commencement Address at Arizona State in May 2009, in response to Arizona State's refusal to award him an honorary degree), and his fashion statements. As a candidate for the presidency, Obama made the news for not wearing the conventional American flag lapel-pin, but then appeared with one that remained on his lapel for the rest of the campaign. Once elected, he allowed himself to be photographed in the Oval Office without his jacket, prompting criticism from former President George W. Bush regarding the "respect" Obama ought to show for the "office". And, of course, Michelle Obama's fashion statements are based on her support of various fashion designers from outside the usual world of *haute couture*, especially ethnic minority designers whose fashions she has worn to considerable publicity. Much of the visibility of Barack Obama has to do with the visualization of the Obama family, with photography and video of the romantic couple and of the family values exemplified by their visible attention to their two daughters, Sasha and Malia.

The visibility of Barack Obama and his family has circulated with considerable speed and frequency around the world, as the two images I

photographed in Tanzania in August 2008 indicate. Two different carts selling tourist trinkets were decked out by the sellers with the famous Obama image.[203]

Like corporate logos and the "branding" businesses are encouraged to develop for recognition, the "Obama logo" achieved considerable trans-national circulation in ways that caused Republicans to protest his lack of "patriotism" and many others to view him as a figure capable of restoring the waning U.S. reputation around the world. Even controversial images, such as the photograph of Obama in Kenya wearing a traditional African headdress, dubbed incorrectly by Repulicans as a "turban", have contrib-uted to the globalization of the Obama logo.

Yet for all the sophistication of Obama's team in employing traditional and new media, it has merely built upon the innovative use of new media in President Clinton's two campaigns and presidencies. The technolo-gies available today are more sophisticated, but the basic digital media are similar to those available to the Clinton team and used with consider-able sophistication and variety at the time. What differs from Clinton's era to Obama's is Barack Obama's cultivation of his global image both for its own sake and for its domestic uses in the U.S. in the aftermath

of 9/11 and contested views of how the U.S. should represent itself internationally.

The Obama team successfully negotiated the different rhetorics of assimilation and multiculturalism, thereby winning enormous support from white voters, many of whom felt particularly threatened by the multicultural and multiethnic cultural politics of the 1990s. Yet in bridging this divide in the U.S., Obama certainly favored a modified assimilationist ideology and a return to consensus-based politics and civil rights. His vaunted "bipartisan" practical politics have not turned out to be very effective, despite symbolic gestures toward opponents, but the rhetoric of "bipartisanship" is central to his image. His presidential campaign and first 100 days are distinguished by his co-optation of neo-liberalism—the conservative strategy exemplified in the "kinder, gentler America" and the "100 Points of Light" slogans employed by the Bush presidents— but that strategy has had some very negative consequences. First, it has produced a considerable and often angry backlash from both sides of the political spectrum. Reverend Wright's radical speeches actually focused on what Marcuse once termed "repressive tolerance" practiced by weepy liberals whose tears take the place of change. Sarah Palin's and Joe the Plumber's meteoric rises to public prominence were driven by the usual white rage at diminished power. Both extremes were driven by Obama's ability to claim the middle ground, pushing them further out of public debates. In the Limbaugh-driven Republican rhetoric of the present, we are witnessing conservative rage consuming itself, but probably without some epiphenomenal problems unpredictable in their grotesque details. Second, Obama has reinvented "American Exceptionalism", repeating the jingoistic rhetoric of conservatives—"America is the greatest country in the world"—and falling into the trap of this mythology in his conduct of foreign policies in Afghanistan and Iraq. We are *still* overtly building Western-style democracies in Iraq, Afghanistan, and Pakistan, so that their peoples can also follow "the American Dream", Iraqi, Afghani, and Pakistani style. We know from the Vietnam War that this "Exceptionalism" is a fatal mythology, as is the silliness of the "American Dream", which is built upon the sands of late-Capitalist entrepreneurial zeal and frontier (colonial) self-reliance.

Many ethnic and other minorities have been casualties of Obama's new "American Exceptionalism", especially those whose specific claims to rights do not fit the profile of the majority and thus have no visibility in consensus-based politics. Native Americans were once again invisible in the presidential campaign. Reverend Joseph Lowery's benediction made one ambivalent appeal to "when the red man can get ahead, man", which unfortunately was heard by many as "when the red man can get a head-man", repeating two notorious stereotypes of Native Americans. Along with all the candidates for the presidency, Obama avoided scrupulously the question of immigration reform, leaving twelve million (and more) undocumented workers in the U.S. to face an uncertain future. Despite a powerful debate across the nation regarding gay marriage during the presidential campaigns, Obama (and the other candidates) took meliorist positions or adopted politically "pedantic" views, treating the issue as a "state's rights" question. Considering the fact that Proposition 108—the Constitutional Amendment banning gay marriage—succeeded in California in part because of strong majorities from African-American and Latino/a voters, Obama should take a stand on such intersectional issues that affect minority rights. But his commitment to a new "American Exceptionalism" makes any such position extremely unlikely.

Tina Fey's "Sarah Palin", together with Palin's ill-advised decision to appear on *Saturday Night Live* with Tina Fey, worked brilliantly to trivialize Palin and thus the McCain-Palin presidential ticket. By transforming the actual Sarah Palin into a "character" in someone else's script, *Saturday Night Live* tapped into the power of what Jean Baudrillard long ago termed the "hyper-real", thereby taking control of Sarah Palin's cultural "narration".[204] Sarah Palin quickly became an "effect" of Tina Fey, both because Tina Fey did an excellent job of impersonation and because the political satire demanded a response that once given by Sarah Palin legitimized the content of the satire. What I once termed the "spinoff rhetoric" of highly self-conscious television—"metavideo"—served to renarrate Sarah Palin and divert the McCain campaign itself.[205] Republican political strategists planning to run Sarah Palin for President in the future seem utterly unaware of this Baudrillardian consequence of postmodern media, despite neo-liberalism's otherwise canny understanding of the media's role in political campaigns. Did Tina Fey or the scriptwriters for *Saturday Night Live* know what they were doing? No, but the semiotic logic of the show, dating back to the 1970s when such strategies first came to prominence, did that work for them. Brava.[206]

In his neglected and brilliant fiction, *Darkwater* (1920), W. E. B. Du Bois complained about a "beauty system" that excluded many African American women, designating them either "ugly" or, worse, invisible.[207] Barack and Michelle Obama have managed successfully this "beauty system" by distinguishing themselves from "beautiful people" and celebrity culture. Of course, both of them are physically attractive, physically fit, and thin. But they have courted working-class voters by claiming their own humble origins and then reproducing these backgrounds in the rhetoric of "family values" they demonstrate with their daughters. Refusing to wear a tuxedo at a recent Washington gala, removing his jacket in the Oval Office, the President emulates the working man. Publicizing the alternative, often minority designers whose fashions she chooses, Michelle Obama underscores the symbolic function of her public appearances while stressing her own modest roots. Their management of fashion semiotics is new, but the convention of presidential "humility" is an old, time-honored one, best exemplified by Obama's role model, Abraham Lincoln.

CHAPTER 9

Don DeLillo and the War on Terrorism
Literature and Cultural Politics

*Oh! The only part of life that matters is contemplation. When
everybody understands that as clearly as I do, they will all
start writing. Life will become literature. Half of humankind
will devote itself to reading and studying what the other half
has written. And contemplation will be the main business of
the day, preserving it from the wretchedness of actual living.
And if one part of human kind rebels and refuses to read the
other half's effusions, so much the better. Everyone will read
himself instead; and people's lives will have a chance to repeat,
to correct, to crystallize themselves, whether or no they become
clearer in the process [...]. I mean to take up writing again.*

– Italo Svevo, "An Old Man's Confessions" (1928),
trans. Ben Johnson and P. N. Furbank

*The Messiah will come only when he is no longer necessary;
he will come, not on the last day, but [at] the very last.*

– Franz Kafka, "The Coming of the Messiah", *Parables and Paradoxes*

Literature before 9/11: *Mao II* (1991)

Shortly after the terrorist attacks on the World Trade Center towers and
the Pentagon, and the crash of hijacked United Airlines Flight # 93 on
September 11, 2001, I received a call from a reporter at the *New York
Times*. Emily Eakin was working on a story about modern literature's response to earlier forms of terror, in particular the fictional representations
of Russian revolutionaries in Fyodor Dostoevsky's *The Possessed* (1871–

72) and European anarchists in Henry James's *The Princess Casamassima* (1886) and Joseph Conrad's *The Secret Agent* (1907).[208] Eakin reasonably assumed that great literature offers us means of coping with crises like September 11 and that this specific event was not historically unique. We talked by phone and email about the national agendas of early modern revolutionary movements and the global terrorist aims of al-Qaeda, including the aesthetic means required to represent these different political cultures and historical periods.

Dostoevsky, James, and Conrad were brilliant practitioners of psychological realism, which located meaning and value in the choices and actions of individuals, even when such individuals act as representatives of political or social groups. James's Hyacinth Robinson "chooses" not to assassinate the Duke, thereby repudiating his relationship with the anarchists, but it is a choice that requires him to take responsibility for his actions by committing suicide.[209] Dostoevsky's *The Possessed* culminates in the murder of Stavrogin's wife, Marya Timofeyevna Lebyadkin, and her brother by the revolutionaries, and the inevitable suicides by Stavrogin and his disciple Kirilov for their responsibility in this bloody conclusion. In Conrad's *The Secret Agent*, Winnie Verloc kills her husband when she discovers that in using her brother, Stevie, in the anarchist plot to blow up the Greenwich Observatory Verloc is responsible for Stevie unwittingly blowing himself up. Just as Winnie judges Verloc as fully responsible for the anarchists' crime against her brother, so Winnie commits suicide both out of desperation and in apparent compensation for her own violent act. Repeating the newspaper story's baffled conclusion about Winnie's leap from a steamer in the middle of the English Channel, Conrad suggests that the *"impenetrable mystery... destined to hang for ever over this act of madness or despair"* can be understood only by way of literary insight into the complex motives of the individual.[210]

What would these literary realists have understood in the acts of the al-Qaeda terrorists who lived in the U.S. suburbs, attended private flight schools, drank and smoked in local bars (while leaving snippets from the Koran for edification of the patrons), worked out at 24-Hour Fitness, and just as routinely hijacked four commercial airliners and drove three directly into their targets and a fourth into the ground? What "realist" account of such behavior is possible, except one that expresses utter bewilderment in the face of the terrorism of al-Qaeda and other Islamic fundamentalist groups around the world committed to a long, even losing struggle against the United States as the leading representative of Western capitalism and its neo-imperialist policies of "globalization"? In today's Western press, "suicide bombers" remain inexplicable and deeply troubling, not merely because of the terrible damage they do to civilians but because conventional explanations that attribute their actions to "madness" or to religious "fanaticism" are obviously wrong.

"The future belongs to crowds", DeLillo writes in *Mao II*, and this prophecy echoes throughout the novel, ushering us from the opening section, "At Yankee Stadium", where a mass wedding presided over by the Reverend Sun Myung Moon displaces the "American Pastime", to Part One.[211] The apocalyptic tone of "the future belongs to crowds" builds on DeLillo's analysis in many previous works of how the postmodern condition has destroyed traditional meanings of the humanist individual, philosophical subjectivity, and psychological selfhood. Although Dostoevsky, James, and Conrad wrote in cultures historically poised on the brink of this transformation, they understood it only in partial, peripheral ways. There is a subliminal glimpse of the vanishing modernist subject in these writers, but at the center of their literary attention is the *problem* of the alienated, fractured, divided self and the various ways the new urban "masses" have contributed to this dilemma.

For these moderns, the self is attenuated and damaged, and they use imaginative means to restore and cure it. Thus their literary works generally conclude with the high drama of either self-sacrifice—the "suicides" that betoken individual responsibility in their three novels about revolution—or self-affirmation: the secular *imitatio Christi* in Dostoevsky's *Crime and Punishment*, Isabel Archer's refusal of Caspar Goodwood and apparent decision to return to Rome at the end of *The Portrait of a Lady*, the possibility of individual idealism and nobility represented by Jim and Nostromo, set off emphatically by their human failure and corruption in *Lord Jim* and *Nostromo*. Embattled, threatened, but finally resilient, the self survives in modern art and literature, often by means of the author's sheer act of imaginative will to repudiate what urban, industrial societies were in fact doing to destroy the self by stripping it of agency and any power to resist complete alienation from its intrinsic power.

DeLillo understands the postmodern condition to involve radically different notions of subjectivity, most of which cannot be simply opposed to or distinguished from mass phenomena and their representation. His characters are "distanced" from themselves and each other, rather than alienated, and this decentering of the self seems to be directly related to the social and cultural mediations through which experience itself is constituted. In *Libra*, Marina Oswald experiences Lee Harvey as "someone you see from a distance", even "when he was hitting her. He was never fully there".[212] Far from being an eccentric or a madman, DeLillo's Lee Harvey Oswald is the prototype of postmodern subjectivity, albeit a dystopic version. In the novel, Oswald's best expression of himself is the famous photograph, taken by Marina and posed by Oswald one day before his assassination attempt on General Ted Walker: "It showed Lee dressed in black, holding a rifle in one hand, some newspapers in the other" (*L*, 290). As Oswald explains the photograph to George de Mohrenschildt: "'It's the kind of picture a person looks at and maybe he understands something he didn't understand before. [...]. Maybe he sees the truth about someone'" (*L*, 289). Inscribed by Lee "*To my friend George from Lee Oswald*" and by Marina in Russian, "*Hunter of fascists—ha ha ha*!!!", the photograph is multiply textual and composes thereby the character of Lee Harvey Oswald, a simulation composed by George, Lee, and Marina among many others (*L*, 290).

Mao II criticizes this sort of simulated identity as symptomatic of a postmodern, globalized world in which no one is at home. The reclusive novelist Bill Gray attempts to resist this tendency and protect the more traditional identity celebrated in the great tradition of the novel, but in his rural Hudson Valley home's vast archive of writing he is surrounded both by his "old handwritten manuscripts, printer's typescripts, master galleys" and by "stacks of magazines and journals containing articles about Bill's work and about his disappearance, his concealment, his retirement, his alleged change of identity, his rumored suicide, his return to work, his work-in-progress, his death, his rumored return" (*M*, 31). Like Nicholas Branch in *Libra* buried alive in the vast and conflicting documents he collects to understand the truth of the Kennedy Assassination, Bill Gray is constituted ontologically by the archive he has built in place of a home.

Sentimentally drawn to an older, mythic America of baseball and books, Gray seems unaware that both professional sports and literary commerce have contributed significantly to the culture of celebrity he has attempted to elude. Long before the Reverend Moon rents Yankee Stadium for his spectacular mass marriages, Gray's childhood heroes are swatting home runs and rounding the bases on radio and in the press in ways legendized by children and novelists. In the novel, Gray recalls how as a child he pretended to announce baseball games, suggesting that such imaginary work prepared him for his career as a novelist. Well before the photojournalist Brita Nilsson arrives at his upstate New York home, Bill Gray is already both effect and cause of the postmodern conditions for subjectivity that give us such historical variants as J. D. Salinger, Thomas Pynchon, Lee Harvey Oswald and Osama bin Laden. Reluctant and intrigued at the same time to be photographed for Brita's "collection" of writers, Bill Gray is far more prepared than he thinks to be framed by this world.

In the eighteenth-century European imaginary, the representative man organized different and conflicting experiences and data by means of his reason or "consciousness". In the postmodern era, such cognitive means are no longer sufficient, as Paul Virilio has pointed out: "Mass phenomena do indeed elude immediate apprehension and can only be perceived by means of the computer and interception and recording equipment which did not exist in earlier times."[213] The "crowd" in De Lillo's future is not constituted by choices made by individuals to join a group movement, as in the collective formed to bring about revolutionary change, but instead by the alienation of individuals from their respective agency and the imposition of order and "belonging" from outside or above. If, as a conscious, rational subject, I choose to join the revolution (or the nation, neighborhood, company), the larger collective is always dependent on the reflective monads constituting it. In the "crowd" or "mass", each subject is merely a synecdoche, which "represents" the whole, however uniquely this subject is employed. In *Mao II*, Bill Gray equates the end of modernity with the death of the novel and with the cognitive and communicative practices on which the novel depends: "'Beckett is the last writer to shape the way we think and see. After him, the major work involves midair explosions and crumbled buildings. This is the new tragic narrative'" (*M*, 157). Bill is speaking in this scene with George Haddad, the character who poses as the negotiator who will exchange Bill for the French Swiss poet, Jean-Claude Julien, the terrorists are holding hostage and will eventually murder.

Bill Gray understands how and why the novel ends with Beckett in late modernity; George Haddad understands how this sort of postmodernity drives us toward the need for some absolute, totalitarian principle or ruler, to govern what no individual can command. Trying to flatter Bill into meeting with the Maoist terrorists in Beirut, George tells him:

> You could have been a Maoist, Bill [...]. I've read your books carefully and we've spent many hours talking and I can easily see you blending into that great mass of blue-and-white cotton. You would have written what the culture needed in order to see itself. And you would have seen the need for an absolute being, a way out of weakness and confusion. This is what I want to see reborn in the rat warrens of Beirut. (*M*, 163).

Because DeLillo's readers never actually *read* Bill Gray's works, we cannot confirm or dispute Haddad's contention, but it is clear that DeLillo thinks that literary representation can and should challenge the totalitarian impulses fueled by postmodern dislocation.

As we read *Mao II*, we learn that literature transforms us only to the extent that we respond to and communicate with it. The terrorist commodifies his hostages, who are targets and victims and symbols; the author compels his readers, those strangers, to talk back, thereby making themselves known, less to him than to each other (as teachers teach and literary critics interpret). DeLillo understands that the commercial and the avant-garde novel, as well as the novelist either celebrated on the talkshow or prized for reclusiveness, are parts of the problem, rather than the solution. The textual situation in which senders and receivers transform each other and accept the historically incomplete character of all communication in fact describes DeLillo's utopian society, not the retreat of a few individuals into book-lined studies or their devoted fans into libraries. In *Libra*, DeLillo indicts Americans for having virtually invented Lee Harvey Oswald as a consequence of their mythic construction of John F. Kennedy as a substitute for their own civic responsibilities. John Johnston has argued that *Libra* deconstructs "the difference between the fictional and historical", not in order to reaffirm the fictional foundations of historical experience, but to "open" fiction and its tidy conventions of coherent characters and meaningful plots "to precisely those forces outside prose fiction that these conventions were meant to internalize, and thereby to contain".[214] In a similar fashion, Ryan Simmons has argued that DeLillo attempts in *Mao II* to demonstrate that "no one has a unique command over language" and that "no one owns language, but everyone is subsumed within language in the postmodern world".[215]

As critics have observed about most of his fiction, DeLillo's internal critique of the novel as an aesthetic form puts him in a very difficult position as a literary author. Simmons discusses how often scholars have confused Bill Gray and DeLillo, and this tendency is undoubtedly reinforced by the nostalgia in contemporary culture for literary and aesthetic "value" (Simmons 677). Given his criticisms in many works of how postmodern culture fetishizes and commodifies literature, DeLillo must take a certain satisfaction from those misreadings of his works that imagine he is mourning the related deaths of the novel and the author, in part because such misreadings expose their readers' deepest fears. Yet such misinterpretations also risk aligning DeLillo with a cultural conservatism he certainly abhors. Nevertheless, it is fair to judge the metafictional double-binds and contradictions on which DeLillo's novels typically rely to be very literary and perhaps too subtle and thus likely to be lost on today's impatient readers.

DeLillo works hard to distinguish his aesthetic practices and values in *Mao II* from what we are told of Gray's more traditional commitments to the "craft" of the novel. Each of the different sections of the novel are introduced by a photograph from the news that reinforces the title-page's photograph of crowded Tiananmen Square in Beijing and its tacit message: "The future belongs to crowds". They also remind us that DeLillo's narrative *follows* global events prominent in the news, including such significant news stories as the 1983 terrorist attacks on the American Embassy and the U.S. Marine barracks in Beirut. Whereas Bill Gray imagines he can escape these media, DeLillo's point is that television, film, photography, music, urban noise, different languages are the ineluctable media in which we live and work. These media makes us, just as they seem to "invade" and then organize the traditional form of the novel.

In *Mao II*, Bill Gray is drawn so relentlessly into the plot of the terrorists that he finally "chooses" exactly what they want without being forced or ordered to do so. Questioning George Haddad about how to find Abu Rashid in Beirut during the revolt of Shiite Muslims and Druse in West Beirut against the Lebanese army in early 1984, Bill follows the directions that will lead him directly into the current site of global anarchy and the control of the terrorists.[216] DeLillo complicates the pattern by making sure Bill Gray dies of "internal injuries" he suffers when a cab hits him in Athens and well before Gray reaches Beirut or the control of Abu Rashid. In a chain of miscommunications and accidents typical of DeLillo's fiction, Brita Nilsson's delivery of Charlie Everson's message to Bill Gray leads Bill to London, where his public speech is postponed by a bomb blast, which directs Bill to Athens, where he is struck by an errant cab and George Haddad talks him into traveling to Beirut by way of Larnaca, Cyprus. By the time Bill dies of his internal injuries on board the ferry he has boarded for his journey to Junieh, Lebanon, the reader knows that Bill Gray has been overtaken by the very contingencies of life he had hoped to avoid by becoming a novelist. The connections of these events are either radically accidental or utterly motivated and plotted, but in both instances they represent Bill Gray's loss of control over his life and its representation.

To be sure, he rationalizes the relentless concatenation of events and other people leading him to Beirut, the hostage, Abu Rashid, and the Maoist terrorists by claiming that he wants to write about the hostage and that this desire is lifting the writer's block that had prevented him from finishing his last novel. But when he reflects on his new interest in the hostage, he betrays a certain futility: "He couldn't remember why he wanted to write about the hostage. He'd done some pages he halfway liked but what was the actual point?" (*M*, 198). Of course, the usual explanations offered by the traditional novelist are available, and Bill Gray imagines he

> could have told George [Haddad] he was writing about the
> hostage to bring him back, to return a meaning that had been
> lost to the world when they locked him in that room. Maybe

that was it. When you inflict punishment on someone who is not guilty, when you fill rooms with innocent victims, you begin to empty the world of meaning and erect a separate mental state, the mind consuming what's outside itself, replacing real things with plots and fictions. One fiction taking the world narrowly into itself, the other fiction pushing out toward the social order, trying to unfold into it. He could have told George a writer creates a character as a way to reveal consciousness, increase the flow of meaning. This is how we reply to power and beat back our fear. By extending the pitch of consciousness and human possibility. (*M*, 200).

Yet he never does say this to George Haddad, and it is just this failure we equate with his willingness to drift toward his own destruction as he wanders into the terrorists' plot.

The terrorist plot in which Bill Gray becomes entangled differs little from the accidents and contingencies of an alienating world, which he cannot control, insofar as both Fate and Chance teach us the same lesson: we no longer have any effective agency. The traditional novelist, no matter how great his craft or genius, is no longer capable of representing those forces that secretly govern ordinary experience. When an old man with the cleaning crew finds Bill Gray's body "lying in the bunk" of the ferry, he takes only Gray's "passport and other forms of identification, anything with a name and a number, which he could sell to some militia in Beirut" (*M*, 216–217).

Bill Gray never reaches Beirut, even though the anarchy of its civil war is for DeLillo a metaphor for postmodern conditions. In the novel, many scenes in New York explicitly foreshadow Beirut, especially DeLillo's treatment of New York City's homeless as equivalent to people displaced by civil war, terrorism, and anarchy. Thus the novel's concluding section, "In Beirut", can easily be read as a pessimistic epilogue, in which the photojournalist Brita Nilsson reappears to confirm another often repeated sentence in the novel: "Our only language is Beirut" (*M*, 239). Arriving one year after Bill's death and "on assignment for a German magazine [...] to photograph" Abu Rashid, she has abandoned her avant-garde project of photographing literary authors, like Bill Gray, and returned to the photojournalism she had given up in the opening pages of the novel, because as she puts it, "'No matter what I shot, how much horror, reality, misery, ruined bodies, bloody faces, it was all so fucking pretty in the end'" (*M*, 229, 235, 24–25).

Is there a way to overcome such aestheticism and its ideology? In the novel, Brita's actions in Beirut have contrary meanings and the reader is left with the radical ambiguity DeLillo often employs to force us to communicate again and overcome our postmodern thralldom. On the one hand, Bill Gray's death on the ferry to Lebanon and Brita's reappearance with her cameras and assignments seem to suggest the triumph of commodity and celebrity culture. DeLillo's account of why Brita decided not to "photograph writers anymore" and return to photojournalism seems characterized by her resignation to contemporary conditions: "She takes assignments now, does the interesting things, barely watched wars, children running in the dust. Writers stopped one day. She doesn't know how it happened but they came to a quiet end. They stopped being the project she would follow forever" (*M*, 229–230). Immediately following this passage, Brita notices "signs for a new soft drink, Coke II,[...] slapped on cement-block walls" and "has the crazy idea that these advertising placards herald the presence of the Maoist group" (*M*, 230). Like Oedipa Maas in Thomas Pynchon's *The Crying of Lot 49*, Brita begins to see coincidences and signs everywhere, driving the characteristic paranoia of the postmodern subject.

Mao II and Coke II are quite rationally related, even if the corporate giant in Atlanta would disavow any ties to terrorist groups or militias in the Beirut civil war. In the ongoing "war on terrorism", declared by President George W. Bush and continued by President Barack Obama, many critics have suggested we have not yet begun to target the transnational corporations whose exploitation of third-world labor and natural resources, manipulation of governments for "favorable" treatment, and aggressive global marketing of products are perceived by many of their subaltern victims as terrorist acts. In DeLillo's response to September 11, 2001, he suggests that what "changed" on that day was the unequivocal identification of such corporate and technological terror with America: "The terrorists who attacked the Pentagon and the World Trade Center were not chanting 'Death to Microsoft.' It is America that drew their fury. It is the high gloss of our modernity. It is the thrust of our technology. It is our perceived godlessness. It is the blunt force of our foreign policy. It is the power of American culture to penetrate every wall, home, life and mind".[217] Whereas "protesters in Genoa, Prague, Seattle and other cities want to slow down the global momentum that seemed to be driving unmindfully toward a landscape of consumer-robots and social instability", the "terrorists of S/11 want to bring back the past" by naming and thereby targeting transnational capitalism "America" (Ruins 35). Of course, insofar as the United States, with its vaunted commitments to democracy and justice for all, has failed to challenge in the name of human rights such globalization, then "America" may well have earned the target it now wears.

In another sense, Brita Nilsson repudiates the technological sublime today exemplified by American foreign and economic policies, albeit endorsed by other first-world nations. Ryan Simmons argues that the character of Karen Janney, the young woman who works for Bill Gray, offers the best alternative to Bill Gray's outmoded aesthetic, but Simmons points out in a footnote that "the photographer, Brita Nilsson, might also be said to fit" his characterization of Karen as better adapted to the postmodern world than Bill Gray: "Karen and the crowds she sees on the streets or on television are all part of a larger system which connects them but which is also limited—which cannot provide the depth of connection that she or Bill or anyone else might want it to. She is not an 'author' as Bill would define one because she does not try to control narrative" (Simmons 694n1, 684).

Simmons does not develop this aspect of Brita Nilsson, preferring to stress Karen Janney as DeLillo's alternative to Bill Gray. DeLillo works out technically effective parallels between Brita's photographic session with Bill Gray at the beginning of the novel and her encounter with Abu Rashid at the end of the novel. For example, Brita communicates with Abu Rashid through an interpreter, even though Abu Rashid speaks English directly to her as the interpreter "interprets" Rashid's meaning, often in bizarre ways. In her earlier photographic session with Bill Gray, his assistant Scott also "interprets", often concluding sentences with the refrain "quoting Bill". Gray's assistant, Karen Janney, leaves her position to surrender her identity to the Moonies early in the novel. In an analogous sense, the hooded young man who guards the door during Abu

Rashid's interview with Brita represents all the "children" who have dedicated their lives to Abu Rashid: "'The boys who work near Abu Rashid have no face or speech. Their features are identical. They are his features. They don't need their own features or voices. They are surrendering these things to something powerful and great'" (M, 234). Abu Rashid tells Brita that the young man is "'my son. Rashid. [...]. I call myself father of Rashid'" (M, 234).

Abu Rashid's conversation with Brita recalls George Haddad's talk with Bill Gray in Athens as the writer prepares to seek out the terrorists. The difference is that Brita resists Abu Rashid's "eloquent macho bullshit", especially his adulation of Mao's leadership (M, 236). In the novel, Brita "says nothing because what can she say", but she swerves suddenly from her assignment to photograph Abu Rashid and "walks over to the boy at the door and removes his hood. Lifts it off his head and drops it on the floor. Doesn't lift it very gently either. She is smiling all the time. And takes two steps back and snaps his picture" (M, 236). The "boy hits her hard in the forearm and reaches in for the camera" as "she throws an elbow that misses and then slaps him across the face" (M, 237). Unlike the resigned, determined, and finally dead novelist, Bill Gray, Brita acts: "Feeling detached, almost out-of-body, she walks over to Rashid and shakes his hand, actually introduces herself, pronouncing her name slowly" (M, 237).

The photojournalist need not, then, merely render "pretty" by explaining and ordering the ugliness of social injustice in our contemporary world. She can expose the identities hidden behind totalitarianisms of all sorts, including those that work through our own psychologies as desires to escape the problems of this world. Brita affirms her own identity in the small but significant gesture of herself looking at the faces of the terrorists. She looks with her camera, because DeLillo knows we cannot escape the media through which we understand, however corrupted they may be. And we look through DeLillo's novel, which refuses to render "pretty" what we see: our own responsibility for "global" problems, whether we name them "transnational capitalism", "American imperialism", or "international terrorism".

Abu Rashid several times commands Brita, "'Don't bring your problems to Beirut,'" but DeLillo invites us to bring all of our problems to the novel. In his essay about 9/11, DeLillo notes that the terrorism that day ended conclusively the Cold War narrative, which "ends in the rubble and it is left to us to create the counter-narrative" (Ruins 35). Brita's symbolic actions at the end of the novel point toward such a counter-narrative, which in his essay DeLillo connects with the "hundred thousand stories crisscrossing New York, Washington and the world" in the aftermath of the terrorists' acts. Interestingly, these stories, including the photographs of the missing and dead posted on buildings and in shop-windows near Ground Zero in New York, have entered formally into the public sphere through the publication of survivors' accounts, the victims' autobiographies, and countless documentaries and docudramas of varying kind and quality: "There are the doctors' appointments that saved lives, the cell phones that were used to report the hijackings. Stories generating others and people running north out of the rumbling smoke and ash. [...]. People running for their lives are part of the story that is left to us" (Ruins 6).

In the novel, some of this storytelling is economically represented in the Beirut wedding Brita witnesses from her balcony in the early morning following her interview with Abu Rashid. The wedding party is preceded by a tank and "followed by a jeep with a recoilless rifle mounted at the rear" (M, 240). Whether the revelers are simply caught in a military action or being protected by some militia we never know, but what is clear is that we are meant to draw hope from an unquestionably ironic scene: "The bride and groom carry champagne glasses and some of the girls hold sparklers that send off showers of excited light. A guest in a pastel tuxedo smokes a long cigar and does a dance around a shell hole, delighting the kids. The bride's gown is beautiful, with lacy appliqué at the bodice, and she looks surpassingly alive, they all look transcendent, free of limits and unsurprised to be here" (M, 240). Brita needs no interpreters to toast the newlyweds from her balcony in a smattering of different languages: "'Bonne chance' and 'Bonheur' and 'Good luck' and 'Salám' and 'Skål,' and the gun turret begins to rotate and the cannon eases slowly around like a smutty honeymoon joke and everyone is laughing" (M, 240).

Literature after 9/11: *Falling Man* (2007)

Sixteen years after Bill Gray in *Mao II* wanders from his aesthetic seclusion in Connecticut to New York City, London, Athens, Cyprus, and then dies in his bunk on the ferry to Beirut, Keith Neudecker in *Falling Man* stumbles blindly out of his collapsing office in the World Trade Center back into his dysfunctional family life, an aimless affair with another 9/11 survivor, and then into the bathos of international poker competitions. Initially sympathetic characters, versions of a waning humanism, Gray and Neudecker degenerate into specters of their terrorist antagonists: aimless, stateless, socially determined beings following others' orders. Sixteen years later, reeling from four years of the U.S. military invasions of Iraq and Afghanistan, ongoing civil and anti-colonial wars in both regions, and a succession of post-9/11 terrorist acts around the globe, U.S. readers have forgotten the cheerful irony of Brita on that balcony in Beirut.

Brita challenges Abu Rashid, unmasks and photographs his faceless "children", introduces herself, asserts her femininity by slapping the "childish" guard, and reaffirms the possibility of subjectivity, even in the differently mediated, postmodern conditions she comprehends in *Mao II*. In 1991, DeLillo still thinks it is possible for Western liberal subjectivity to "survive". The wedding party Brita toasts must be Christian, of course, because they are drinking Champagne, so the Druse Christians DeLillo uses at the end of *Mao II* anticipate his more sustained reversion to Western concepts, including Christianity, in *Falling Man*. Both Gray and Neudecker are far more existentialist than their terrorist *Doppelgänger*; each meditates on the randomness that terrorism both exposes and exploits. However goal-oriented Abu Rashid and Mohamed Atta, the historical al-Qaeda terrorist fictionalized in *Falling Man*, may be in the cause of radical Islam, DeLillo makes clear that both serve the much higher purpose of metaphysical contingency. Against his best intentions, DeLillo ends up contributing to the cultural colonialism whereby global terrorism is internalized and accommodated. *Falling Man* is a classic instance of the famous Pogo aphorism: "We have met the enemy, and he is us!"[218] On the one hand, such a recognition offers the possibility of engaging the issues that global "terrorists" insist we repress unless they are brought violently home to us. On the other hand, DeLillo may be offering us yet another "misrecognition", in which all we see are reflections of ourselves, rendering the non-Western subject as invisible. Just how we sort out these cultural representations of the other remains crucial work for the cultural critic and the primary task of cultural politics.

In *Falling Man*, Atta is clearly identified in the novel by DeLillo by his given name "Amir"—"Amir spoke in his face. His full name was Mohamed Mohamed el-Amir el-Sayed Atta".[219] Yet despite his effort to *personalize* the best-known of the 9/11 hijackers with this "given" name, DeLillo represents al-Qaeda primarily through the character, Hammad, not Mohammed Atta. An Iraqi veteran of the Iran-Iraq War (1980–1988), "a baker, here in Hamburg maybe ten years", who "prayed in the same mosque" as Hammad, tells him his war stories, especially about the boys the Iranians sent in waves of assault on the contested borderland between Iraq and Iran (*FM*, 77). The nameless baker concludes that "Most countries are run by madmen", and as Hammad listens distractedly "was grateful to the man" (78). Hammad's attention is not on macropolitical issues but women and sex—"he kept thinking that another woman would come by on a bike, someone to look at, hair wet, legs pumping" (78), even though he knows he must suppress such desires, especially for German women. When he does satisfy his sexual desires, he does so with a Syrian immigrant to Germany, but even that relationship seems foreign to him. Hammad's gratitude to the baker seems less for the specific lessons to be learned from the futile Iran-Iraq War and more from the bare human contact such conversation provides.

DeLillo's analyses of al-Qaeda's motives and the personal and social psychologies of the terrorists are brief, scattered through the novel in two chapters ("On Marienstrasse", 77–83; "In Nokomis", 171–178) and a portion of the concluding chapter "In the Hudson Corridor" (237–243), in which the actual impact of Hammad's flight on the World Trade Center is represented. DeLillo is careful, however, to make sure each of the three parts of the novel—1. Bill Lawton, 2. Ernst Hechinger, 3. David Janiak—includes some part of the terrorists' story. Even so, less than twenty pages of a 246-page novel deal with al-Qaeda, most of them focusing on Hammad's distraction and confusion, torn between basic human desires for social and sexual contact and the false society of al-Qaeda. DeLillo seems to stress Hammad's ordinariness, his lack of intellectual sophistication, both as part of his common humanity and his willingness to be recruited. When Hammad asks Amir Atta about "the others, those who will die?" he is told: "[T]here are no others. The others exist only to the degree that they fill the role we have designed for them. This is their function as others. Those who will die have no claim to their lives outside the useful fact of their dying". DeLillo can only conclude: "Hammad was impressed by this. It sounded like philosophy." (*FM*, 176)

DeLillo trivializes the terrorists by minimizing the attention he pays to them in the novel, reinforcing his arguments in *Underworld* (1997) and *Cosmopolis* (2003) that first-world, hypercapitalist nations, especially the U.S., have created their own antagonists in al-Qaeda and any other "terror" (domestic or foreign) we might experience in our postmodern condition. The currency trader in *Cosmopolis* smugly watches on television the Seattle demonstrators opposing the global economic policies of the World Trade Organization and International Monetary Fund as they chant, "*A specter is haunting the world...*"[220] For the currency speculator, the symbolic action of the demonstrators is pure theater, mere entertainment, not a symptom of the impending collapse of global credit markets, admittedly historically ahead of any of these novels and yet systemically predictable, given the conditions of vastly growing disparities in wealth and poverty dividing individuals, institutions, and nations. Unintentionally recalling Jacques Derrida's *Specters of Marx* (1993), DeLillo approximates its argument: we need a new intellectual-activist paradigm and a new international to overcome the failures of Marxism *and* the impending collapse of global capitalism. There is no difference between the home-grown American assassin, Lee Harvey Oswald, and the imported terrorists of al-Qaeda: terror is the inevitable by-product of a system built upon unstable master-servant relations that inevitably prompt the servant's rebellion. Keith Neudecker's son, Justin, hearing the endlessly repeated news stories about Osama bin Laden begins looking for "Bill Lawton", the homophonic resemblances between the Arabic and Anglo-American name at first lost on his family.

"There is no purpose, this is the purpose" are Atta's words, and they echo in Hammad's head throughout his brief appearances in the novel, but they also function as a sort of horrible *leitmotif* in the same way "The future belongs to crowds" organizes *Mao II* (*FM*, 177). Once the veneer of social organization and the symbolic structures of affiliation—family, neighborhood, religion, nation, et al..—collapse, then each of us is exposed to what Giorgio Agamben has termed "bare life", a condition that can be simulated by totalitarian regimes but is also the fundamental condition to which we respond in our efforts to "be human". Of course, the application of Agamben's term "bare life" to the characters in DeLillo's novel seems at first immoral, insofar as Agamben uses the phrase to represent how the Nazis reduced their victims to the most minimal existences to justify their extermination. Atta's contention that the "others" exist only for al-Qaeda's purposes recalls Nazi rationalizations of their genocide.

Agamben develops the concept of "bare life" in part out of Hannah Arendt's notion in *The Origins of Totalitarianism* (1951) of the "naked life" experienced by refugees of all sorts displaced by World War II.[221] Even before we witness Keith Neudecker escape the World Trade Center after the 9/11 attacks, we know him to be a "refugee", deeply traumatized and displaced, incapable of dealing with his family life and work, finally driven relentlessly by forces he does not understand to the triviality of competitive poker. Drifting from pre-9/11 poker games with friends as a mere social pastime to the gambling parlors of Atlantic City and Northeastern Indian casinos after 9/11, finally pursuing competitive poker as his vocation in Las Vegas, "Neudecker" does indeed get a "new deck" or "new cover" that actually exposes to the reader the randomness of everyday life. The existentialist as fundamentally alienated can thus connect with other "refugees", such as the African American woman Keith meets when he identifies her name inside a briefcase he has carried out of the Tower.

The brief affair between Florence Givens and Keith Neudecker is possible only because of their shared bond of post-traumatic stress:

> She talked about the tower, going over it again, claustrophobically, the smoke, the fold of bodies, and he understood that they could talk about these things only with each other, in minute and dullest detail, but it would never be dull or too detailed because it was inside them now and because he needed to hear what he'd lost in the tracings of memory. (*FM*, 90–91)

Florence is described as a "light-skinned black woman", whose "odd embodying of doubtful language and unwavering race" suggest a community outside Neudecker's society, even though she lives just across Central Park (admittedly a proximity that also suggests class distinctions of the East and West sides of New York). DeLillo just barely eroticizes her ethnic identity, albeit strictly through Neudecker's perspective: "[W]hen she laughed there was a flare in nature, an unfolding of something half hidden and dazzling" (92). And she is predictably in tune with the Brazilian music she plays on her CD player for him, "clapping her hands to the music" and finally dancing "arms up and away from her body, nearly trancelike, [...] facing him now, mouth open, eyes coming open" until Neudecker "began to crawl out of his clothes" (92–93).

"'I've never been to Brazil,'" Florence admits, but it is her racial identity in the novel that permits her to respond, however awkwardly, to music that finally moves Neudecker out of his middle-class propriety. The music (and thus this possible contact between the two characters) was what was inside the briefcase Neudecker returns to Florence: "'This is the disc that was in the player that you carried out of there,'" she tells him (93). Three pages from the end of the novel, as Neudecker makes his way down the stairways of the Tower, an "old man, smallish, sitting, [...] resting", hands him the briefcase, explaining, "'I don't know what I'm supposed to do with this. She fell and left it'" (244). Parodying some classic detective plot, DeLillo gives us the "treasure" inside that briefcase as the Brazilian rhythms of Samba or some hybrid musical form, intended to liberate us from the confines of capitalism, print-knowledge, Western Civilization: "He heard the music change to something that had a buzz and drive, voices in Portuguese rapping, singing, whistling, with guitars and drums behind them, manic saxophones" (92). Neudecker, the real estate investment banker—"'[s]mall outfit called Royer Properties [...]. We were Royer and Stans. Then Stans got indicted'" (53)—can only respond professionally: "'I'm talking to somebody. Very early in the talks. About a job involving Brazilian investors. I may need some Portuguese'" (93).

Like the white man drumming his fingers methodically on the juke joint's table in Zora Neale Hurston's "How It Feels to Be Colored Me" (1928), Neudecker never really makes contact with Florence, even if they do have a brief sexual relationship. "Music. The great blobs of purple and red emotion have not touched him", Hurston writes, "He has only heard what I felt [...]. He is so pale with his whiteness then and I am *so* colored".[222] But DeLillo does not draw this conclusion, even if he gestures in the direction of Keith's and Florence's cultural, ethnic, and class differences, overlooked briefly as a consequence of a shared, but passing post-traumatic stress. Their undeveloped interlude is strange indeed in the novel, because it is one of the very few times characters in the novel actually cross the boundaries of their small worlds, apart from the framing act of al-Qaeda's attack, in itself a fundamental transgression of realms. At some level, DeLillo suggests that these personal failures—Keith's inability to hear the Brazilian rhythms Florence so clearly feels—are symptomatic of our national problem and explain in part our susceptibility to terror.

The other instances of transgression in the novel are either fantastic, trivial, or merely reinstate the boundaries they threaten. Hammad longs for the German women cycling in the street, but then sleeps with a Syrian woman. Lianne angrily tells her neighbor, Elena, to turn down the Arabic sounding music—"women in soft chorus, singing in Arabic" (119)—shortly after 9/11, complaining, "'The whole city is ultrasensitive right now. Where have you been hiding?'" (*FM*, 120). Lianne's mother, Nina, has a twenty-year long relationship with a mysterious German art-dealer, Martin Ridnour, aka Ernst Hechinger, who is rumored to have been associated with Kommune 1 in Berlin and the Red Brigades in Italy (146). Linda Kauffman has argued convincingly that *Falling Man* draws on DeLillo's nonfictional prose, both before and after 9/11, to comment on the relationship between 1960s radical protest movements in Europe and the U.S. to contemporary global terrorist movements.[223] Like Antonio Negri, convicted *in absentia* for his role in the Italian Red Brigades' kidnapping and murder of Christian Democratic Prime Minister Aldo Moro, Ridnour/Hechinger represents the intersection of radical politics and culture.

DeLillo explicitly identifies Ridnour/Hechinger with "Kommune 1", not Baader-Meinhof, although Nina also suggests "he was in Italy for a while, in the turmoil, when the Red Brigades were active. But I don't know" (146). Kommune 1, or "K 1", was a short-lived political commune founded in Berlin in 1967 by a group of radicals led by Dieter Kunzelmann, Rudi Dutschke, Bernd Rabehl, and including Hans Magnus Enzensberger's ex-wife, Dagrun, and his brother, Ulrich. By 1969, this anti-government student activist group had fallen apart, but in its heyday was known for planning and occasionally carrying out Dadaist style "performance" acts of social satire. Such acts included the planned "Pudding Assassination" of Vice President Hubert Humphrey during his visit to Berlin in April 1967—so-called because one plan called for attacking him with pudding, yogurt, and flour—and the famous K 1 photograph of communards' buttocks posed against a wall with the headline: "*Das Private ist politisch!*" ("The personal is political!"). The symbolic actions of Kommune 1 were usually linked to specific political acts, such as their demonstration against the Shah of Iran's visit to Berlin on June 2, 1967, but they were often criticized by German left-activists as more interested in publicity than in political change.

Kommune 1 nevertheless comes close to DeLillo's earlier versions of the radical artist, and their leaders were headlined as "Eleven Little Oswalds" in *Die Zeit*'s coverage of the abortive "Pudding Assassination" plot. Thanks to their members' connections with well-known German writers, Kommune 1 members lived for a time in Hans Magnus Enzensberger's Berlin apartment and later in Uwe Johnson's studio apartment until Johnson, abroad in the U.S., grew alarmed at the negative publicity Kommune 1 had attracted and asked his neighbor, Günter Grass, to have them evicted. Whereas the Red Brigades in Italy and the Baader-Meinhof in Germany really did commit urban terrorist acts with lasting consequences, Kommune 1 worked primarily through symbolic actions. However different these political activist groups are, they still have in common their origins in 1960s European left politics and their associations with the 1960s Left in the U.S.

DeLillo includes very few political debates in the novel and all of them take place among the scholars and artists surrounding Lianne's mother, Nina, the distinguished Professor of Art History, and her lover, Martin/ Ernst, the cosmopolitan art-dealer and former radical. At the lunch following the memorial service for Nina, Martin announces "the thought [...] of American irrelevance", of "the day [that] is coming when nobody has to think about America except for the danger it brings", that "America is losing the center" (191). Martin's different thoughts are in fact the same for DeLillo: irrelevance equals marginal; marginal equals dangerous. These equivalences suggest the ultimate one: America = terrorism. This conclusion, of course, comes predictably from the suspected 1960s' radical, Ernst Hechinger (aka Martin Ridnour), pontificating on a subject we are led to believe he knows too well.

But what, then, should we conclude about the brief, undeveloped relationship between Florence Givens and Keith Neudecker, whose German surname adds to his vague family relationship to Ernst Hechinger through Keith's mother-in-law, Nina? Michael Hardt and Antonio Negri conclude *Empire* (2000) with a final section, "The Multitude against Empire", in which they predict an emerging coalition of oppressed peoples rising against the EuroAmerican Empire that has caused so much human misery in the names of modernization, progress, freedom, and selfhood in the previous 500 years.[224] If it does arrive, Hardt and Negri argue, it will not come from within the system of EuroAmerican hegemony and privilege. "What comes after America?" Martin asks Nina's mourning friends and her daughter, but he has no more idea what to do with this knowledge than did the historical members of Kommune 1 (192). Lianne understands the problem: "Maybe he was a terrorist but he was one of ours, she thought, and the thought chilled her, shamed her—one of ours, which meant godless, Western, white" (195).

Why, then, does DeLillo so marginalize his other characters, his characters of *otherness*, ranging from the ordinary but nonetheless ethnically specific Florence to Hammad and Amir Atta, the terrorists? Florence Givens' surname suggests the various gifts with which she is associated, ranging from the suitcase (with its CD player and its Brazilian music) to the human contact she gives Keith, perhaps hinting at a new "gift economy" of human relations, rather than social relations based on property and commodities. Yet DeLillo, like Keith, seems merely to entertain her as an impossible alternative, a means to non-Western knowledge she implies in her yearning, albeit clumsy, dance to those Brazilian rhythms. Keith Neudecker's response is finally trivial, personal: he will confess his affair to his estranged wife, Lianne, and she will "get a kitchen knife and kill me". Trivializing any revolution from within the first-world system, DeLillo refuses to explore the possibility of any transvaluation from *outside*, apart from the dogmatism of the terrorists, represented as the nearly perfect opposite, the inevitable product, of Western ambiguity and doubt.

In his representation of a specific terrorist, DeLillo gives some human definition to Hammad only to westernize him, a strategy reinforced by the fact that Hammad is fictional, whereas the historical Amir Mohammed Atta is dogmatic and totalitarian. Hammad stumbles along in Hamburg, Afghanistan, Nokomis (Florida), even on board the jetliner hurtling down the Hudson Corridor toward the North Tower of the World Trade Center. He has his doubts about the use of children in the Iran-Iraq War, the promise of salvation to all martyrs in the *jihad* against the West, the prohibition against sex for the terrorists, even the demand that Muslim men grow beards. Critical of most of these lessons, he nonetheless accepts the basic premises: that the West is making war on Islam and that a blow against Western dominance shows "how a great power can be vulnerable. A power that interferes, that occupies" (46). And yet those final words are spoken by Martin/Ernst, the descendant of the 1960s EuroAmerican left, not by Islamic fundamentalists or such groups as Hezbollah and Hamas, who repeatedly condemn EuroAmerican support of what they consider Israeli imperialism in the Middle East.

DeLillo understands fully how the existentialist aura of modernity, in which he and I were both educated, does not adequately motivate the social bond. To argue as philosophical existentialism did that the fundamental absurdity of our existence as humans, our insurmountable alienation from the external world, is what calls us together and thus should motivate us passionately to create human habitation and social institutions, is too abstract and paradoxical to motivate the ordinary person. DeLillo cannot transcend his earlier education, and he still believes in the fundamental abyss, the randomness of existence that the mind transforms into patterns, plots, characters, destinies, and empires. Behind the dogma of Amir Atta lies the skepticism of Hammad, so that even the *jihadists* will be tricked into nothingness in the end. But DeLillo no longer believes that this universal truth of human contingency can motivate anything beyond the ceaseless history of a will-to-power that thrives on warfare and the production of subalterns who deserve our domination (whoever "we" may be in the particular historical moment).

Lianne "loved Kierkegaard in his antiqueness, in the glaring drama of the translation she owned, an old anthology of brittle pages with ruled underlinings in red ink [...].He made her feel that her thrust into the world was not the slender melodrama she sometimes thought it was" (118). But Lianne's life *is* "a slender melodrama", only expanded into significance by the suffering of untold others, victims of foreign policies, wars, economic cheats, whereby Lianne lives in relative comfort and Hammad remembers nothing but crowding, narrow rooms filled with other lodgers, and ceaseless displacement. Yemen, Saudi Arabia, Afghanistan, Hamburg, Florida, New York, the Hudson Corridor—Hammad is always in some foreign place, experiencing to be sure the fundamental estrangement of DeLillo's and modernity's existentialist thesis. Are we *all strangers*? Yes and no; Hammad more than Lianne. Does Lianne recognize this impasse when she turns oddly, unpredictably, casually to religion in chapter 14, just a few pages before Hammad and Atta begin their fateful flight toward the North Tower? "She wanted to disbelieve", perhaps because her father, Jack, a suicide, believed so passionately and contradictorily "that God infused time and space with pure being, made stars give light", as if this gave purpose to his own career as "an architect, an artist", someone in the business of producing order (232).

But it is not the "will to disbelieve" that motivates her; instead, Lianne turns to Catholicism, as if in direct reply to the passionate will to believe DeLillo attributes to Atta: "Others were reading the Koran, she was going to church. [...]. She followed others when they stood and knelt and she watched the priest celebrate the mass, bread and wine, body and blood. She didn't believe this, the transubstantiation, but believed something, half fearing it would take her over" (233). Lianne's religious conversion is still some version of Christian existentialism, a lingering trace of the antiquated Kierkegaard she loved in college and before 9/11, but it is nonetheless Catholicism, especially when it says: "God is the voice that says, 'I am not here'" (236). Although Lianne waffles between several versions of Christianity in a few pages, her conversion does enable her "to be alone, in reliable calm, she and the kid", apart from Keith, who has chosen the radical contingency of hyper-capitalism (236).

Displaced from the North Tower to Florence's apartment "across the Park" to the Sport and Gambling clubs of Atlantic City, then finally to Las Vegas, where he "works" fitfully as a competitive, compulsive poker player, Keith Neudecker acts out hyper-capitalism's response to the existentialist predicament. If it is all a lie, merely a passing game, then we can only expose the fiction by ceaselessly demonstrating it, always living on the edge, facing every day the sheer contingency thinly veiled in the "risks" of the stock, credit, and currency markets of the Wall Street world where Keith once felt secure. Almost forty years ago, Robert Venturi, Denise Scott Brown, and Steven Izenour's *Learning from Las Vegas* (1972) appeared as a postmodern manifesto, even if its title underscores the irony that serious architecture and urban planning should follow the lead of Las Vegas' *kitsch*.[225] DeLillo's conclusion in *Falling Man* is that Las Vegas has only led us to the bathos of capitalism, the absolute point of contradiction when the system can no longer hold, and he turns Las Vegas into the capital of America's "own shit" (191), recalling the main argument of *Underworld* (1997).[226]

The dilemma staged in DeLillo's *Falling Man* is exemplified in the eponymous act of David Janiak, whose repeated enactment of "falling" reminds New Yorkers of the pathos of the American "fall". Of course, what he stages is literally a "memento mori", that old poetic trope, of the several victims of 9/11 who chose to throw themselves from the top of the towers, rather than be incinerated or asphyxiated within. Much has been written about these "falling" people, whose peculiar positions were primarily the consequence of the basic physics involved, rather than any final gesture in response to the horrifying events of 9/11. Lianne witnesses one of Janiak's performances when she picks up Justin at school and chances on Janiak "falling" from an elevated subway platform visible from the schoolyard. Years later, she comes across his obituary, then searches his history on the web. A trained actor with "a heart ailment and high blood pressure" (230), he is found dead at 39 years old in Saginaw County, Michigan, "more than five hundred miles from the site of the World Trade Center" (223), perhaps preparing to perform his "last jump" without a harness.

The performance art DeLillo stages in the novel invokes the rich history of street performance in New York City and recalls the specific act of the French aerialist, Philippe Petit, who on August 7, 1974 defied security at the World Trade Center, still under construction, to stretch a cable between the towers and tight-rope walk between them. Celebrated and criticized in James Marsh's recent documentary, *Man on Wire* (2008), in which no reference to 9/11 is made, Petit anticipates DeLillo's

Janiak, just as Marsh's documentary offers an unwitting commentary on DeLillo's mysterious figure. Both call attention to the human being in the overwhelming scale of late-modern urban space; both depend upon the World Trade Center as a symbol of modernist dehumanization, pitting either Petit's daring or Janiak's victimized human form against such a cityscape.

Yet even as news photographs of Petit's daring act circled the globe and Janiak leaves New York City, presumably to spread his own news to the Midwest and across America, both figures occlude the events of 9/11. Americans did not attack themselves on September 11, even if DeLillo argues convincingly that Americans contributed to the global conditions that have prompted the rise of numerous anti-imperialist, non-state affiliated, politically radical groups at war with first-world nations and global financial powers since the end of the Cold War in 1989. Understanding "our fall" as a powerful nation, which has abused its moral and political authority in that same historical period, is certainly an important task. *Falling Man* contributes to this ongoing analysis by left intellectuals around the globe by detailing the instability of the values on which the U.S. has based that moral authority: religious tolerance, the nuclear family, intellectual and cultural criticism of the state, equal opportunity, anti-imperialism, and universal human rights. Janiak "falls" in the novel to demonstrate our failings in each of these areas. Islamic terrorism drives Lianne to Catholicism. Lianne and Keith's shaky marriage only briefly recovers after his escape from the North Tower; as he struggles with post-traumatic stress, the marriage totters and falls again. Nina and Martin/Ernst's artistic circle typifies the "radical chic" that no longer has any traction in global politics. Neither Kommune 1's pranks nor serious art can change the system from within. The white walls of the art-dealer Martin Ridnour's apartment suggest not only his impermanence but also the erasure of aesthetic and intellectual critique. Postmodern intellectuals and artists have been contained by a pervasive U.S. anti-intellectualism, as well as by their own complicity in the global class/caste system. Like those elegant Giorgio Morandi paintings that hang in Nina's apartment in which slender bottles and spare boxes barely appear against white backgrounds, contemporary art criticizes late capitalism merely by stressing our impoverishment and commodification. In Morandi's paintings, *we* are those bottles and boxes, still-lives without natural referents, distilled into useless, expensive objects in a shop window.

But none of this explains Atta and al-Qaeda. Hammad's westernized desires and confused soul do not adequately represent the rage or the violence directed against the U.S. by groups and individuals who are willing to die for the barest chance to "speak out" against first-world arrogance. The ten rural peasant youth who carried out the attack on Mumbai between November 26 and 29, 2008, paused in the lobby of Taj Mahal Hotel and Tower to wonder at the television screens, personal computers, and vast array of technological devices available to the hotel guests. Those young revolutionaries were witnessing a disparity of global wealth also evident in the social and economic inequities of rapidly modernizing Mumbai. Of course, the motives of their Pakistani-based militant organization, Lashkar-e-Taiba, are in part driven by religious differences between Muslims and Hindus in South Asia, but the attack also indicated how these local religious politics are now inflected with a deep anti-Semitism that seems to bind together globally Islamic terrorist groups. The religious, political, economic, social, and personal cathexes of global terrorism cannot be represented adequately, much less successfully analyzed and criticized, entirely within the framework of EuroAmerican ideologies. British imperialism in the Subcontinent, U.S. neo-imperialism around the world, and global capitalism of the first-world nations are all to blame for the production of terrorism, but terrorism is neither a unified global movement nor entirely the *effect* of these causes.

Written before 9/11 and published in the same year, Salman Rushdie's *Fury* (2001) does attempt to understand the psychology of the minoritized non-European faced with first-world economic, political, and personal hegemony. Rushdie's protagonist, Malik Solanka, is not a poor peasant from an undeveloped country but a Cambridge-educated Bombay millionaire, whose invention of the doll, "Little Brain", has brought him fortune and fame. Perhaps for all of these reasons, Solanka feels an overpowering "fury", which he fears he will wreak violently on his own family, so he exiles himself from London to New York. Yet in New York City, he reads compulsively newspaper stories about a serial killer Solanka fears may be himself, acting out his uncontrollable rage in some repressed or somatic state.[227]

Malik Solanka turns out not to be that psychopathic killer, but Rushdie makes clear that his character's anger against the West is so real, so palpable even to him, that it may erupt at any moment. When on November 5, 2009, Nidal Malik Hasan, a U.S. Army major serving as a psychiatrist at Fort Hood, Texas entered the Soldier Readiness Center, shouted "*Allahu Akbar!*" and opened fire, wounding forty-three and killing thirteen people, his fury adds to that of the 9/11 terrorists and others, whether al-Qaeda inspired or not, bombing trains in Madrid and London, nightclubs in Bali, foreign naval ships in Yemen, resorts in Egypt and Israel, as well as the countless foiled attempts to bomb public transport and spaces throughout the imperialist first-world. Was Major Hasan a "terrorist"? Did his cell-phone and email contacts with Anwar al-Awlaki in Yemen *prove* that Hasan was part of this "global war", or was he just another psychopath, a "madman" ironically trained to treat others' post-traumatic stress disorder?

Rushdie's pre-9/11 attempt at a literary interpretation of the "consciousness" of third-world fury by no means "covers" the issue, which today is at the center of our global anarchy. John Updike's *Terrorist* (2006) brilliantly captures the inner fury of Ahmad Ashmawy Mulloy, the eighteen-year-old Northern New Jersey convert to Islam who was raised by an Irish-American mother abandoned by her Egyptian husband when Ahmad was three. Sentimental in its conclusion when Ahmad changes his mind while driving a truckload of explosives into the Lincoln Tunnel, *Terrorist* nevertheless is a valiant effort by a thoroughly bourgeois writer to employ the techniques of the novel to help American readers comprehend this otherworldly fury. It is not, then, the "failure" of the novel as a genre that makes it so difficult for us to "represent" terrorism and terrorists. Whatever its limitations, the novel can still help us think through an "other", however fraught with problems of language, style, cultural and religious differences, and reader competency this process may be.

The fatal impasse in DeLillo's *Falling Man* is not the fault of the literary genre, but DeLillo's excessive reliance on the U.S. national form. Throughout his career, DeLillo has been one of our greatest critics of the limitations of thinking only from inside the U.S. I began this essay by arguing that DeLillo's Lee Harvey Oswald cannot be understood in exclusively national terms. America "changed" the day Oswald assassinated John F. Kennedy, because from that moment on we could never again understand "America" apart from Mexico, Cuba, Japan, the Soviet Union. Should we *ever* have thought of "America" in a culturally isolationist way? In recent years, American Studies has turned significantly toward transnational and international work to demonstrate that "national" knowledge—the old "American Exceptionalism"—has blinded us to the historical and geopolitical scope of U.S. imperialism, its global deployment of domestic racial and ethnic and sexual stereotypes, class and related economic inequities, and its extension of slavery "by other means".

Rushdie's Malik Solanka in *Fury* is never tricked into believing that New York City is some cosmopolitan or multicultural utopia. Worse even than that old imperial metropole, London, New York City poses as egalitarian, inclusive, diverse, and functional, when in fact Solanka clearly sees it as a microcosm of the inequities, political barriers, and occupied territories that continue to enrage so many outside the "first world". In "Edward Said and American Studies", I argued that even Said, one of our most important postcolonial theorists, was himself lured by the cosmopolitan promise of New York City. But Rushdie understands New York to be a thoroughly *American* metropolis, well before it was targeted as such by al-Qaeda. DeLillo's *Harper's* essay, "In the Ruins of the Future", published in December 2001, only three months after 9/11, predicts accurately what he would write in *Falling Man*: a searching criticism of our national failings without a complementary understanding of the global forces we have helped to produce and yet have exceeded our cultural, political, and military control. In this respect, both his nonfictional and fictional responses to 9/11 contribute to, rather than challenge, what I have termed the "hypernationalism" whereby the U.S. state has attempted to incorporate and thereby domesticate global problems. That one of our most powerful social critics and insightful writers could be so captivated by the national form is another reason why we so desperately need ways of thinking beyond the nation to theorize anew the political, economic, and human relations of a genuinely global order of things.

The agenda for a progressive cultural politics, whether in the established discipline of American Studies or such related fields as Ethnic, Postcolonial, Indigenous, and Cultural Studies, must be post-nationalist and offer models of social, political, and economic affiliation that exceed the national form. The contact zones with other, non-U.S. communities need to be determined by scholars working together in a variety of fields, but for a cultural politics conceived in post-national terms we need a new comparatism that will go far beyond an older, Eurocentric "world litera- ture" and consider the relations between exilic, dissident, and marginal- ized writers and intellectuals within the U.S. and beyond its borders. By the same token, we cannot ignore the importance of studying the U.S. as a global power, especially as it exercises such power through cultural practices. It is no longer sufficient to criticize "American Exceptional- ism" at home, but today we must also reveal how such Exceptionalism is exported and thereby works its way through many different local net- works beyond our borders. How are U.S. films and literature received in Iraq, Israel, Pakistan, Jerusalem, and Nicaragua? Which consumer goods, computer software, Internet content, and related "cultural work" are available in those nations with large U.S. military bases and balance-of- trade imbalances? Demystification of U.S. power, especially in the guise of "freedom and opportunity", remains a central task, even as we must learn more about those communities, states, and peoples most threat- ened by U.S. global hegemony. As we have learned from the enormous immigrant populations displaced by the Vietnam War, our military, po- litical, and economic powers of globalization often bring significant new populations to our nation, so that immigration and its cultural conse- quences must be studied in conjunction with the cultural foreign policy I have proposed. The "American novel" can no longer be read in isolation or in terms solely of its representations of a national symbology that is impossible to think apart from its transnational, postnationalist circuits.

Notes

Preface

1. Gerald Graff, *Beyond the Culture Wars: How Teaching the Conflicts Can Revitalize American Education* (New York: W. W. Norton and Co., 1992).

Introduction

2. George W. Bush, *Decision Points* (New York: Crown Publishers, 2010), pp. 275, 320.

3. Mark Levine, *Why They Don't Hate Us: Lifting the Veil on the Axis of Evil* (Oxford: Oneworld Publishing, 2005).

4. Donald E. Pease, *The New American Exceptionalism* (Minneapolis: University of Minnesota Press, 2009); Amy Kaplan, "Where Is Guantanamo?" *American Quarterly* 57:3 (September 2005), 831–858.

5. Chalmers Johnson, *The Sorrows of Empire: Militarism, Secrecy, and the End of the Republic* (New York: Metropolitan Books, 2004), pp. 151–186.

6. The recent humanitarian aid in Haiti following the 2010 earthquake seems to be an exception to the history of U.S. neglect of Haiti, but it actually follows a history in which the U.S. has occupied the nation (1915–1934), routinely interfered in its internal politics, and exploited its labor. Along with non-governmental agencies and other nations, the U.S. provided substantial relief to Haiti in the aftermath of the earthquake, but today as cholera sweeps through camps occupied by more than one million displaced Haitians, their desperate circumstances are once again neglected in the U.S. media.

7. Available on http://www.whitehouse.gov/blog/NewBeginning/

8. Fareed Zakaria, "The Capitalist Manifesto: Greed Is Good (To a point)", *Newsweek* (June 13, 2009), p. 7.

9. Ruth Wilson Gilmore, *Golden Gulag: Prisons, Surplus, Crisis, and Opposition in Globalizing California* (Berkeley: University of California Press, 2007).

10. William D. Cohan, *House of Cards: A Tale of Hubris and Wretched Excess on Wall Street* (New York: Doubleday, 2009).

11. Louis Althusser, "Ideology and Ideological State Apparatuses", in *Lenin and Philosophy and Other Essays*, trans. Ben Brewster (London: New Left Books, 1971), pp. 127–189; Slavoj Žižek, *For They Know Not What They Do: Enjoyment as a Political Factor* (London: Verso Press, 2008).

12. See John Carlos Rowe, *The New American Studies* (Minneapolis: University of Minnesota Press, 2002), pp. 3–63.

13. William Readings, *The University in Ruins* (Cambridge, MA: Harvard University Press, 1997); Christopher Newfield, *Ivy and University: Business and the Making of the American University, 1880–1980* (Durham, N. C.: Duke University Press, 2003) and *Unmaking the Public University: The Forty Year Assault on the Middle Class* (Cambridge, MA: Harvard University Press, 2008).

14. Gary Hall, *Digitize This Book! The Politics of New Media, or Why We Need Open Access Now* (Minneapolis: University of Minnesota Press, 2008).

Chapter 1

15. Said's Wellek lectures were published as *Musical Elaborations* (New York: Columbia University Press, 1991).

16. Said's revised dissertation was published two years later as *Joseph Conrad and the Fiction of Autobiography* (Cambridge, MA: Harvard University Press, 1966).

17. Indeed, James is part of the representative trinity in F. R. Leavis, *The Great Tradition: George Eliot, Henry James, Joseph Conrad* (New York: New York University Press, 1967), whereas Charles Dickens warrants only "An Analytic Note" on *Hard Times* in the concluding chapter.

18. Ernest Hemingway, *The Dangerous Summer*, intro. James A. Michener (N. Y.: Scribner, 1985); Said, *Reflections on Exile and Other Essays* (Cambridge, MA: Harvard University Press, 2000), p. 238. Further references in the text as: *R*.

19. Although he refers briefly to Henry Adams, Said does so in numerous places, especially in his essays on Blackmur. Blackmur never finished his book on *Henry Adams* (New York: Harcourt Brace Jovanovich, 1980), which was edited and published after Blackmur's death by Veronica Makowsky. Without a specialist's knowledge of Adams, Said had an uncanny understanding of the social meaning of what Adams termed his own "conservative Christian anarchism"—that is, his thoroughly paradoxical politics—as a symptom of the impasse facing many modern American

liberals as their enthusiasm for democratic vistas turned into a crucial tool of the modern American Empire. See Rowe, *Literary Culture and U.S. Imperialism*, 165–194.

20. Said, *Orientalism* (New York: Random House, Inc., 1978), pp. 294–295. Further references in the text as: *O*.

21. I recall Said repeating on several occasions how he had conceived *Orientalism* in angry response to the liberal western scholarship represented by Frances FitzGerald's *Fire in the Lake: The Vietnamese and the Americans in Vietnam* (New York: Random House, 1972), which relies heavily on the Orientalist scholarship of her mentor, the French Indochina specialist, Paul Mus, to whose memory FitzGerald shares with her father the dedication of her book. In particular, Said repeated this story during his challenge of my use of FitzGerald's work in my "Eye-Witness: Documentary Styles in the American Representations of Vietnam", which I delivered at "The Mediation of Received Values", conference sponsored by University of Minnesota in October 1984 to inaugurate the journal *Cultural Critique*. His criticism of my paper took me by complete surprise, but it also led me to reread and reconsider FitzGerald's work in ways that led to the revision of the published version of my essay in *The Vietnam War and American Culture*, eds. John Carlos Rowe and Rick Berg (New York: Columbia University Press, 1991), pp. 148–174.

22. Said, *Culture and Imperialism* (New York: Random House, Inc., 1993), p. 63. Further references in the text as: *CI*.

23. Amy Kaplan, *The Anarchy of Empire in United States Culture* (Cambridge, MA: Harvard University Press, 2002), p. 14. I make a similar gesture in *Literary Culture and U.S. Imperialism: From the Revolution to World War II* (New York: Oxford University Press, 2000), pp. 13–15.

24. Lawrence Buell, "Are We Post-American Studies?" in *Field Work: Sites in Literary and Cultural Studies*, eds. Marjorie Garber, Paul B. Franklin, and Rebecca Walkowitz (New York: Routledge, 1996); C. Richard King, *Postcolonial America* (Urbana: University of Illinois Press, 2000); John Carlos Rowe, *Post-Nationalist American Studies* (Berkeley: University of California Press, 2000). These theoretical discussions have been supplemented by many historically specific studies of the United States from postcolonial perspectives, including Katherine Kinney, *Friendly Fire: American Identity and the Literature of the Vietnam War* (New York: Oxford University Press, 2001) and Christina Klein, *Cold War Orientalism: Asia in the Middlebrow Imagination, 1945–1961* (Berkeley: University of California Press, 2003)

25. Rowe, *The New American Studies* (Minneapolis: University of Minnesota Press, 2002), pp. xxii–xxviii.

26. Spivak, "The Politics of Interpretations" (1982), *In Other Worlds: Essays in Cultural Politics* (New York: Routledege, 1988), p. 131.

27. Said, *The World, the Text, and the Critic* (Cambridge, MA: Harvard University Press, 1983), pp. 45, 28. Further references in the text as: *WTC*.

28. Said, *Out of Place: A Memoir* (New York: Alfred A. Knopf, 1999), p. 295.

29. See my critique of Auerbach as a transhistorical cosmopolitan ideal in *The New American Studies*, pp. 211–212n.8, 213n.17.

30. For an excellent account of how the New York Intellectuals of the 1940s and 1950s anticipated and in some cases participated in the debates in critical theory of the late 1960s and after, see Klaus J. Milich, *Die frühe Postmoderne: Geschichte eines europäisch-amerikanischen Kulturkonflikts* (Frankfurt: Campus Verlag, 1998).

31. On Trilling's anticipation of contemporary neo-liberalism, see John Carlos Rowe, *Afterlives of Modernism: Liberalism, Transnationalism, and Political Critique* (Hanover, N.H.: University Press of New England, 2011).

32. F. W. Dupee, *Henry James: His Life and Writings*, 2nd edition (Garden City, N. Y.: Doubleday and Co., Inc., 1956) was the first critical study of Henry James I ever read and for many in my scholarly generation a book that deeply influenced our understanding of Henry James as modernist. (I confess this understanding of Dupee's book came to me much later; I first read it when I was sixteen and hastily completing a high school report!).

33. W. J. T. Mitchell, "Remembering Edward Said," *The Chronicle of Higher Education* (October 10, 2003), B11.

34. Vijay Prashad, "Confronting the Evangelical Imperialists," *CounterPunch* (November 13, 2003), (www.counterpunch.org/prashad111320003.html/)

35. Said, *Covering Islam: How the Media and Experts Determine How We See the Rest of the World* (New York: Pantheon Books, 1981) and *Blaming the Victims: Spurious Scholarship and the Palestinian Question*, eds. Edward W. Said and Christopher Hitchens (London: Verso, 1988).

36. Said, "The Palestinian Experience," in *Reflections on the Middle East Crisis*, ed. Herbert Mason, Studies in the Behavioral Sciences, 7 (The Hague: Mouton, 1970), pp. 127–147; "A Palestinian Voice," *The Middle East Newsletter* (October-November 1970), 4:8: 11–15.

37. Said, *The Palestinian Question and the American Context*, Institute for Palestine Studies, # 1 (E) (Beirut: Institute for Palestine Studies, 1979), p. 7.

38. Jonathan Krakauer, *Where Men Win Glory: The Odyssey of Pat Tillman* (New York: Doubleday and Co., 2009), represents much of this contradictoriness in the competitive accounts of Tillman's athletic celebrity, his military service, and death in Afghanistan.

Chapter 2

39. Christina Klein, *Cold War Orientalism: Asia in the Middlebrow Imagination, 1945–1961* (Berkeley: University of California Press, 2003), p. 276.

40. *Ibid.*, pp. 273–276.

41. Donna Przybylowicz and Abdul JanMohamed, "Introduction: The Economy of Moral Capital in the Gulf War", in "Economies of War" special issue, *Cultural Critique* 19 (Fall 1991), 5–13.

42. Noam Chomsky, "After the Cold War: U.S. Foreign Policy in the Middle East", *Cultural Critique* 19 (Fall 1991), 15–31.

43. See George C. Herring, "America and Vietnam: The Unending War", *Foreign Affairs* (Winter 1991/92).

44. Harvard Sitikoff, "The Postwar Impact of Vietnam", *The Oxford Companion of American Military History*, ed. John Whiteclay Chambers, II (New York: Oxford University Press, 1999).

45. General David Shuter, former commander of the El Toro Marine Corp Air Station, told an audience at the University of California, Irvine on January 23, 1991 that anti-war protesters were "encouraging the enemy" and that "dissent" is no longer appropriate once the war had begun. "Protesters 'Encouraging Hussein,' Retired General Tells UCI Forum", *Los Angeles Times*, Orange County Edition (January 24, 1991), B12.

46. *All-Star Salute to the Troops*, dir. Dwight Hemion (CBS-TV, April 3, 1991).

47. Robert Divine, "Historiography: Vietnam Reconsidered," *Diplomatic History* (1988), 83.

48. *Ibid.*, 82–3.

49. Since 1991, estimates of civilian and combat casualties on both sides of the First Gulf War have continued to vary quite widely, but the most recent figures seem to support my approximations in 1991. "Two to three times the American casualties in the Vietnam War" would mean 116,000 to 174,000 total casualties, if the approximate number of 58,000 American casualties in the Vietnam War is used for comparison. In 2010, Wikipedia (http://en.wikipedia.org/wiki/Gulf_War#casualties) cites several U.S. military sources for the following casualty figures: Iraqi civilian 103,500; Iraqi combat 30–37,500; U.S. combat-related 148; non-combat related 145; other Coalition forces' combined casualties 100. These figures would give totals in a range of 133,893 to 141,393. My purpose in combining the casualty figures both in my original essay and in this updated note is to counter the U.S. state's desire to divide casualty figures in order to minimize their impression. Civilians, combatants, Iraqis, and Coalition forces all should be "counted" in the human damage of war.

50. Harold Meyerson, "Gulf-Conflicted," *LA Weekly* (February 22–28, 1991), 18.

51. Truong Nhu Tang, with David Chanoff and Doan Van Toai, *A Viet Cong Memoir* (New York: Random House, 1985), p. 75.

52. George C. Herring, *America's Longest War: The United States and Vietnam, 1950–1975*, 2nd ed. (New York: Alfred A. Knopf, 1986), p. 86. Herring points out that our military aid was "four times greater than economic and technical assistance" between 1955 and 1959 (p. 62).

53. This is one of the few places I leave my recommendation made in 1991 in the present tense, because it still seems relevant and imaginable to global politics.

54. Meyerson, "Gulf-Conflicted", 18.

55. Bob Woodward, *Obama's Wars* (New York: Simon and Schuster, 2010).

56. See Gold-Panner, "Obama's Wars—Vietnam Redux", *My Auburn (California)* blog (9/22/10). Woodward's book was released on 9/27/10.

Chapter 3

57. Ernest Hemingway, *In Our Time* (New York: Boni and Liveright, 1925).

58. Ernest Hemingway, *in our time* (Paris: Three Mountains Press, 1924).

59. Carlos Baker, *Ernest Hemingway: A Life Story* (New York: Charles Scribner's Sons, 1969), p. 116.

60. For a discussion of Dos Passos's use of the news media in *Manhattan Transfer*, see John Carlos Rowe, *Afterlives of Modernism: Liberalism, Transnationalism, and Political Critique* (Hanover: University Press of New England, 2011).

61. "Images from Fallujah Will Stir Debate, But ... Won't Alter Policy", Op-Ed, *Newsday* (April 2, 2004).

62. Operation Phantom Fury has been accused of causing long-lasting environmental damage by employing white Phosphorus shells during combat. Sigfrido Ranucci and Maurizio Torrealta, directors of the Italian documentary, *Fallujah, the Hidden Massacre*, make a strong case for the impact of white Phosphorus on the dramatic increase of rates of cancer in Fallujah, as well as the immediate casualties caused in this particular military assault to retake the city from Iraqi dissidents. *Fallujah, the Hidden Massacre* (11/08/2005, Radiotelevisione Italiana [RAI, Italian State Television] production, English and Italian versions).

63. Edward Said, *Covering Islam: How the Media and Experts Determine How We See the Rest of the World* (New York: Pantheon, 1981).

64. Edward Said, *Orientalism* (New York: Random House, 1978).

65. "Xe" apparently caused various search engines to generate a large number of unrelated Internet sites, a strategy that did little to improve the company's image as paramilitary, secretive, and paranoid.

66. Jeremy Scahill, *Blackwater: The Rise of the World's Most Powerful Mercenary Army* (New York: The Nation Books of the Avalon Publishing Group, Inc., 2007).

67. "Erik Prince" (Wikipedia).

Chapter 4

68. Wallerstein, Immanuel; Juma, Calestous; Keller, Evelyn Fox; Kocka, Jürgen; Lecourt, Dominique; Mudimbe, V. Y.; Mushakoji; Prigogine, Ilya; Taylor, Peter J.; Trouillot, Michel-Rolph, *Open the Social Sciences*. Report of the Gulbenkian Commission on Restructuring of the Social Sciences (Stanford: Stanford University Press, 1996), pp. 44–45.

69. Martin W. Lewis and Kären Wigen, "A Maritime Response to the Crisis in Area Studies," *The Geographical Review* 89:2 (April 1999), 162.

70. Walter D. Mignolo, *Local Histories/Global Designs: Coloniality, Subaltern Knowledges, and Border Thinking* (Princeton: Princeton University Press, 2000), pp. 278–280.

71. Walt Whitman, *Democratic Vista*, in *Leaves of Grass*, eds. Sculley Bradley, Harold W. Blodgett, and Michael Moon, Norton Critical Edition (New York: W. W. Norton and Co. 2004), represents most of the nineteenth-century U.S. national myths regarding gender divisions (especially maternity and the "separate spheres" ideology), Anglo-Saxon superiority, the "western" (and tacitly "southern") march of European civilization. Whitman's prose, a complement to his poetic corpus, suggests how nineteenth-century U.S. literary culture (and the subsequent twentieth-century scholarly establishment that canonized it) helped shape the "exceptional areas" of "American" and "European" Studies as disciplinary tools of imperialism's "civilizing mission".

72. Carl E. Guthe, "The Ethnogeographic Board," *The Scientific Monthly*, 57:2 (August 1943), 188.

73. *Ibid*. Board membership also included scholars who held positions on two relevant private foundations, Mortimer Graves, the Sinologist who was also Secretary of the ACLS, and Wilbur A. Sawyer, a specialist on the treatment of malaria, who was Director (1935–1944) of the Rockefeller Foundation's International Health Division (IHD), and one governmental agency,

the National School of Modern Oriental Languages and Civilizations, also chaired by Mortimer Graves. The Board in 1943 consisted of: William Duncan Strong (Director), an anthropologist; Carl E. Guthe (chair), an anthropologist from the University of Michigan; Wendell C. Bennett, an archaeologist; Carter Goodrich, a historian; John E. Graf, an anthropologist; Mortimer Graves, a Sinologist, who was also Secretary of the American Council of Learned Societies and Chair of the National School of Modern Oriental Languages and Civilizations; Robert B. Hall, a geographer; Wilbur A. Sawyer, a specialist on Yellow Fever, especially its treatment in Latin America, who directed (1935–1944) the Rockefeller Foundation's International Health Division; Douglas M. Whitaker, a biologist.

74. "William Duncan Strong," *Wikipedia*.

75. Carter Goodrich was a member of the faculty at the Wharton School of the University of Pennsylvania. Trained as an economic historian, he specialized in modernization and development, and was on the faculty of the "Industrial School" at Wharton.

76. The original Board (1942) seems to have no representation from sociology or political science, and only Goodrich suggests an explicit connection with economics. Isaiah Bowman, the geographer to whom Lewis and Wigen refer, was not a member of the original Board and must have been a later addition.

77. Donald Pease, "*Moby-Dick* and the Cold War," *The American Renaissance Reconsidered*, eds. Walter Benn Michaels and Donald E. Pease (Baltimore: The Johns Hopkins University Press, 1985), pp. 113–155. Pease specifically traces the Cold-War interpretation of *Moby-Dick* back to Matthiessen, as in Pease's conclusion: "Ever since Matthiessen's reading of [*Moby-Dick*] as a sign of the power of the freedom of figures in the American Renaissance to oppose totalitarianism, *Moby-Dick* has been a Cold War text, one that secures in Ishamel's survival a sign of the free world's triumph over a totalitarian power" (153).

78. Martin Lewis and Kären Wigen, the cultural geographers on whom I have relied earlier in this essay, direct the "Oceans Connect" initiative at Duke, which redefines area studies in terms of maritime connections. As they themselves acknowledge, one of the weaknesses of this new area studies model is that it privileges older sites of transport, immigration, and commerce without taking sufficiently into account such new sites, such as "Internet sites and airports" (Lewis and Wigen, 168). Even in the historical contexts in which oceans were the defining contact-zones or "flows," the maritime model ends up proliferating ever-more complicated "areas"—the Black Atlantic is now complemented by the Green Atlantic, the Red Atlantic, the North Atlantic (which also includes Black, Green, and

Red), et al.—that suggest the inherent problem with "area" as a structural, geographical, or conceptual unit.

79. Technically, of course, Emerson, Hawthorne, and Whitman are not "Creoles," because they are born after U.S. independence from England, whereas Franklin, Adams, Jefferson, et al. do qualify as "Creoles".

80. Bolívar's famous "The Jamaica Letter: Response from a Southern American to a Gentleman from This Island" (September 6, 1815), in *El Libertador: Writings of Simón Bolívar*, trans. Frederick H. Fornoff, ed. David Bushnell (New York: Oxford University Press, 2003), p. 13, renews the revolutionary project against Spain in part by indicting the Spanish as a "wicked stepmother," in part by transferring the "atrocities" and "perversities" of Spain against Amerindians to the Creole rebels who he claims Spain wishes to make "slaves". José Martí's "The Indians in the United States" (1885), in *Selected Writings*, ed. and trans. Esther Allen (New York: Penguin Books, 2002), pp. 157–164, reports on the Mohonk Conferences begun in 1883 and out of which came the passage of the hated Dawes General Allotment Act of 1887. Martí's conclusion, albeit written two years before the passage of the Dawes Act, is perfectly in keeping with the Dawes Act's goals of "allotment and assimilation" of Native American lands and peoples to the U.S. nation.

81. Alejo Carpentier, *The Lost Steps*, trans. Harriet de Onís (New York: Farrar, Straus and Giroux, 1956).

82. Félix Varela, *Jicoténcal*, eds. Luis Leal y Rodolfo J. Cortina (Houston: Arte Publico Press, 1995). Leal and Cortina make the case for Varela's authorship of the novel in the "Introducción," pp. vii–xlvii. Authorship of the novel remains disputed, as Guillermo I. Castillo-Feliú points out in his "Introduction" to the English language translation of the novel, *Xicoténcatl: An Anonymous Historical Novel about the Events Leading up to the Conquest of the Aztec Empire*, trans. Guillermo I. Castillo-Feliú (Austin: University of Texas Press, 1999), pp. 1–6. In her fascinating account of the transnational significance of this neglected "American" novel, Anna Brickhouse, *Transamerican Literary Relations and the Nineteenth-Century Public Sphere* (New York: Cambridge University Press, 2004), pp. 37–83, stresses the "Pan-American" and "anti-imperialist" features of the novel, but she does not read the allegory of nineteenth-century nationalism as an ideologically loaded way of "using" Amerindians for nationalist purposes.

83. Gustavo Pérez Firmat, ed., *Do the Americas Have a Common Literature?* (Durham, NC.: Duke University Press, 1990); Marshall C. Eakin, "Does Latin America Have a Common History?"

84. Shelley Streeby, *American Sensations: Class, Empire, and the Production of Popular Culture* (Berkeley: University of California Press, 2002).

85. John Carlos Rowe, *Literary Culture and U.S. Imperialism: From the Revolution to World War II* (New York: Oxford University Press, 2000), pp. 174–175.

86. Spain did not sign the international agreement until 1817, and even after that date Cuba continued to be a source of illegal shipments of slaves from Africa. Cirilo Villaverde's Cuban nationalist novel, *Cecilia Valdés or El Angel Hill: A Novel of Nineteenth-Century Cuba* (1882), trans. Helen Lane, ed. Sibylle Fischer (New York: Oxford University Press, 2005), builds its plot around illegal slave shipments to Cuba, U.S. planters living in Cuba, and the generally entangled political and economic fortunes of nineteenth-century U.S. and Cuba.

87. Marc Shell and Werner Sollors, *The Multilingual Anthology of American Literature: A Reader of Original Texts with English Translations* (New York: New York University Press, 2000), which includes only four Native American selections out of the twenty-nine in the anthology; Walter Mignolo, *The Darker Side of the Renaissance: Literacy, Territoriality, and Colonization*, 2nd ed. (Ann Arbor: The University of Michigan Press, 2003), pp. 136–160.

88. Charles C. Mann, *1491: New Revelations of the Americas before Columbus* (New York: Vintage Books, 2006).

89. Jared Diamond, *Guns, Germs, and Steel: The Fates of Human Societies* (New York: W. W. Norton, 1997).

90. "North American Studies" developed in post-World War II European universities, especially in Germany, as part of the "area studies" model, as has "European Studies" been formulated more recently in Europe and the U.S. "North American Studies" clearly displays in most instances the Cold-War "area studies" model, whereas "European Studies" seems to have emerged specifically in reaction to the limitations of such an area studies model while still preserving its basic terms. A thorough consideration of these two "area studies" categories would require a more developed and independent argument.

91. Paul Gilroy, *The Black Atlantic: Modernity and Double Consciousness* (Cambridge: Harvard University Press, 1993), p. 4.

92. Peter D. O'Neill and David Lloyd, eds., *The Black and Green Atlantic: Cross-Currents of the African and Irish Diasporas* (Basingstoke: Palgrave Macmillan, 2009).

93. Ngũgĩ wa Thiong'o, *Decolonising the Mind: The Politics of Language in African Literature* (New York: New York University Press, 1986), p. 7.

Chapter 5

94. Max Horkheimer and Theodor Adorno, *Dialectic of Enlightenment*, trans. John Cumming (New York: Continuum, 1988), p. 122.

95. *Ibid.*, p. 120.

96. See the website: http//www.informationclearinghouse.info/article2842.htm.

97. Peter Maass, "The Toppling: How the Media Inflated a Minor Moment in a Long War", *New Yorker* (1/10/2011), 47–60.

98. Chalmers Johnson, *The Sorrows of Empire: Militarism, Secrecy, and the End of the Republic* (New York: Henry Holt and Co., 2004), p. 30. Further references in the text as: Johnson.

99. "In Search of Al-Qaeda", *Frontline*. PBS (21 November 2002).

100. Anne Friedberg, *Window Shopping: Cinema and the Postmodern* (Berkeley: University of California Press, 1993), p. 120.

101. Karl Marx, *Capital: A Critique of Political Economy*, trans. Ben Fowkes, 2 vols. (New York: Random House, 1977), I, 125–177; Georg Lukács, *History and Class Consciousness: Studies in Marxist Dialectics*, trans. Rodney Livingstone (Cambridge: MIT Press, 1971), pp. 91–92.

102. Mark Poster, *What's the Matter with the Internet?* (Minneapolis: University of Minnesota Press, 2001), p. 20.

103. Anna McCarthy, *Ambient Television: Visual Culture and Public Space* (Durham, NC: Duke University Press, 2001), pp. 226–251.

104. Karl Marx and Friedrich Engels, *The German Ideology*, ed. C. J. Arthur. (New York: International Publishers, 1988), p. 47. Further references in the text as: *GI*.

105. Francis Fukuyama, *The Ends of History and the Last Man* (New York: Bard Press, 1998), p. 127.

106. John Gallagher and Ronald Robinson, "The Imperialism of Free Trade", *Economic History Review*, 2nd series, 6 (1953): 1–25. Further references in the text as: Gallagher and Robinson.

107. Today China is the source of the greatest imbalance of trade in U.S. trade relations globally.

108. Robert Kagan, *Of Paradise and Power: America and Europe in the New World Order* (New York: Random House, 2003), pp. 157–158.

109. John Carlos Rowe, *The New American Studies* (Minneapolis: University of Minnesota Press, 2002), pp. 180–186. Further references in the text as: *NAS*.

110. Anthony Swofford, *Jarhead: A Marine's Chronicle of the Gulf War* (New York: Scribner, 2003), p. 210.

111. The English translation by Paul Patton, *The Gulf War Did Not Take Place*, was published in 1995.

112. Lynn Spigel, "Entertainment Wars: Television Culture after 9/11", *American Quarterly* 56.2 (June 2004), 239. Further references in the text as: Spigel.

113. "Lynch: Military Played Up Rescue Too Much", CNN (11/7/2003).

114. "Rambo Image Was Based on Lie, Says US War Hero Jessica Lynch", *Guardian* (London) (April 25, 2007).

115. Susan Faludi, *The Terror Dream: Myth and Misogyny in Insecure America* (New York: Metropolitan Books, 2007), p. 191.

116. Mohamed Odeh al-Rehaief with Jeff Coplon, *Because Each Life Is Precious: Why an Iraqi Man Came to Risk Everything for Private Jessica Lynch* (New York: HarperCollins, 2003). Al-Rehaief's version of events has been disputed by many, including Jessica Lynch. See Rick Bragg, *I Am a Soldier Too: The Jessica Lynch Story* (New York: Vintage, 2004).

117. One of my points in this essay and in *Literary Culture and U.S. Imperialism* is that when we view U.S. imperialism in its full historical scope, rather than as a recent "neo-imperialism" dating either from World War II or from the Spanish-American War, we see such features as U.S. Orientalism as relatively unchanged, except for the specific peoples employed. From the Barbary Pirates of nineteenth-century Tripoli to the Philippine revolutionaries led by Aguinaldo in the Philippine-American War (1898–1902) who resisted U.S. annexation to the Viet Cong and North Vietnamese Army regulars and more recently to the Libyans, Palestinians, Iraqis, Iranians, and transnational al-Qaeda style revolutionaries, diverse groups around the globe have been consistently Orientalized by the U.S. For an interesting discussion of U.S. Orientalism in these contexts, see Klein, 1–19.

118. I am indebted to Thomas LeClair of the University of Cincinnati for this interpretation of the Kurdish elements in the dissident group represented in *Three Kings*.

119. Lisa Lowe, "Imagining Los Angeles in the Production of Multiculturalism". In *Mapping Multiculturalism*, eds. Avery F. Gordon and Christopher Newfield (Minneapolis: University of Minnesota Press, 2001), p. 420.

120. "I Made a Mistake by Joining the Taliban", *Washington Post* (5 Oct. 2002), A 1.

121. *Crossing Jordan* (NBC television), "Death Toll" (March 12, 2006) (http://www.imdb.com/title/tt0284718/episodes)

122. Talal Asad, *Genealogies of Religion: Disciplines and Reasons of Power in Christianity and Islam* (Baltimore: The Johns Hopkins University Press, 1993), p. 18. Further references in the text as: Asad.

Chapter 6

123. Azar Nafisi, *Reading Lolita in Tehran: A Memoir in Books* (New York: Random House, 2003). Further references in the text.

124. John Carlos Rowe, "Culture, U.S. Imperialism, and Globalization," *American Literary History* 16:4 (Winter 2004), 575–595.

125. John Carlos Rowe, "European Lessons in Imperialism: A Letter to America," *Transatlantic Studies*, special issue ed. Charles Gannon 6:2 (August 2008), 183–198.

126. Frank Norris, "The Frontier Gone at Last," *The Complete Works of Frank Norris*, vol. 4 (New York: P. F. Collier and Son, 1899), p. 283, is just one example of *fin-de-siècle* writings defending the superiority and inevitable global domination of the Anglo-Saxon "race". Norris predicts that "this epic of civilization" ends in "the true patriotism [that] is the brotherhood of man" and the knowledge that "the whole world is our nation and simply humanity our countrymen" (289). Reginald Horsman's *Race and Manifest Destiny: The Origins of American Racial Anglo-Saxonism* (Cambridge, MA: Harvard University Press, 1981) is the classic study of this cultural tradition.

127. Richard Byrne, "A Collision of Prose and Politics," *Chronicle of Higher Education*, LIII:8 (10/13/06), A12–14, 16.

128. Elaine Scarry, *On Beauty and Being Just* (Princeton: Princeton University Press, 1999). Other titles include Michael Clark, ed. *The Revenge of the Aesthetic: The Place of Literature in Theory Today* (Berkeley: University of California Press, 2000) and several of the contributions to *Aesthetics in a Multicultural Age*, eds. Emory Elliott, Louis Freitas Caton, and Jeffrey Rhyne (New York: Oxford University Press, 2002).

129. Elaine Scarry, *Dreaming by the Book* (New York: Farrar, Straus, Giroux, 1999) and *Who Defended the Country?* Eds. Joshua Cohen and Joel Rogers (Boston, MA: Beacon Press, 2003).

130. *dKosopedia, the Free Political Encyclopedia* (www.dkosopedia.com/index.php/ Smith_Richardson_Foundation)

131. Website for Smith Richardson Foundation (http://www.srf.org).

132. *Ibid.*

133. *dKosopedia, the Free Political Encyclopedia* (www.dkosopedia.com/index.php/ Smith_Richardson_Foundation)

134. The Dialogue Project website (http://dialogueproject.sais-jhu.edu).

135. "Paul D. Wolfowitz," *Wikipedia* (http://en.wikipedia.org/wiki/ Paul.Wolfowitz).

136. "About the Author" front-matter in *Reading Lolita in Tehran* and "Roundtable: Three Women, Two Worlds, One Issue," *SAIS Review* (Summer-Fall 2000), 31.

137. Johns Hopkins University website (http://webapps.jhu.edu). As far as I can determine, there is no home-page for Azar Nafisi in the numerous home-pages for individual faculty at the Johns Hopkins University.

138. Nafisi's *Anti-Terra: A Critical Study of Vladimir Nabokov's Novels*, credited to her as a book with that English title in "About the Author," *Reading Lolita in Tehran*, n.p., has not been published in English. In response to my email inquiry, she wrote that the book was published in Persian in Tehran in 1994 and that "[...] I have been trying to get some copies myself, but the publisher claims the book is out of print and they cannot obtain permission to reprint" (Azar Nafisi email to John Carlos Rowe on June 4, 2005). On facing title page, "Also by Azar Nafisi," of her new book, *Things I've Been Silent About: Memories of a Prodigal Daughter* (New York: Random House, 2008), n. p., *Anti-Terra* is listed parenthetically in its Farsi title: *On Donya-Ye Deegar: Taamoli Daar Assar-E Vladimir Nabokov*. An Iranian scholar with whom I have corresponded informs me that this scholarly study was indeed published in Tehran under this Farsi title, but that he has not seen a copy.

139. "Praise for *Reading Lolita in Tehran*," front-matter in *Reading Lolita in Tehran*. The Book Sense Award (formerly the "Abby Award") was inaugurated on June 2 at BookExpo America 2000; the "winners are chosen by independent booksellers across the country who vote for the titles they most enjoyed handselling to their customers in the previous year" (http://www. booksense.com/readup/awards/bsby.jsp). Mira Rastegar, "Reading Nafisi in the West: Authenticity, Orientalism, and 'Liberating' Iranian Women," *Women's Studies Quarterly*, "The Global and the Intimate," eds. Geraldine Pratt and Victoria Rosner, 34:1–2 (Spring-Summer 2006), 108–128, assesses the Anglophone reviews of *Reading Lolita in Tehran*, concluding that most rely on liberal and Orientalist assumptions about theocratic Iran.

140. First-year undergraduates at Mount Holyoke College were asked to read *Reading Lolita in Tehran* for their orientation program in the Fall of 2005. Azar Nafisi, "Selections from *Reading Lolita in Tehran*," in Richard E. Miller and Kurt Spellmeyer, eds., *The New Humanities Reader*, Second Edition (Boston: Houghton Mifflin, 2006), pp. 334–356.

141. *People Planet Purpose: Leading the Way to a Sustainable Future,* conference brochure for National Association of Independent Schools' Annual Conference (February 28—March 3, 2007), Denver, Colorado, p. 4.

142. Frank Lentricchia, *The Edge of Night: A Confesssion* (New York: Random House, 1994); Edward Said, *Out of Place: A Memoir* (New York: Knopf, 1999); Marianna Torgovnick, *Crossing Ocean Parkway: Readings by an Italian American Daughter* (Chicago: University of Chicago Press, 1994).

143. Steven Mailloux, "Judging and Hoping: Rhetorical Effects of Reading about Reading," in *New Directions in American Reception Study,* eds. James Machor and Philip Goldstein (New York: Oxford University Press, 2008), 23–32.

144. Susan Stanford Friedman "Unthinking Manifest Destiny: Muslim Modernities on Three Continents," *American Literature and the Planet,* eds. Lawrence Buell and Wai-Chee Dimock (Princeton: Princeton University Press, 2007).

145. Mitra Rastegar, "Reading Nafisi in the West," 126n6, notes that *Reading Lolita in Tehran* has not been translated into Farsi, is virtually unknown in Iran, and is dismissed by those Iranians familiar with it as Western propaganda.

146. The first reference is section 12 in "Part II: Gatsby," and it deals with Nafisi's gradual alienation from the Confederation of Iranian Students at the University of Oklahoma, especially "the most radical group," which at one point accuses "one of their members, a former running champion, [...] of being an agent of the Iranian secret police, SAVAK. Some zealous members had decided to 'extract' the truth from him. They had lured him into a room at the Holiday Inn and tried to get him to confess by means of torture, including burning his fingers with a cigarette. When they had left the room and were in the parking lot, their victim managed to escape" (113). The next day, "several FBI agents with dogs and the 'culprit'" arrive on campus looking for the "assailants," but the victim of the Iranian students' torture refuses "to expose his tormentors," allowing Nafisi to comment on how the radical students' reaction to this event "frightened me," because it seems to indicate a tendency on the part of Iranian students in the U.S. to emulate "Comrade Stalin" and to anticipate the behavior of Iranian students in Tehran during the Islamic Revolution (114). The accusation of the "victim" as an agent of SAVAK is neither confirmed nor denied, and the odd fact that the FBI appears, rather than representatives of the Norman Police Department, is not explained.

147. Nafisi, "Roundtable: Three Women, Two Worlds, One Issue," 45.

148. Just how Nafisi's special arrangement with her sole male student, Nima, manages to preserve the "secrecy" of her private seminar from the authorities goes unexplained.

149. Mitra Rastegar, "Reading Nafisi in the West," 113.

150. Lisa Yonemaya, "Liberation under Siege: U.S. Military Occupation and Japanese Women's Enfranchisement," *Legal Borderlands: Law and the Construction of American Borders*, eds. Mary L. Dudziak and Leti Volpp, special issue of *American Quarterly* 57:3 (September 2005), 886.

151. Robert W. Johannsen, *To the Halls of the Montezumas: The Mexican War in the American Imagination* (New York: Oxford University Press, 1985), pp. 68, 170.

152. Martha Nussbaum, "Introduction," *Women, Culture, and Development: A Study of Human Capabilities*, eds. Martha C. Nussbaum and Jonathan Glover (New York: Oxford University Press, 1995), p. 4.

153. Mitra Rastegar, "Reading Nafisi in the West," 111.

154. *Ibid.*, 119.

155. *Ibid.*, 35.

156. Linda J. Nicholson, ed., *Feminism/ Postmodernism* (New York: Routledge, 1990) is a good anthology representing such third-wave, postmodern feminist approaches, indicating clearly how they depart from second-wave feminist views.

157. Nafisi, "Roundtable: Three Women, Two Worlds, One Issue," 35.

158. *Ibid.*

159. Paul Berman, *Power and the Idealists, or, The Passion of Joschka Fisher and Its Aftermath* (Brooklyn, N.Y.: Soft Skull Press, 2005), p. 172.

160. *Ibid.*, p. ix; *A Tale of Two Utopias: The Political Journey of the Generation of 1968* (New York: W. W. Norton and Co., 1996). Berman is also the editor of *Debating PC: The Controversy over Political Correctness on College Campuses* (New York: Dell, 1992).

161. Nafisi's 1979 doctoral dissertation at the University of Oklahoma is catalogued by Dissertation Abstracts International under "Naficy," Azar as *The Literary Wars of Mike Gold, A Study in the Background Development of Mike Gold's Literary Ideas, 1920–1941*, DAI, 40, no. 08A (1979): 4599. According to her dissertation director at Oklahoma, David S. Gross, "Naficy" was the way she spelled her surname during her graduate work. Alan Velie also served on the dissertation committee.

162. Theodore Adorno, *Aesthetic Theory*, trans. C. Lenhardt, eds. Gretel Adorno and Rolf Tiedemann (London: Routledge and Kegan Paul, 1984), p. 7; Bertholt Brecht, *Brecht on Theater: The Development of an Aesthetic*, ed. and trans. John Willett (New York: Hill and Wang, 1964), pp. 91–99.

163. Showing little interest in Nafisi's literary interests, except insofar as they represent the West's liberal individualism, Paul Berman gives special

attention to her treatment of Bellow: "She quotes Saul Bellow on the value of literature in the face of political oppression—on literature's ability to reach 'the heart of politics.' And what is the heart of politics? It is the precise spot where, in Bellow's phrase, 'the human feelings, human experiences, the human form and face, recover their proper place—the foreground" (*Power and the Idealists*, p. 171).

164. Murray Krieger, "The Existential Basis of Contextual Criticism," in *The Play and Place of Criticism* (Baltimore: Johns Hopkins University Press, 1967), pp. 239–251; Sarah N. Lawall, *Critics of Consciousness: The Existential Structures of Literature* (Cambridge: Harvard University Press, 1968); Wolfgang Iser, *The Act of Reading: A Theory of Aesthetic Response* (Baltimore: Johns Hopkins University Press,1978); David Bleich, *Readings and Feelings: An Introduction to Subjective Criticism* (Urbana, Ill.: National Council of Teachers of English, 1975); Steven Mailloux, *Rhetorical Power* (Ithaca: Cornell University Press, 1989).

165. See Michael Denning, *The Cultural Front: The Laboring of American Culture in the Twentieth Century* (New York: Verso, 1998) and Cary Nelson, *Repression and Recovery: Modern American Poetry and the Politics of Cultural Memory, 1910–1945* (Madison: University of Wisconsin Press, 1992).

166. Philip Roth, *The Great American Novel* (New York: Penguin Books, 1973).

167. R. W. B. Lewis, *The American Adam: Innocence, Tragedy, and Tradition in the Nineteenth Century* (Chicago: University of Chicago Press, 1955).

168. Rowe, *At Emerson's Tomb: The Politics of Classic American Literature* (New York: Columbia University Press, 1997), p. 3.

169. F. Scott Fitzgerald, *The Great Gatsby* (New York: Scribner, 1925), p. 3.

170. *Ibid.*, pp. 179–180.

171. Victor Shklovsky, "Art as Technique" (1917), in *Critical Theory Since Plato*, rev. ed., ed. Hazard Adams (New York: Harcourt Brace Jovanovich, 1992), pp. 751–759, offers one of the typical Russian Formalist definitions of literary "estrangement".

172. Rowe, *The New American Studies* (Minneapolis: University of Minnesota Press, 2002), pp. 76–77.

173. John M. Ellis, *Literature Lost: Social Agendas and the Corruption of the Humanities* (New Haven, Conn.: Yale University Press, 1997). See my review of Cary Nelson, *Manifesto of a Tenured Radical* and John M. Ellis, *Literature Lost: Social Agendas and the Corruption of the Humanities, Academe: Bulletin of the A.A.U.P.*, (May—June 1998), 76–77.

174. "Vow for 'Freedom in All the World': Text of the Inaugural Address," *Los Angeles Times* (1/21/05), A22.

175. I admit this may be a somewhat tenuous reading, insofar as Nafisi uses multiple literary examples in the James and Austen parts. Nevertheless, Daisy in James's *Daisy Miller* and Elizabeth Bennet in Austen's *Pride and Prejudice* are the privileged characters in their respective parts of Nafisi's book. Those parts might have just as easily been entitled: "Daisy" and "Elizabeth" (or "Eliza").

176. Nafisi's unnamed confidante, tagged her "magician," first comes to her attention during debates between students and faculty at the University of Tehran regarding changes in the curricula. A Professor of Drama (and apparently Film), he refuses to teach in a university which has eliminated Racine from the curriculum and voluntarily resigns his position, arguing that "there was no one [...], certainly no revolutionary leader or political hero more important than Racine" (139). He gives no thought apparently to the possibility that the French culture represented by Racine might have some complicity with French colonialism in the Middle East. "When he spoke again, it was to say that he felt one single film by Laurel and Hardy was worth more than all their revolutionary tracts, including those of Marx and Lenin" (140). Although he is also enamored of Russian films, the "magician" is clearly a western-style Professor, whose defense of EuroAmerican classics sounds much like those American conservatives, such as William Bennett, who insisted so stridently on the importance of Shakespeare in the U.S. liberal arts education.

177. Daniel Bell, *The End of Ideology: On the Exhaustion of Political Ideas in the Fifties* (Cambridge, MA: Harvard University Press, 2000) and Francis Fukuyama, *The End of History and the Last Man* (New York: Free Press, 1992). Fukuyama is one of Nafisi's colleagues at the School for Advanced International Studies.

178. Nafisi includes a brief "Suggested Reading" list of thirty-one authors, all of whom are mentioned in *Reading Lolita in Tehran* (355–356).

179. Azar Nafisi, *Things I've Been Silent About*, pp. 319–320. Further references in the text as: *Things*.

Chapter 7

180. Michael B. Oren, *Power, Faith, and Fantasy: America in the Middle East, 1776 to the Present* (New York: W. W. Norton and Co., 2007), p. 77.

181. Robert Stam and Ella Shohat, *Flagging Patriotism: Crises of Narcissism and Anti-Americanism* (New York: Routledge, 2007), is an excellent example of this work by intellectuals to challenge the rhetoric of U.S. patriotism.

182. In the historical and imaginary "revisions" of the Vietnam War worked out in U.S. culture after 1975, conservative critics of our military and political failure in the Vietnam War often cited the American public's failure to "support the troops." In *Coming Home*, Sally (Jane Fonda) picks up her demobilized husband, Bob Hyde (Bruce Dern), at the Oakland Naval Air Station (check this) driving a sporty and classic (and expensive!) Porsche Speedster. As he upshifts out the gate of the military base, he turns to the assembled anti-war demonstrators outside the fence and gives them the finger. Audiences cheered Hyde's "rebellious" gesture of contempt for the anti-war demonstrators. During the 2005 NFL Super Bowl broadcast on the Fox Network on February 6, 2005, the St. Louis brewing company Anheuser-Busch showed U.S. troops returning from Iraq and walking through an airport to the spontaneous applause of strangers, culminating in a black-out screen with the words, "Thank you", followed by "Anheuser-Busch." The next day's NBC Evening News (February 7, 2005) did a special story on this advertisement and the overwhelmingly positive response it received from viewers, even though some critics noted that the advertisement was still designed to urge consumers to "buy beer." Capitalizing on the "moral values" and "social responsibility" displayed in this advertisement, the Anheuser-Busch Co. assured Americans that the advertisement would be shown only once, marking thereby its special purpose. Written by Steve Bougdanos of DOB Chicago Advertising, the sixty-second advertisement clearly attempts to reverse the "Vietnam-Effect" of protesters challenging veterans returning from the Vietnam War.

183. Benedict Anderson, *Imagined Communities*, rev. ed. (London: Verso, 1995), pp. 37–46, suggests that in print cultures much of this work is done by a shared national language and by the cultural work—from literary texts to daily journalism and news—that reinforces the "official language" or, in the cases of nations with several languages, reinforces the bilingual or polylingual character of that "imagined community."

184. Trace Adkins, "Arlington", *Songs about Me* (Liberty, 2005). Adkins declares himself a singer of "working class anthems", so his sentimentalizing of death in the Second Gulf War helps legitimate the ongoing U.S. military exploitation of working-class military personnel (www.traceadkins.com/bio).

185. Samuel P. Huntington, *Who Are We? The Challenges to America's National Identity* (New York: Simon and Schuster, 2004), p. 274.

186. *Ibid.*, p. 192.

187. *Ibid.*, p. 273.

188. Pheng Cheah and Bruce Robbins, eds. *Cosmopolitics: Thinking and Feeling beyond the Nation* (Minneapolis: University of Minnesota Press, 1998).

189. Kwame Anthony Appiah, *Cosmopolitanism: Ethics in a World of Strangers* (New York: W. W. Norton, 2006), p. xv.

190. *Ibid.*, p. 153.

191. Edouard Glissant, *Caribbean Discourse: Selected Essays* (1981; rpt. Charlottesville, Virginia: University Press of Virginia, 1989), p. 64, makes a similar claim about how "Literature" and "History" serve the "functional fantasy" of Western Civilization.

192. Steve Earle, *The Revolution Starts Now* (Sarangel Music, 2004).

193. "Home to Houston", *The Revolution Starts Now*, lyrics from www. steveearle.com/ .

194. "Rich Man's War", *The Revolution Starts Now*, lyrics from www. steveearle.com/ .

195. Walter D. Mignolo, *The Darker Side of the Renaissance: Literacy, Territoriality, and Colonization* (Ann Arbor: University of Michigan Press, 1995), p. 20, describes his method as "a pluritopic hermeneutic", which allows the differences between Mexica (Aztec) and Spanish national knowledges, for example, to appear, thus challenging the hegemony of Eurocentric knowledge.

196. Neil Young, "Living with War", *Living with War* (Reprise Records/Silver Fiddle Music, 2006).

197. W. E. B. Du Bois, *The Souls of Black Folk* (New York: Penguin Books, 1989), p. 207.

198. Ariel Dorfman, "Waving the Star-Spanglish Banner", *Washington Post* (May 7, 2006).

199. "Nuestro Himno", *Wikipedia* (http://en.wikipedia.org/wiki/ Nuestro_Himno)

200. Gustave Kobbé, *The New Kobbé's Complete Opera Book*, ed. and rev. The Earl of Harewood (New York: G. P. Putnam's Sons, 1976), p. 1181.

201. "Nuestro Himno", *Wikipedia*.

Chapter 8

202. Marquard Smith and the JVC Editorial Group, "Editorial: Questionnaire on Barack Obama," *Journal of Visual Culture*, The Obama Issue, vol. 8:2 (August 2009), 123.

203. *Ibid.*, pp. 23–24.

204. Both photographs were taken by the author in northern Tanzania in August 2008.

205. Jean Baudrillard, "Simulacra and Simulations," in *Selected Writings*, ed. Mark Poster (Stanford: Stanford University Press, 1988), pp. 166–184.

206. John Carlos Rowe, *The New American Studies* (Minneapolis: University of Minnesota Press, 2002), pp. 151–171.

207. Sarah Palin's subsequent decision to resign early from the Governorship of Alaska and assume an "at-large" position as national political celebrity, supportive of Republican and more narrowly Tea Party causes, also follows this logic of the "spinoff effect" and the Baudrillardian hyper-real. Palin is clearly a political phenomenon *produced* by these cultural constructions of her. Her celebrity on the McCain-Palin ticket doomed McCain's bid for the presidency, and her own continuing celebrity, haunted by Tina Fey's satire, appears to be having the same negative effect on Palin's chances for higher political office.

208. W. E. B. Du Bois, "The Damnation of Women," in *Darkwater: Voices from within the Veil*, in Eric Sundquist, ed., *The Oxford W. E. B. Du Bois Reader* (New York: Oxford University Press, 1996), pp. 564–576.

Chapter 9

209. Emily Eakin, "Novels Gaze into Terror's Dark Soul", Arts and Ideas, *New York Times* (9-22-01).

210. John Carlos Rowe, *The Theoretical Dimensions of Henry James* (Madison: University of Wisconsin Press, 1984), pp. 147–188.

211. Joseph Conrad, *The Secret Agent* (Garden City, NY: Doubleday and Co., Inc., 1921), p. 249.

212. Don DeLillo, *Mao II* (New York: Penguin Books, 1991), p. 16. Further references in the text as: *M*.

213. Don DeLillo, *Libra* (New York: Penguin Books, 1989), p. 241. Further references in the text as: *L*.

214. Paul Virilio, *The Virilio Reader*, ed. James Der Derian (Malden, MA: Blackwell Publishers, Inc., 1998), p. 107.

215. John Johnston, "Superlinear Fiction or Historical Diagram?: Don DeLillo's *Libra*", *Modern Fiction Studies* 40:2 (Summer 1994), 338.

216. Ryan Simmons, "What Is a Terrorist? Contemporary Authorship, the Unabomber, and *Mao II*", *Modern Fiction Studies* 45:3 (Fall 1999), 683. Further references in the text.

217. DeLillo makes references to Shiite and Christian militias battling in Beirut and to the conflict among Syrian, Israeli, and Lebanese military forces (*M*, 195), so we can conclude that the scenes in the novel set in Beirut take place between Israel's invasion of Lebanon in June of 1982 and its military withdrawal in 1985. More precisely, DeLillo refers to the extreme violence of different militias between February and September 1984, the year after the terrorist car bombers attacked the U.S. Embassy and U.S. Marine headquarters in Beirut. Abu Rashid's terrorist group is probably intended to represent a Palestinian group, such as Hamas, even though the Maoist associations are purely fictional. In the novel, Abu Rashid tells Brita: "'I had a wife I loved killed by the Phalange'" (*M*, 234). Thomas Friedman, *From Beirut to Jerusalem* (New York: Doubleday, 1989), pp. xiii-xiv, provides a good summary of how the Phalangist militia leader Bashir Gamayel was assassinated on September 14, 1982, shortly after his election as President of Lebanon. Phalangist militamen subsequently massacred Palestinians in the Sabra and Shatila refugee camps surrounded by the occupying Israeli army.

218. DeLillo, "In the Ruins of the Future: Reflections on Terror and Loss in the Shadow of September", *Harper's* (December 2001), 34. Further references in the text as: Ruins.

219. Walt Kelly, *The Pogo Papers* (New York: Simon and Schuster, 1953), p. 35.

220. DeLillo, *Falling Man* (New York: Scribner, 2007), p. 80. Further references in the text as: *FM*.

221. DeLillo, *Cosmopolis* (New York: Scribner, 2003), p. 89. Further references in the text as: *C*.

222. Giorgio Agamben, *Homo Sacer: Sovereign Power and Bare Life*, trans. Daniel Heller-Roazen (Palo Alto: Stanford University Press, 1998); Hannah Arendt, *The Origins of Totalitarianism* (1951) (New York: Harcourt, 1976).

223. Zora Neale Hurston, "How It Feels to Be Colored Me", *A Zora Neale Hurston Reader*, ed. Alice Walker (Old Westbury, NY: Feminist Press, 1979), p. 154.

224. Linda S. Kauffman, "The Wake of Terror: Don DeLillo's 'In the Ruins of the Future,' 'Baader-Meinhof,' and *Falling Man*", *Modern Fiction Studies* 54:2 (Summer 2008), 353–377.

225. Michael Hardt and Antonio Negri, *Empire* (Cambridge, MA: Harvard University Press, 2000), pp. 393–413.

226. Robert Venturi, Denise Scott Brown, and Steven Izenour, *Learning from Las Vegas* (Cambridge, MA: MIT Press, 1972).

227. DeLillo, *Underworld* (New York: Scribner, 1997).

228. Salman Rushdie, *Fury* (London: Jonathan Cape, 2001).